From Sequences to Graphs

SCIENCES

Computer Science, Field Directors –
Valérie Berthé and Jean-Charles Pomerol

Bioinformatics, Subject Heads – Anne Siegel and Hélène Touzet

From Sequences to Graphs

Discrete Methods and Structures for Bioinformatics

Coordinated by
Annie Chateau
Mikaël Salson

WILEY

First published 2022 in Great Britain and the United States by ISTE Ltd and John Wiley & Sons, Inc.

ISTE Ltd
27-37 St George's Road
London SW19 4EU
UK

www.iste.co.uk

John Wiley & Sons, Inc.
111 River Street
Hoboken, NJ 07030
USA

www.wiley.com

Library of Congress Control Number: 2022940907

British Library Cataloguing-in-Publication Data
A CIP record for this book is available from the British Library
ISBN 978-1-78945-066-8

ERC code:
PE6 Computer Science and Informatics
 PE6_13 Bioinformatics, biocomputing, and DNA and molecular computation

Contents

Chapter 2. Sequence Indexing   49

Thierry LECROQ and Mikaël SALSON

Chapter 3. Sequence Alignment 87
Laurent NOÉ

Chapter 4. Genome Assembly 113
Dominique LAVENIER

Chapter 5. Metagenomics and Metatranscriptomics

Cervin GUYOMAR and Claire LEMAITRE

Chapter 6. RNA Folding

Yann PONTY and Vladimir REINHARZ

Preface

Scientists have long been interested in studying living organisms, both at a macroscopic scale, by analyzing their external appearance or their overall internal functioning, and at a more microscopic scale. Taken to its extreme, their observation consists of studying the nucleus of cells and the molecules of living organisms that define their functioning: namely DNA and RNA. In an organism, DNA is actually the carrier of genetic information, which is called the *genome*, thus playing an important role. However, the genome is not everything; it is composed of genes that allow for RNA production which have various functions such as protein synthesis or regulation of cell activity. In digital form, these DNA or RNA molecules are most often represented as text from four-letter alphabets (A, C, G and T for DNA; A, C, G and U for RNA). Using these DNA and RNA sequences, computer-based methods are able to answer a number of biological questions. This is the heart of this book. In the chapters of this book, we will find the answers to these questions, as well as their limitations to some fundamental questions that have been, and are still being, addressed by bioinformatics. How can a short sequence of a few hundred nucleotides quickly be searched for in a genome that can make a few billion of them? How can sequences be compared with one another? How can the complete sequence of a genome be reconstructed? How can the bacteria that make up our intestinal flora be identified? Based on their sequences, how can the structure that certain RNAs will adopt be predicted?

The methods that are described in this book have their roots anchored in two fields with long-standing foundations, which have long evolved alongside each other without any significant interaction: computer science and biology. It was during the 20th century that the symbiosis between computational methods and biological problems led to combined modeling and the design of bioinformatics algorithms, methods and tools.

From Sequences to Graphs,
coordinated by Annie CHATEAU and Mikaël SALSON.
© ISTE Ltd 2022.

DNA was first sequenced in the late 1970s, with low volumes and incurring huge costs. The need to store and manipulate this data automatically soon became very pressing. As a result, the mid-1980s witnessed the development of the first sequence databases. These databases are pooled by the community who feeds them sequencing experiments, which are increasingly growing and require more efficient methods. This is how sequence alignment methods are implemented, which are *dedicated* to these genomic sequences, and designed for optimizing the time and space used for this operation. These databases are not only maintained, but also expanded and made public internationally, further accelerating access to knowledge. Data acquisition is also accelerating since the first complete bacterial or yeast genomes in the mid-1990s, as well as with the human genome project, which has kept many teams busy for over a decade. Access to knowledge about these genomes leads to questioning living organisms from a completely new point of view, and opens up new avenues for several fields of application, particularly in the health sector, and also in ecology and evolution, along with the enrichment of the fundamental knowledge of organisms and how they function.

Since the mid-2000s, genomic data have been acquired at a much faster pace following the advent of *high-throughput sequencers*, which enable, to a certain extent, the transformation of DNA or RNA molecules into short sequences of letters at a low cost and at an increasingly frenetic pace. There is an ongoing discussion of projects involving several thousand, or even tens of thousands, complete genomes of individuals of interest. These developments make it now possible to question living organisms in a finer manner, at the scale of varieties and individuals of the same species, but also at the scale of the different tissues that make up an organism, or even at the scale of a natural environment sample containing thousands of different organisms. With these new questions emerges the need to model data as a whole, in a structured way, and to develop methods for the purpose of answering them.

At the same time, storage and information processing capacities, as well as computational performance allowed by increasingly powerful processors and exploiting increasingly complex parallelism, have accompanied an extraordinarily rapid progress in the field of algorithmics and problem modeling based on the use of elaborate discrete structures. Some particular operations that seemed inaccessible have become commonplace at a lower cost in modern programs, and it is not uncommon today to run calculations over a grid whose capacities far exceed what could be imagined some 20 years ago.

Nonetheless, this is not enough to make feasible all the studies that we would like to achieve on sequencing data and their derivatives.

The data produced by the sequencers, due to their quantity (up to 10 million nucleotides per second) and their particularities (whose lengths and types of errors vary according to sequencing technologies), require the appropriate use of methods in order to extract relevant information therefrom in a reasonable amount of time without resorting to gigantic computing infrastructures.

Although the methods developed are generally independent of the technology, they must take into account the constraints of the technology in order to yield solutions for practical applications. In particular, the increase in the volume of data to be processed makes some solutions impractical and requires the use of much more faster heuristics. Therefore, the methods used in bioinformatics are most often at the crossroads between exact and approximate methods.

In order to better understand the specific terms and tools of bioinformatics, we have introduced most of them in Chapter 1. This chapter also covers in detail the data (DNA, RNA and proteins) which we are working with, and the way they are obtained. Moreover, this chapter presents some algorithmic notions that are useful for understanding this book, and addresses the concepts used in bioinformatics more broadly. The remaining chapters present the most commonly studied problems in bioinformatics from genomic data. Some chapters focus more on tools, others on methods and still others on a more detailed description of data. We briefly present the questions which the following chapters of this book will answer.

Sequence indexing. In order to address the influx of data, how can these be easily stored, queried and manipulated? This is the subject of Chapter 2, which explains how to respond to these different aspects. The crucial issues here are the conservation of information, the flexibility of the structure and its ability to answer in a reasonable time the most common question, namely "Is this sequence indeed in my genome?"

Sequence alignment. When studying one or more sequences, a question arises very quickly: how can we tell whether the sequences are similar if a sequence is approximately found in another, and also can a score that allows for classifying these comparisons between them be determined? A crucial point in bioinformatics is to be able to answer the question "What are the most significant occurrences of my pattern in my sequence?" This is what is called the sequence alignment, which is the subject of Chapter 3. This chapter also deals with the aspects of alignment-free comparison where, in order to cope with the volume of data and sometimes significant error rates, making use of an alignment is not feasible and heuristics are developed.

Genome assembly. In Chapter 4, the following question is addressed: "How can the complete sequence of an organism be obtained based on the reads produced by sequencing?" This fundamental problem thus arose from a technical difficulty that makes it impossible to read the genome of an organism in one piece from its cells. This technical difficulty will most likely disappear if advances in sequencing make it possible to read the genome in a single pass; however, the assembly is for the moment essential to the knowledge of the genome and raises many problems, such as "how to choose between two possibilities to assemble the reads?" or "how could the quality of the reconstruction be evaluated?" Graphs prove to be very interesting models in this context of reconstruction.

Metagenomics and metatranscriptomics. When several organisms are mixed in a sample, for example, of soil, from a marine environment or from the internal environment of an organism (the well-known microbiota), additional problems can occur along with those already existing during the assembly. For example, "how can we determine which species are present?" or still "how can genomes be assembled when they are mixed together?" This is the subject of Chapter 5.

RNA folding. RNA data are particular data because their secondary structure plays a fundamental role in the functioning of organisms. Chapter 6 proposes an overview of methods for modeling and inferring this secondary structure from sequence data. Here the fundamental question is "how can the folding of a word on itself be found and evaluated, taking into account the affinities between the characters of this word?"

Apart from the solutions provided to answer this large number of questions, it now becomes all the more necessary to take a step back from the methods capable of processing these data. What does it mean when we "find the same piece of sequence" of one organism in another, and what is the significance of this assertion with regard to the parameters chosen, the methods used and their limitations in terms of modeling? What is the place of this method in the landscape of methods already developed and of the problems raised by current data and knowledge?

It is this critical thinking, which can only be developed with full knowledge of the facts, that we also wish to cultivate in our readers. Indeed, the discrete structures used are models that we build, mathematical objects that are not absolute truths, that we design according to an objective, while keeping in mind that these models may have their limitations. Those limitations are expressed in terms of data representativeness, power of expression and classical methods that can be applied. We finally make trade-offs between these limitations and the need to obtain quick answers to crucial questions for the purpose of increasing the knowledge of living beings. The research presented in this book illustrates this explorative process. It is certainly an illusion to understand each of the mechanisms that underlie all of these methods, but the underlying general scheme can be a useful guide for our scientific practice.

This book is part of a series dedicated to methods in bioinformatics; in particular, it is related to the analysis of sequences characterizing genetic information in organisms. This book is intended for all students from the master's level upwards, doctoral students, young and senior researchers. This book focuses on examples of modeling and problem solving using discrete structures. Far from being exhaustive, this book is intended to be a reminder and an opening for those who are dedicated to one of the fields covered, and an introduction for the future generation of bioinformaticians. Written by researchers in the field, coming from various backgrounds, with most of them significantly involved in bioinformatics training, this book has been conceived with a pedagogical effort that makes it accessible to less informed readers. We sincerely hope that you will enjoy reading this book.

In order to make this book, it was necessary to harness the energy and will of several people, whom we would like to thank in particular. First of all, we would like to thank the researchers who agreed to write the various chapters, an exercise that added to their already busy schedules, and with a quality which we applaud. Second, we would like to thank our coordinators, Hélène Touzet and Anne Siegel, for their kindness, advice and support throughout this adventure. Finally, we would like to thank ISTE for having trusted us and given us complete freedom in the organization and coordination of this book.

May 2022

Author Biographies

Annie Chateau has been a lecturer at the University of Montpellier since 2006. She switched to bioinformatics in 2004 after a thesis in mathematical logic. Her interests include algorithms and combinatorial structures related to various problems such as sequence alignment, genomic rearrangements, genome scaffolding, articulation between phylogeny and synteny, and more generally NGS data manipulation. She has been teaching algorithms in bioinformatics for about 15 years, at all levels, and is currently in charge of the Master's in Bioinformatics in Montpellier.

Tom Davot-Grangé is currently a temporary teaching and research associate at the University of Montpellier. He defended his thesis on genome scaffolding in 2020. His area of research relates to the fields of fundamental computer science, such as graph theory and algorithmic complexity, as well as to bioinformatics within particular sequence contig scaffolding, a problem he studied during his PhD.

Cervin Guyomar is a research engineer at INRAE, in the UMR GenPhySE based in Toulouse. He defended a thesis in bioinformatics in 2018 on the metagenomics of the pea aphid holobiont. He was particularly involved in proposing innovative methods to assemble genomes and characterize microbial species variation in bacterial communities. Since then, he has been developing analyses for many types of genomic data, in particular for the functional annotation of animal genomes.

Dominique Lavenier is a senior researcher at the CNRS, IRISA, Rennes, France. After working in the field of machine architectures, and more particularly with specialized parallel architectures for genomic data processing, he joined the Symbiose bioinformatics group in Rennes in 2000.

From Sequences to Graphs,
coordinated by Annie CHATEAU and Mikaël SALSON.
© ISTE Ltd 2022.

He created and co-directed the DEA in genomics and computer science (2000–2004), and then the Master's in Bioinformatics in Rennes (2004–2008). Between 2008 and 2010, he was seconded as a university professor at ENS Cachan, Brittany branch. In 2012, he created the GenScale bioinformatics team, IRISA/Inria, Rennes. From 2016 to 2021, he was a member of the CoNRS in the computer science section (06) and in the interdisciplinary commission (CID 51): modeling and analysis of biological data and systems. His current research activities include the processing of genomic data volumes, and more specifically data structures and associated parallel algorithms.

Thierry Lecroq obtained a thesis in computer science from the University of Orleans in 1992. In the same year, he was appointed as a lecturer at the University of Rouen Normandy, France. He was then appointed as a professor at the same university in 2002. He is currently the director of the research team Information Processing in Biology and Health (TIBS) of the Laboratory of Informatics, Information and System Processing (LITIS). He is the co-author of several books and chapters on text algorithmics. He was one of the coordinators of the CNRS working group focused on this field for more than 10 years (2008–2018). He teaches in the Computer Science Department of the University of Rouen Normandy, France, and mainly in the Master's of Bioinformatics.

Claire Lemaitre has been an Inria Research Fellow in the Genscale team of the Inria Rennes Bretagne Atlantique center and the IRISA computer science laboratory in Rennes since 2010. She has a multidisciplinary background in bioinformatics, which she completed with a PhD in 2008. Since her thesis on genomic rearrangements in mammalian genomes, she has been interested in the organization and evolution of genomes. For this purpose, she has developed algorithms and computational methods for comparing and analyzing DNA sequences, whether they are complete genomes or data from massive sequencing. In particular, she has developed software for genome assembly, detection of genomic variants and comparison of metagenomic data.

Laurent Noé has been a lecturer at the University of Lille since 2006. He is currently focusing on algorithms and models related to sequence comparison, NGS data and spaced seeds. He teaches networks, information coding and programming, and has been teaching bioinformatics for 15 years. He is currently co-responsible for the reinforced research course in computer science at the University of Lille.

Yann Ponty has been a senior researcher since 2020. He is responsible for the AMIBio team of the Computer Science Laboratory of the Ecole Polytechnique, where he has been conducting research in bioinformatics since his admission to the CNRS in 2009. He discovered RNA bioinformatics during his thesis and defended in 2006 at the University of Paris-Saclay. He developed original algorithmic methods for folding prediction according to the thermodynamic or kinetic principles, the research in structured RNA in genomes and the design of functional RNAs. His works are inspired, on the one hand, by algorithmic techniques, including dynamic programming and parameterized algorithms, and, on the other hand, by enumerative and analytical combinatorics through the random generation and analysis of algorithms on average. During his spare time, he teaches RNA bioinformatics in training courses for the Master's in Bioinformatics at Paris-Saclay and Sorbonne University.

Vladimir Reinharz has been a professor at the University of Quebec in Montreal and a member of the Laboratory of Algebra, Combinatorics and Mathematical Computing since 2020. He has been conducting research in bioinformatics since his thesis in 2015 at McGill. He develops algorithmic methods to understand the relationship between sequence, structure and function in RNA, as well as the evolution and modularity of its three-dimensional structure. To this end, he uses various techniques and representations, from dynamic programming and integer programming including graphs. He teaches bioinformatics at all levels.

Mikaël Salson has been a lecturer in computer science at the University of Lille since 2010. He defended a thesis on full-text compressed indexes. He then developed with his colleagues algorithmic methods and software programs for the analysis of high-throughput sequencing data (RNA-Seq, V(D)J recombinations, microRNAs, etc.) or for their indexation (V(D)J recombinations, sequencing datasets). He is also responsible for the first year of the master's degree in bioinformatics in Lille.

1

Methodological Concepts: Algorithmic Solutions of Bioinformatics Problems

Annie CHATEAU **and Tom** DAVOT-GRANGÉ

University of Montpellier, CNRS, UMR 5506 – LIRMM, France

In this book, we strive to describe models and solutions applied to various problems in bioinformatics, using discrete structures. These structures are characterized as being defined by an inductive or natural process, and as being capable of carrying information in a more or less structured form. After covering a brief overview of the different types of data that we might encounter in these problems, we recall in this chapter the definitions essential to the understanding of modeling in the form of graphs, before presenting a few conventional solution principles in algorithmics with these structures. This chapter is intended to be a reminder, however, not exhaustive.

1.1. Data, models, problem formalism in bioinformatics

1.1.1. *Data*

1.1.1.1. *Genomic data*

Genomic data, which the methods presented in this book essentially deal with, originate from the capture of information on the DNA or RNA molecule.

From Sequences to Graphs,
coordinated by Annie CHATEAU and Mikaël SALSON.
© ISTE Ltd 2022.

Without going back to molecular basics, we will consider in all that follows that we are dealing with polymers composed of *nucleotides*. A reference book in molecular biology can enlighten the novice reader on the complexity of the mechanisms that underlies the involvement of these molecules in the functioning of organisms (Alberts 2004). The acquisition of the sequence of nucleotides is achieved by means of *sequencing*. Sequencing technologies have evolved enormously in recent years, and it is widely accepted that sequencing is no longer a real barrier to the study of a living organism, in the sense that it is relatively easy to obtain these data when you have a good quality sample of the DNA of this organism. Of course, depending on the technology used, the quality of the data obtained, called *reads*, will be different, with possible errors of sometimes quite different nature. Sequencing data are characterized by their *volume*, which imposes challenges in terms of storage, handling, processing, as well as in the interpretation of results. They are also *incomplete* because current technologies do not allow access to certain areas of the genome, for example, near the centromere, the area where the chromosome arms converge, when dealing with a chromosome. Finally, they are *noisy* because the precision of sequencing machines is not perfect, as well as the extraction and purification phases can generate contaminations, biases, and errors which can subsequently be propagated at the time of the "reading" of the DNA molecule. A presentation of the different sequencing methods summarized here below can be found in Heather and Chain (2016). They are also analyzed and presented in detail, from the point of view of their use in assembly problems, in Chapter 4.

The first generations of sequencing methods, from the 1970s onwards, produce data with relatively few errors, but are expensive and time-consuming to produce. They represent only a tiny minority of the data available today. We will not consider them, even if they were on the basis of the first bioinformatics methods.

The second generation of sequencing data appeared around 2005 and triggered the explosion of sequencing organisms, both in volume and in diversity. This is known as *high-throughput sequencing*. It has also made it possible to shift from inter-species comparative analyses to intra-species analyses, to analyze the genomes of certain populations. These data are characterized in particular by their size (short reads, of the order of a few hundred base pairs) and their quality (error rate on average less than 1%). We will not address the precise characteristics of these technologies, but the vast majority of the data accessible in public databases are originating from this second generation.

The third generation of sequencing data, which emerged in the 2010s, produces longer reads, with the ultimate goal of reading the molecule in a single run, while eliminating the amplification step employed by the second-generation technologies. As the length of the reads obtained evolves every time these technologies are improved, we will only indicate that they make it possible to obtain sequences that are a few orders of magnitude longer than the short reads. In doing so, they capture structures that were not accessible to short reads, such as genomic repeats whose length is shorter than the size of long reads, or the resolution of haplotypes, that is, variations that can be observed between two copies of the same chromosome.

In recent years, these sequencing data have become instrumental in the analysis of living organisms at all levels, whether in the therapeutic field, in agronomy, in environmental and biodiversity monitoring, and also in human societies more generally speaking. Nevertheless, they are only the first step in acquiring the knowledge of living organisms, as they offer a static view of an organism.

1.1.1.2. *Protein data*

Proteins are at the heart of the functioning of living organisms. They are the result of the translation of messenger RNA (mRNA) into chains of amino acids, themselves synthesized in the cell by means of the transcription from DNA, and are subject to a delicate machinery which regulates their expression, their form and their interactions. They can be found in several forms, depending on the aspect taken into consideration. The primary structure of proteins, that is, the sequence of amino acids in the protein, represents raw information that can be derived from the corresponding mRNA sequence. Associated with this representation of proteins, we can find all the problems related to the division of proteins into identified *domains*, and to the annotation of proteins, that is, the attachment of a function to the protein sequence. The complexity of this task and the related issues are outlined in Letunic and Bork (2017).

The secondary structure is defined as the way a polymer folds on itself due to the affinities between its molecular constituents. For proteins, this secondary structure identifies the areas of helix α and sheet β folding, indicating the areas of functional activity inside the protein. For RNAs, the folding induced by hydrogen bridges between nucleotides is significant in how RNA will interact with surrounding proteins inside the cell, especially those responsible for translation.

Finally, the tertiary structure of proteins describes how the protein is arranged in three dimensions. It can be determined using different technologies, which associate the different amino acids of the protein with their coordinates in space. Steric hindrance is a key factor in areas concerned with protein activity, and in particular in drug design. For more details on the structure of proteins, the reader can refer to Petsko et al. (2009).

1.1.2. *Genome modeling*

The different types of accessible data are the object of various scientific problems (comparison, extraction of particular structures, or statistical relations between the data and an observable phenomenon). In order to provide answers to these problems, we use models that allow us to formalize these data. Formalizing is the act of defining and naming structures to represent the manipulated concepts. To analyze sequences, whether they are nucleotidic or proteinic, they will be modeled using the concepts and vocabulary of text algorithmics.

We denote by $\mathcal{A}_{DNA}$ (respectively, $\mathcal{A}_{RNA}$ and $\mathcal{A}_{Prot}$) the alphabet (see section 1.3), that is, a set of symbols, consisting of the nucleotides $\{A, C, G, T\}$ (respectively, $\{A, C, G, U\}$ and the alphabet of 20 amino acids). Any word from the alphabet $\mathcal{A}_{DNA}$ is called a *genomic sequence*, and a *transcriptomic sequence* designates a word from the alphabet $\mathcal{A}_{RNA}$. A word from the alphabet $\mathcal{A}_{Prot}$ is a *protein sequence*. A genomic sequence can be a *gene*, that is, it might correspond to a sequence coding for a protein, or not. A word or set of words from alphabet $\mathcal{A}_{DNA}$ is called a *genome*. The difference with a sequence is that a genome is characteristic of a given organism.

This very general definition covers different concepts that are context-dependent. The genome of an organism is accessed through different reading windows, which can be, for example:

- the set of *reads* produced by a sequencing experiment for an organism;

- the set of *contigs* produced by an assembly of sequencing data;

– the set of chromosome sequences produced as a result of scaffolding the contigs;

– the set of *genes* present in the organism.

A transcriptome is then comparable to a genome from the RNA alphabet. A proteome can be assimilated to a genome from the amino acid alphabet. A metagenome (respectively, metatranscriptome, metaproteome) is defined as a set of genomes (respectively, transcriptomes, proteomes) belonging to several organisms, originating usually from the same environment.

1.1.3. *Problems in bioinformatics*

Modeling problems is one of the major steps that contribute to proposing a solution to a given biological problem. The formalism makes it possible to apply generalist methods, to recognize the similarity between different problems and thus the propensity to be able to adapt the solutions of any problem to another and finally to manipulate mathematically the structures and the algorithms dedicated to this problem. There is sometimes a significant difference between the initial biological problem and its mathematical modeling. This difference concerns the complexity of the data taken into account, the assumptions made about the nature and quality of these data, as well as the expression of the expected result. Data or problem modeling is therefore subject to evolution, the latter being guided by the needs of the time. The genome can be taken as an example. Before the era of high-throughput sequencing, genetic information was accessed through the characteristics expressed, the phenotypes and their associated genes. Then, with access to RNA expression data, variations in expression of the same gene could be studied. Moreover, access to the non-coding genetic message has opened up very important perspectives in the study of evolution, particularly by taking repeated elements into account. And there is a growing interest in the information that the "dark matter" of DNA can reveal. The "genome" model is thus enriched over time, and is bound to become more and more complex as needs arise, as well as in terms of the capacity to process this complexity.

In the rest of this chapter, we introduce the fundamental notions of text algorithmics and graph theory, in order to model the questions that the following chapters answer.

1.2. Mathematical preliminaries

In this section, we describe some basic elements to help readers understand the foundations of mathematics useful for the manipulation of the models used in bioinformatics.

1.2.1. *Propositional logic preliminaries*

In propositional logic, the basic objects manipulated are called *propositions*. A proposition is a statement that can either be true or false. In the first case, a proposition will take the value TRUE and in the second case, it will take the value FALSE. For example, the proposition "$3 < 5$" is a proposition that takes the value TRUE, conversely the proposition "3 is an even number" takes the value FALSE. A proposition which depends on parameters is called a *predicate*. Therefore, the proposition $x = y$ is a predicate which depends on the values of x and y. A proposition can be constructed from other propositions by using the following operations:

– **Negation.** Let p be a proposition; the *negation* of p, denoted by $\neg p$, is the proposition whose value is equal to TRUE if and only if the value p is equal to FALSE.

– **Conjunction.** Let p_1 and p_2 denote two propositions. The *conjunction* of p_1 and p_2, denoted $p_1 \wedge p_2$, is the proposition whose value is equal to TRUE if and only if the values of p_1 and p_2 are equal to TRUE. In everyday language, this operator can be replaced by "AND".

– **Disjunction.** Let p_1 and p_2 denote two propositions. The *disjunction* of p_1 and p_2, denoted by $p_1 \vee p_2$, is the proposition whose value is equal to FALSE if and only if the values of p_1 and p_2 are equal to FALSE. In everyday language, this operator can be replaced by "OR".

The order of priority of the operators is given by $\neg, \wedge$ and $\vee$. We use parentheses when this order must be modified. A proposition taking the value TRUE is said to be *satisfied*, and in the opposite case, it is said to be *unsatisfied*. In order to simplify certain operations, we also introduce the following operators:

– **Implication.** Let p_1 and p_2 denote two propositions. The *implication* of p_2 by p_1, denoted $p_1 \Rightarrow p_2$, corresponds to the proposition $\neg p_1 \vee p_2$.

– **Double implication.** Let p_1 and p_2 denote two propositions. The *double implication* of p_2 by p_1, denoted $p_1 \Leftrightarrow p_2$, corresponds to the proposition $(p_1 \Rightarrow p_2) \wedge (p_2 \Rightarrow p_1)$.

The book by Cori and Lascar (2003) is a reference work in propositional logic.

1.2.2. *Preliminaries on sets*

A *set* is a collection of unique objects, and may be finite or infinite. The most commonly accepted notation for describing the contents of a set uses curly braces. These curly braces can surround the list of objects directly; this is then referred to as a description in *extension*, or as a predicate characterizing all the objects in the collection, in which case it is called a description in *comprehension*. For example, for a set E containing the integers $1, 2, 3, 4$ and 5, we can either write $\{1, 2, 3, 4, 5\}, \{1, \ldots, 5\}$ or $\{i \mid i \in \mathbb{N}^+ \wedge i \leq 5\}$ (it should be understood as E contains all non-zero natural numbers less than or equal to 5). The set of natural numbers is denoted $\mathbb{N}$ and the set of strictly positive natural numbers, used in the previous example, is denoted $\mathbb{N}^+$. The set of real numbers is denoted $\mathbb{R}$ and the set of strictly positive real numbers is denoted $\mathbb{R}^+$. Finally, the empty set, that is, the set containing no elements, is denoted $\emptyset$. The *cardinality* of a finite set E, denoted by $|E|$, is the number of elements that E contains.

To construct propositions, the following notations will be used. To indicate that an object x belongs to a set E, we use the symbol $\in$. Thereby, $1 \in E$ means that the integer 1 belongs to the set E. The symbol $\forall$ is used to express that all the elements x of a set E verify a property $P(x)$, which will be denoted $\forall x \in E, P(x)$. For example, the proposition $\forall x \in \{1, \ldots, 5\}, x \leq 5$ is satisfied. The symbol $\exists$ is a mean to indicate that there exists at least one element x of the set E which verifies a property $P(x)$, which will be denoted $\exists x \in E, P(x)$. Therefore, the proposition $\exists x \in \{1, \ldots, 5\}, x = 6$ is unsatisfied. The symbols $\forall$ and $\exists$ are called *quantifiers* and can be replaced in everyday language by "for any" and "there exists", respectively. A set E' is *included* in a set E if all the elements of E' belong to E and this is denoted by $E' \subseteq E$. In other words, the two propositions $E' \subseteq E$ and $\forall x \in E', x \in E$ are equivalent. If there exists at least one element of E which does not belong to E', this is then referred to as *strict inclusion* and it is denoted by $E' \subset E$. If E' is included in E, strictly or not, it is said that E' is a *subset* of E.

Sets can be created by using operations on other sets. A *union* of two sets E_1 and E_2, designated by the operator $\cup$, is the set containing all the elements of E_1 and E_2: $E_1 \cup E_2 = \{x \mid x \in E_1 \lor x \in E_2\}$. For example, we have $\{1, 2, 3\} \cup \{3, 4, 5\} = \{1, 2, 3, 4, 5\}$. An *intersection* of two sets E_1 and E_2, designated by the operator $\cap$, is the set containing the elements contained in both E_1 and E_2: $E_1 \cap E_2 = \{x \mid x \in E_1 \land x \in E_2\}$. For instance, we have $\{1, 2, 3\} \cap \{3, 4, 5\} = \{3\}$, two sets whose intersection is zero are said to be *disjoint*. The *difference* between a set E_1 and a set E_2, designated by the operator $\setminus$, is the set containing the elements of E_1 which are not in E_2: $E_1 \setminus E_2 = \{x \mid x \in E_1 \land x \notin E_2\}$.

A *multiset* is a collection of objects that are not necessarily unique. A *n-uplet* is a multiset of cardinality n including an order on its elements. For such a set, we replace the curly braces by parentheses when describing the content of an n-uplet, and the position of the objects in the notation then corresponds to its position in the order. As such, the two 3-uplets $(1, 2, 3)$ and $(3, 2, 1)$ are not equal because their orders are not the same.

A *map* f is a relation between the elements of a starting set and an ending set. The notation $f : D \rightarrow A$ allows specifying the starting set D and the arrival set A. Each element of the starting set is related to a single element of D. There is no constraint on the number of elements with which each element of the arrival set must be associated. For an element $x \in D$, we denote by $f(x)$ the element of A associated with x by the map f. For an element $y \in A$, $f^{-1}(y)$ denotes the subset of D containing the elements associated with y by f. The mapping $f : D \rightarrow A$ is a *bijection* if for any element $y \in A$, we have $|f^{-1}(y)| = 1$.

For two sets E_1 and E_2, the *Cartesian product* of E_1 and E_2, denoted $E_1 \times E_2$, is defined as the set of 2-uplets containing an element of each set. Formally, $E_1 \times E_2 = \{(e_1, e_2) \mid e_1 \in E_1, e_2 \in E_2\}$. For a Cartesian product involving n sets $E_1, \ldots, E_n$, it should be in principle considered that the resulting set contains 2-uplets of the form $(e_1, (e_2, (\ldots, e_n)))$ but in order to simplify the notation, it will be preferable to consider that the resulting set is constituted of n-uplets of the form $(e_1, \ldots, e_n)$. The Cartesian product of a set E by itself is denoted E^2, which can be generalized with the notation E^n if the Cartesian product is performed $n - 1$ times. As an example, if we take the sets $E_1 = \{1, 2, 3\}$ and $E_2 = \{a, b\}$, we have the

Cartesian products $E_1 \times E_2 = \{(1,a),(1,b),(2,a),(2,b),(3,a),(3,b)\}$ and $E_2^2 = \{(a,a),(a,b),(b,a),(b,b)\}$.

1.3. Vocabulary in text algorithmics

An *alphabet* Σ is a non-empty, finite or infinite set of *symbols*. A *word* (also called string of characters or sequence) of the alphabet Σ is a list of symbols from Σ. If w is a finite word, its *length* (i.e. the number of symbols contained in w) is denoted $|w|$. For example, 3425 is a word of length 4 of the alphabet $\Sigma_6 = \{0,1,2,3,4,5\}$. A few remarks:

– a word can be finite or infinite;

– a finite word of length n can be seen as a mapping from the set $\{1,\dots,n\}$ into the set Σ;

– a word of length $n = 0$ is the word *empty*, denoted ε.

The set of finite words of an alphabet Σ is denoted Σ^*. The set of *non-empty* finite words of the alphabet Σ is denoted Σ^+. For example, if $\Sigma = \{a,b\}$, then $\Sigma^* = \{\varepsilon, a, b, aa, ab, bb, aaa, aab, \dots\}$.

If $a \in \Sigma$ and $w \in \Sigma^*$, then $|w|_a$ represents the number of occurrences of the symbol a in the word w.

The *concatenation* of two finite words w and x is the juxtaposition of the symbols of w and the symbols of x, denoted wx. Concatenation is not *commutative*, generally speaking $wx \neq xw$ is not true, but it is *associative*: we always have $(xy)z = x(yz)$. Concatenation is expressed as multiplication, that is, w^n denotes $w \dots w$ (n times).

It is said that a word y is a *factor* of a word w if there exist words x and z such that $w = xyz$. The word x is a *prefix* of the word w if there exists a word y such that $w = xy$. The word z is a *suffix* of the word w if there exists a word y such that $w = yz$. A prefix or suffix x of a word w is said to be *proper* if $x \neq w$. For example, if we consider $w =$ barbappa. The word $x =$ bar is a prefix of w, $y =$ papa is a suffix of w and $y =$ rbapa is a factor of w.

If $w = a_1a_2\dots a_n$, then for $i \in \{1,\dots,n\}$, we define: $w[i] = a_i$. If $i \in \{1,\dots,n\}$ and $i - 1 \le j \le n$, we define: $w[i\dots j] = a_i\dots a_j$. It should be noted that $w[i\dots i] = a_i$ and $w[i\dots i-1] = \varepsilon$.

If $w = a_1 a_2 \ldots a_n$ is a finite word of Σ, then the word $a_n a_{n-1} \ldots a_1$ is called a *mirror word* of w, denoted by $\overline{w}$. A finite word w that is identical to its mirror word is called a *palindrome word*. For example, the word `kayak` is a palindrome. In bioinformatics, we also introduce the problem of the *reverse complement*, that is, for a word w from the alphabet $\{A, C, G, T\}$, the word obtained by considering the mirror word of w and the substitution of the nucleotides by their complementary: $A \leftrightarrow T$ and $C \leftrightarrow G$. For example, the reverse complement of the word `AATGCC` is the word `GGCATT`. The reverse complement of a sequence would then correspond to the read of the other DNA strand (therefore in the opposite direction of reading). In this context, the palindrome will be defined with respect to the reverse complement rather than with respect to the mirror word. Reverse complements can play an important role when searching for patterns in a sequence whose orientation is not known a priori.

A *well-parenthesized word* from an alphabet containing the characters ' (' and ') ' is a word that can be defined by structural induction in the following way:

– words that do not contain parentheses are well parenthesized;

– if u is a well-parenthesized word, then (u) is a well-parenthesized word;

– if u and v are two well-parenthesized words, then uv is a well-parenthesized word.

When the alphabet does only contain parentheses, it is called *Dyck words*.

A *period* of a word w is an integer $0 < p \leq |w|$ such that for all $i \in \{1, \ldots, |w| - p\}$ $w[i] = w[i + p]$. The smallest period of w is denoted $period(w)$. For example, the periods of `aabaaabaa` (of length 9) are 4, 7, 8 and 9. An *edge* of the word w is a factor of w which is both a prefix and a suffix of w. Edge and period are dual notions, which are involved in the processing of repeated patterns. We can quote Crochemore et al. (2001) as a reference work in text algorithmics.

1.4. Graph theory

In this section, we define some notions and properties which have graph theory at their basis. Graphs have been introduced by the mathematician Leonhard Euler to solve the problem of Königsberg's bridges (Euler 1736).

Figure 1.1 briefly presents this problem. However, it should be noted that the graph presented in this figure is a loose interpretation compared with the historical truth. Graphs are relatively simple mathematical objects that can be used to model a large number of real-life problems. They enable, among other things, the modeling of binary relations between several entities: this can be relations between people (friends on social networks, kinship relations, etc.), machines in a network or classes in a program.

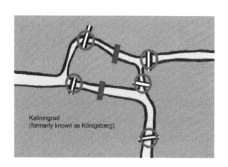 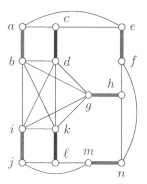

Figure 1.1. *The problem of the seven bridges of Königsberg. The problem consisted of finding a route for a stroll crossing each of the bridges only once and returning to the starting point. Left: schematic view of the city of Königsberg. The city is now called Kaliningrad and only five of the seven bridges remain today (circled in red) because two bridges were destroyed during World War II; their locations are drawn in blue. Right: a way to model the problem without using a multigraph. Each vertex represents one end of a bridge; the presence of an edge between two vertices indicates that there is a path between these two ends. The edges drawn in bold represent bridges. The vertex a is adjacent with the vertices b, c and e. Thereby, its neighborhood is denoted $N(a) = \{b, c, e\}$ and we have $deg(a) = 3$. For a color version of this figure, see www.iste.co.uk/chateau/graphs.zip*

Formally, a *graph* G is an object consisting of two sets: a set of *vertices*, denoted $V(G)$, and a set of *edges*, denoted $E(G)$, consisting of unordered pairs of vertices. These are then *undirected* graphs. *Directed* graphs are defined in a similar way, but the set of edges is then replaced by a set of *arcs* consisting of pairs of ordered vertices. We focus this presentation of graphs on the undirected case, but models using directed graphs are also frequently used.

The notation uv is used to designate an edge between the two vertices u and v, if both vertices are known. The set notation $\{u, v\}$ is also sometimes found in the literature. It is said that the vertices u and v are the *endpoints* of uv and that uv is *incident* to u and v. Two vertices u and v are *adjacent* or *neighbors* if there exists an edge incident to u and v. Similarly, two edges e_1 and e_2 are *adjacent* if they share an endpoint, namely, if $e_1 \cap e_2 \neq \emptyset$. For a vertex u, $N(u)$ denotes the set of the neighbors of u. The *degree* of a vertex u, denoted $deg(u)$, corresponds to the number of neighbors of u, in other words, $deg(u) = |N(u)|$. $\Delta(G)$ denotes the maximum degree of the vertices of graph G. The graph *order* is the number of vertices of the graph.

We present some definitions and properties of graph theory that will be used in this book. We refer the reader to more complete works such as Bondy and Murty (1985) and Diestel (2017).

1.4.1. *Subgraphs*

Let G be a graph. It is sometimes necessary to only consider some parts of the graph to define an algorithm or a property. For this, the notion of *subgraph* is introduced. A graph H is a subgraph of G if $V(H) \subseteq V(G)$ and $E(H) \subseteq E(G)$. In this case, it is said that G is a *supergraph* of H. There are two particular types of subgraphs:

– H is an *induced subgraph* if it is restricted to a subset of vertices. Formally, let $V' \subseteq V(G)$ be a set of vertices of G; it is said that H is induced by V' if $V(H) = V'$ and $E(H) = \{uv \mid uv \in E(G) \land uv \subseteq V(G)\}$. The subgraph of G induced by the vertices of V' can be denoted by $G[V']$;

– H is a *partial subgraph* of G if it contains all the vertices G (only some edges have been removed from the original graph).

Figure 1.2 gives examples of subgraphs.

Figure 1.2. *Illustration of the definition of subgraphs. Left: the original graph G. Center: a partial subgraph of G. Right: the subgraph of G induced by the set $\{a, b, d, e, f, h, i\}$*

1.4.2. *Path in a graph*

An n-*path* is a graph consisting of a sequence of consecutive edges such that $\Delta \leq 2$. In other words, a graph is a path if there exists an n-uplet $(u_1, \ldots, u_n)$ of unique vertices such that for any pair of integers (i, j) with $0 < i < j \leq n$, there exists an edge between u_i and u_j if and only if $j = i+1$. The two vertices u_1 and u_n are the *ends* of the path. Moreover, this n-uplet will be used to designate such a path. A *cycle* is a path in which an edge has been added between the two ends. A graph G is *connected* if for each pair of vertices (u, v), there exists a path with u and v as ends. Intuitively, this means that from a vertex u, all the other vertices of the graph can be reached by traveling through the edges. A *connected component* of a graph is a maximal induced connected subgraph. An edge e of a graph G is called a *bridge* if the partial subgraph including edges $E(G) \backslash \{e\}$ has one more connected component than G, in other words, if deleting e results in splitting a connected component in two. A similar notion for a vertex is the *articulation point*. A vertex v of a graph is an articulation point if the graph induced by the vertices $V(G) \backslash \{v\}$ contains one more connected component than G.

A graph such that all possible edges are present is called a *complete graph*. It should be noted that a *clique* is a maximal set of vertices such that the graph induced by this set is a complete graph. A *stable*, on the other hand, is a set of vertices of degree zero, otherwise called *isolated vertices*.

A *tree* is a connected graph for which there is no induced cycle; an example of a tree is given by the middle graph in Figure 1.2. It is possible to *root* a tree at one of its vertices, denoted r, and called the *root* of the tree. In this case, for any vertex u, the parent of u is its neighbor in the path having u and r as extremities. The children of a vertex u are the vertices having u as parent. Vertices with no children are called *leaves*. The *height* of a tree is the length of the longest path between the root and one of the leaves.

1.4.3. *Matching*

In a graph, a *matching* is a set of edges which share no vertices in common. A *perfect matching* of a graph G is a set of edges M^* such that the partial subgraph G' with $E(G') = M^*$ is a matching. In other words, for each vertex

u of G, there exists exactly one edge incident to u in M^*. Therefore, in G', each vertex u possesses exactly one neighbor, which is denoted $M^*(u)$. It is said that u is *matched* with $M^*(u)$. Given a matching of G, an *alternating element* is a path or cycle $(u_1, \ldots, u_n)$ of G where n is even such that all for $i < n$ odd, $M^*(u_i) = u_{i+1}$. More specifically, the terms *alternating path* or *alternating cycle* can be used. As an example, we can observe Figure 1.1: the edges representing the bridges form a matching and in order to solve the problem raised by Euler, it is necessary to find an alternating cycle containing all the matching edges. In this example, there is no such cycle. A *walk* in a graph is a sequence of consecutive edges which, unlike a path or a cycle, can "cross" the same vertex or the same edge several times. Similarly, a walk can be defined by exhibiting an n-uplet $(u_1, \ldots, u_n)$ of vertices, not necessarily unique, such that for any $i < n$, the vertices u_i and u_{i+1} are neighbors. A walk is said to be *open* if $u_1 \neq u_n$ and *closed* otherwise. Similarly, a walk is *alternating* if n is even and for any odd $i < n$, the edge $u_i u_{i+1}$ belongs to the matching. Coming back to our example of the Königsberg bridges, a walk can be found traversing all the bridges if crossing the same bridge several times is allowed. The solution will then consist of a closed alternating walk. The number of edges constituting a walk, a path or a cycle is called *length* of this object (it will be assumed that the length is finite).

1.4.4. *Planarity*

A graph is *planar* if it is possible to draw it in a plane without its edges crossing one another. In the classes of graphs we presented earlier, paths, cycles and trees are planar graphs. Conversely, complete graphs are most of the time not planar. A graph G is said to be *dense* if its number of edges is close to that of the complete graph with $|V(G)|$ vertices. Planar graphs are generally considered to be sparse graphs. The graph is said to be *outerplanar* if it is planar and can be drawn in the plane without crossing any of its edges, such that all vertices belong to the outer face of the graph, in other words, such that no vertices are surrounded by edges. It can be shown that a graph G is outerplanar if and only if the graph formed by adding to G a new vertex and all the edges connecting it to the vertices of G is a planar graph. An example can be seen in Figure 1.3.

Figure 1.3. *Planarity in graphs: the left graph is non-planar (it is the complete graph with five vertices K_5), the middle one is planar but not outerplanar (the light red vertex is not on the outer face of the graph) and the right graph is outerplanar. For a color version of this figure, see www.iste.co.uk/chateau/graphs.zip*

Planar and outerplanar graphs are special classes of graphs in which difficult problems in the general case can fall into another complexity class when restricted to these classes of graphs.

1.4.5. *Tree decomposition*

A widely used tool for solving problems with graphs is *tree decomposition*. This tool was discovered independently by several authors. It was especially popularized by Neil Robertson and Paul Seymour in their work on graph minors (Robertson and Seymour 1986). Its definition is as follows:

DEFINITION 1.1 (Tree decomposition).– *Let G be a graph. A tree-decomposition of G is a tree T presenting the following properties:*

– each vertex $B \in V(T)$ of T is a subset of $V(G)$. The vertices of T are called bags*;*

– for each edge uv of G, there exists a bag B such that $uv \subseteq G(B)$;

– for each vertex u of G, the subgraph induced by the bags containing u is connected.

The width *of T, denoted $w(T)$, is equal to the cardinality of the smallest bag of $V(T)$. Let T_{min} be a tree decomposition of G such that its width be minimum. The* tree width *G, denoted $tw(G)$, is equal to $w(T) - 1$.*

The tree width is a means to see how close a connected graph is to a tree: as matter of fact, a graph is a tree if and only if its tree width is equal to one. An interesting property of a tree decomposition T of a connected graph G is that each bag B is a *separator*: if we remove the vertices of B in G, then the graph is no longer connected, that is, $G[V(G) \setminus B]$ has two connected components. As an example, we can refer to Figure 1.7.

1.5. Algorithmic problems

1.5.1. *Definition*

A *problem* is a central notion in the field of fundamental computer science. It is a question depending on a certain number of parameters which must be answered. A distinction is made between two main types of problems: *decision problems* for which it will be necessary to answer YES or NO and *optimization problems* for which it will be necessary to find a "better" solution, with respect to one or more parameters. The parameters of a problem can take several possible values which determines a certain number of potential entries for the problem, which are then called *instances*. Solving an instance of a problem will consist of answering the problem question for that instance. As an example, we can revisit the Königsberg bridge problem. Euler wanted to know if there was a stroll traversing all the bridges; this is therefore a decision problem. This problem can be generalized and formulated as follows:

Problem 1.1. Bridge stroll

Input: A graph G equipped with a perfect matching M^*.
Question: Is there an alternating cycle containing all the edges of the matching?

The graph in Figure 1.1 is an instance of this problem and the answer for this instance is NO. This is then referred to as a *negative instance*. For instances where the answer is YES, it is called a *positive instance*. If we wish to make a stroll that goes through as many bridges as possible without crossing twice through the same bridge, an optimization problem can be formulated.

Problem 1.2. Maximum bridge stroll

Input: A graph G with a perfect matching M^*.
Output: An alternating path of maximum length.

The criterion to be optimized here is the length of the alternating path, which we seek to maximize. This is thus known as a maximization problem. A minimization problem could be formulated in the same way, in which an alternating path containing all the matching edges minimizing its length would have to be found.

The term *solution* takes on different meanings depending on the type of problem. For a decision problem, the object making it possible to answer favorably to the question will be the main focus. For Problem 1.1 (BRIDGE STROLL), the point will be to identify an alternating cycle of length $2|M^*|$. This is actually a misnomer; complexity textbooks rather referred to it as a *certificate*. For an optimization problem, the goal is the object answering the problem but not necessarily optimizing the desired criterion. For Problem 1.2 (MAXIMUM BRIDGE STROLL), any alternating cycle is a solution. For the solution that optimizes the desired criterion, this will be referred to as *optimal solution*. It should be noted that it is always possible to "transform" an optimization problem into a decision problem by allowing a maximum or minimum value on the criterion to be optimized. For example, Problem 1.2 can be transformed (MAXIMUM BRIDGE STROLL) as follows:

Problem 1.3. k-Maximum bridge stroll

Input: A graph G with a perfect matching M^* and an integer k.
Question: Is there an existing alternating path of length at least k?

This is then called the *associated decision problem* with the optimization problem. It is easy to see that we know how to find an optimal solution to an optimization problem if and only if a solution to the associated decision problem can be found for any value of k.

In the following two sections, we present classical problems in theoretical computer science.

1.5.2. *Graph problem*

We present here classical optimization problems on graphs. Let G be a graph; a *cover* $V' \subseteq V(G)$ of G is a set of vertices such that $\forall uv \in E(G), uv \cap V' \neq \emptyset$, in other words, such that each edge of G is incident to at least one vertex of V'. For any set of vertices V', it is said that the edge uv is *covered* by V' if either u or v belongs to V'. Finding the smallest cover in a graph is a classical problem which can be formulated as follows:

Problem 1.4. VERTEX COVER

Input: A graph G.
Output: A minimum size cover V'.

It should be noted that, given a cover V' of a graph G, the vertices of G not belonging to this cover induce a stable. Similarly, for any set of vertices I of G, inducing a stable, the vertices of G not belonging to I form a cover. A set of vertices inducing a stable is called an *independent set*. The following problem can be formulated.

Problem 1.5. INDEPENDENT SET

Input: A graph G.
Output: A maximum size-independent set V'.

Figure 1.4 shows an example of cover and independent set.

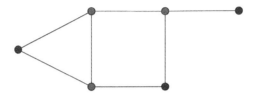

Figure 1.4. *Example of the complementarity of a cover and of an independent set. The red-colored vertices form a cover, while the blue-colored vertices form an independent set. For a color version of this figure, see www.iste.co.uk/chateau/ graphs.zip*

For the following problem, we use a *directed graph*. For a vertex u of a directed graph, an arc of the form (v, u) is an *incoming arc* and an arc of the form (u, v) is an *outgoing arc*. The set of arcs of a directed graph is denoted by $A(G)$. We should bear in mind that for two vertices u and v, it is possible that both the arc (u, v) and the arc (v, u) exist. When indicating a path or a cycle $(u_1, \ldots, u_k)$ in a directed graph, it must respect the orientation of the arcs: that is, for two consecutive vertices u_i and u_{i+1}, the arc (u_i, u_{i+1}) must exist in the graph.

Given a directed graph, one of the problems in graph theory consist in finding a path or cycle through all vertices.

Problem 1.6. Directed Hamiltonian path (respectively cycle)

Input: A directed graph G.
Output: A path (respectively cycle) containing all of the vertices of G.

Finally, the last problem on graphs that we introduce is the TRAVELING SALESMAN (Problem 1.7), which originally is not a graph problem. In this problem, a traveler must visit a set of cities and return to his starting point while minimizing the total time needed to complete the journey. We can model this problem using a complete directed graph G where each vertex represents a city. To represent the distance, we use a cost function $c : E(G) \to \mathbb{N}$ returning the time used when traveling the edge between two vertices. The path is modeled using a cycle $C = (u_1, \ldots, u_n)$ (with $u_1 = u_n$) and the cycle cost corresponds to the value $\sum_{i<n} c(u_i, u_{i+1})$.

Problem 1.7. Traveling salesman

Input: A complete graph G and a cost function $c : E(G) \mapsto \mathbb{N}$.
Output: A cycle containing all vertices of G, such that the cost of C is minimized.

1.5.3. *Satisfiability problems*

The second type of problem we may encounter when addressing complexity is that of satisfiability problems. This type of problem involves propositional formulas. A *Boolean variable* is a variable that can be assigned either the value TRUE or the value FALSE. A *literal* is a proposition that is either equal to a Boolean variable or equal to the negation of a Boolean variable. A *clause* is a disjunction of literals, for instance, given three Boolean variables x_1, x_2 and x_3; the predicate $x_1 \lor \neg x_2 \lor x_3$ is a clause involving the three literals $x_1, \neg x_2$ and x_3. A *Boolean formula* in *conjunctive normal* form is a propositional formula composed of conjunctions of clauses. Thereby, the formula $\varphi = (x_1 \lor x_2) \land (\neg x_2 \lor \neg x_3) \land (\neg x_1 \lor \neg x_3)$ is a Boolean formula composed of the three clauses $C_1 = x_1 \lor x_2, C_2 = \neg x_2 \lor x_3$ and $C_3 = x_1 \lor \neg x_3$. A β assignment of the variables φ is an assignment of values TRUE or FALSE to each of the Boolean variables that compose the formula. The value assigned to the variable x_i in β is denoted by $\beta(x_i)$. The formula φ is *satisfiable* if there is an assignment which satisfies φ and *unsatisfiable* otherwise. Knowing whether or not a formula is satisfiable is a very important problem in theorical computer science. It can be formulated as follows:

Problem 1.8. Satisfiability

Input: A Boolean formula φ in conjunctive normal form.
Question: Is φ satisfiable?

The SATISFIABILITY problem has been extensively studied and many variants exist for which constraints are given on the instances. For unsatisfiable formulas, it may be interesting to find an assignment that maximizes the number of satisfied clauses. As such, the following optimization problem can be formulated.

Problem 1.9. Maximum satisfiability

Input: A Boolean formula in conjunctive normal form φ.
Output: An assignment β of the variables of φ such that the number of clauses satisfied by β is maximum.

1.6. Problem solutions

1.6.1. *Algorithm*

To find a solution to a problem, we make use of an *algorithm*. An algorithm is simply a finite sequence of instructions that are not ambiguous, in other words, that do not require the reader's interpretation. An algorithm generally requires an input and returns an output that answers the desired problem. Some storage space is required to perform intermediate computations. This storage space appears in the form of variables for which values can be assigned. There are several ways to write algorithms. For example, for an algorithm meant to be executed by an operating system, a programming language will be used (C, C++, Java, etc.). Here, we use a language called *pseudo-code* which is a language close to natural language.

As an example, an algorithm answering Problem 1.1 (BRIDGE STROLL) can be built. For an instance from a real example, it can be assumed that for every vertex u, the vertices in $N^*(u) \cup \{u\}$ form a clique (because all the endpoints of the bridges are located on the same island). We will call such a graph a *realistic bridge graph*. For a realistic graph of bridges, the BRIDGE STROLL problem can be answered by running the following algorithm:

We will not formally prove the correctness of this algorithm, but the general idea is that every time we enter an island, we must be able to leave it, and as such the number of bridges on each island must be even (and so the neighborhood of each bridge endpoint must be odd).

Let A be an algorithm. Since an algorithm takes as input an instance and gives a solution on output, it can be seen as a function. The same notation can be used: thus, $A(I)$ will designate the solution returned by the algorithm A for the instance I. Similarly, it will be said that an application $f : D \mapsto S$ is *computable* if there exists an algorithm A such that $\forall I \in D, f(I) = A(I)$.

ALGORITHM 1.1. Algorithm answering to BRIDGE STROLL for realistic instances.

Input: A realistic graph of G bridges
Output: TRUE if G is a positive instance of BRIDGE STROLL, FALSE otherwise.

1 **For all** $u \in V(G)$ **do**
2   **If** $|N^*(u)|$ *is pair* **then**
3   **return** FALSE

4 **return** TRUE

1.6.2. *Complexity*

There are several criteria for evaluating the performance of an algorithm: average execution speed, worst-case execution speed, memory requirements, possibility of parallelization and so on. Most often, algorithmic performance is measured according to the criterion of execution speed in the worst-case scenario. This depends in part on the hardware being used. Therefore, in order not to be overwhelmed by technological considerations, it proves more relevant to look at the number of elementary operations to be performed as a function of the input size: this is known as *time complexity*.

To agree upon the number of elementary operations of an algorithm, we take the number of steps necessary for executing when the algorithm is simulated on a *Turing machine*. A Turing machine is a theoretical object that enables following algorithmic procedures. It is composed of a tape of infinite size, broken down into squares in which symbols are inscribed. A read/write head is placed on this tape. It also contains a state register for memorizing the state of the machine and an action table, which according to the state of the machine and the symbol read by the head, indicates which symbol is to be written in the current square, the new state of the machine as well as the direction in which the head must move. There are several definitions for a Turing machine; the following definition described in Lewis and Papadimitriou (1981) can, for example, be given.

A *deterministic Turing machine* is defined by the 5-tuple $(Q, \Gamma, q_0, \delta, F)$ where:

- Q is a finite set of states;

- Γ is a set of possible symbols for the squares of the tape, including a white symbol \$;

- $q_i \in Q$ is the initial state of the machine;

- $\delta : Q \times \Gamma \mapsto Q \times \Gamma \times \{\leftarrow, \rightarrow\}$ is the transition function;

- $F \subseteq Q$ is the set of terminal states.

Operating a Turing machine means that the transition function is successively applied until the machine reaches a terminal state. The transition function is applied as follows. We assume that a Turing machine T is in a state q_i, that the read head is located at the square c_x containing the symbol S_1 and that $\delta(q_i, S_1) = (q_j, S_2, \rightarrow)$. When we say that the transition function is applied it means that the state q_j is registered in the state register, the symbol S_2 is written into the square c_x and finally, the read head is moved to the square c_{x+1}. The number of steps before reaching a terminal state is simply the number of times the transition function is applied. We should note that there are also *non-deterministic* Turing machines for which the transition function is not a function: in this case, for a state q_i and a symbol S_j, there are several existing possibilities for the transition function and the machine will have to make a choice among these transitions.

As an example, consider the following Turing machine $T = (Q, \Gamma, q_0, \delta, F)$. This one reads a binary word (i.e. from the alphabet $\{0, 1\}$) and indicates if it is alternately composed of 1 and 0. It is composed of an initial state q_i and two final states q_{true} and q_{false}, which indicate if the word verifies the property or not, respectively. Two intermediate states q_0 and q_1 will also be used which indicate whether the last read symbol is a 0 or a 1, respectively. The transition function δ is given in the following table.

	q_i			q_0			q_1		
	Q	Γ	direction	Q	Γ	direction	Q	Γ	direction
\$	q_{true}	$-$	$-$	q_{true}	$-$	$-$	q_{true}	$-$	$-$
0	q_0	0	$\rightarrow$	q_{false}	$-$	$-$	q_0	0	$\rightarrow$
1	q_1	1	$\rightarrow$	q_1	1	$\rightarrow$	q_{false}	$-$	$-$

As soon as the machine reads two consecutive identical symbols, it goes into the final state q_{false} because the property is not verified. Otherwise, if it reaches a white symbol, it means that it has not come across two consecutive identical symbols and therefore that the property holds for this word. An example of how this machine works is illustrated in Figure 1.5.

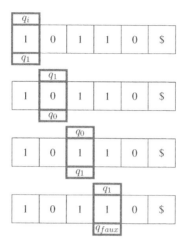

Figure 1.5. *Example of the functioning of the Turing machine given as an example with the word* 10110. *The head is symbolized by the red rectangle. The state above the head is the current state of the machine and the state below the head is the state returned by the transition function. For a color version of this figure, see www.iste.co.uk/chateau/graphs.zip*

Naturally, the algorithms presented here will not be described by a Turing machine. It may therefore be difficult to know exactly how many elementary operations are necessary for their execution. To mitigate this problem, we use the Landau notation $\mathcal{O}$ to get the time complexity of an algorithm. This notation is defined as follows:

Let $f : \mathbb{N} \to \mathbb{N}$ and $g : \mathbb{N} \to \mathbb{N}$ denote two functions. It is said that f is *bounded* by g if there exist two constants K and N such that:

$$\forall n > N, f(n) < K \cdot g(n).$$

To indicate that f is bounded by g, the notation $f = \mathcal{O}(g)$ will be used. This notation is used to describe the general appearance of a function. To designate the time complexity, the smallest function bounding the number of elementary operations during execution will be given. An example can be given, by calculating the complexity of Algorithm 1.1. It can be assumed that the set $N^*(u)$ is provided with the input for each vertex u. In the worst case, we have to travel every vertex to execute the instruction at line 2, which makes a total of $|V(G)|$ instructions. We thus have a time complexity of $\mathcal{O}(|V(G)|)$. To simplify, it will be said that an algorithm is polynomial (respectively, exponential, factorial, etc.) if its time complexity is polynomial (respectively, exponential, factorial, etc.).

Another Landau notation that can be used is the o notation.

Let two functions be $f : \mathbb{N} \mapsto \mathbb{R}^+$ and $g : \mathbb{N} \mapsto \mathbb{R}^+$; f is said to be *dominated* by g if for any constant C, there exists a constant N such that for any

$$n > N, \frac{f(n)}{g(n)} < C$$

In other words, the quotient of f by g tends to zero when n tends to infinity. To indicate that f is dominated by g, the notation $f = o(g)$ will be used.

Finally, the notation Θ is used to indicate a complexity that is upper bounded, as well as lower bounded, by the indicated function, up to a constant. Thereby, if $f = \Theta(g)$, where f and g are two $\mathbb{N} \rightarrow \mathbb{N}$, then f is bounded by g and g is bounded by f.

1.6.3. *Runtime*

In terms of operation use, it is important to get the best possible time complexity. Let us take for example Problem 1.4 (VERTEX COVER). A somewhat naive algorithm can be formulated which consists of looking at all possible subsets of vertices of the graph and of selecting the minimum cover among them. This algorithm is called *brute force algorithm* and can be adapted to solve any problem. It is described by Algorithm 1.2.

The complexity of this algorithm is equal to $\mathcal{O}(2^{|V(G)|})$. Let us consider a practical point of view and assume that this algorithm is implemented on a system that can perform an instruction every 10 nanoseconds. If it takes less than a second to find a minimum solution in a graph with less than

30 vertices, it will take about 36 years to find a minimum solution in a graph with 60 vertices and more than 10^5 billion years in a graph with 100 vertices. In comparison, the age of the universe is estimated to be about 13.8 billion years (Planck Collaboration et al. 2018). This kind of algorithm is therefore not usable when the size of the instances becomes too large. Table 1.1 gives orders of magnitude of runtimes for different time complexities. It can be seen that only polynomial complexities are usable in practice when the size of the input becomes important.

ALGORITHM 1.2. brute-force algorithm for VERTEX COVER

Input: A graph G

Output: A cover $V' \subseteq V(G)$ of the vertices of G of minimum size

1 $V' \leftarrow V(G)$

2 **For all** $V'' \in \mathcal{P}(V(G))$ **do**

3   **If** $|V''| < |V'|$ *and* V'' *is a vertex cover of* G **then**

4          $V' \leftarrow V''$

5 **return** V'

Complexity time	Adjective	Runtime according to n				
		$n = 10$	$n = 30$	$n = 50$	$n = 100$	$n = 10^6$
$\mathcal{O}(1)$	Constant	10ns	10ns	10ns	10ns	10ns
$\mathcal{O}(\log n)$	Logarithmic	10ns	14ns	17ns	20ns	80ns
$\mathcal{O}(n)$	Linear	100ns	300ns	500ns	1µs	10s
$\mathcal{O}(n^2)$	Quadratic	1µs	9µs	25µs	100µs	116 days
$\mathcal{O}(n^3)$	Cubic	10µs	270µs	1.25ms	10ms	$10^5 y$
$\mathcal{O}(n^7)$		100ms	218s	2 hours	11 days	10^{20}By
$\mathcal{O}(2^n)$	Exponential	10µs	10s	130 days	10^5By	–
$\mathcal{O}(n!)$	Factorial	36ms	10^7By	10^{39}By	10^{133}By	–

Time units: nanoseconds (ns), milliseconds (ms), seconds (s), hours, days, year (y) or billion years (By).

Table 1.1. *Runtime comparison for polynomial (green, the first six lines) and exponential or factorial (red) time complexities. It is assumed that the machine running the algorithms can perform an elementary instruction every 10 nanoseconds. For a color version of this figure, see www.iste.co.uk/chateau/graphs.zip*

1.7. Complexity classes

Problems that share common properties in their resolution will be grouped in the form of sets called *complexity classes*. These classes are used to characterize the intrinsic difficulty of algorithmic problems. The focus will be on classes using two types of algorithms: exact algorithms and approximate algorithms. Here again, we will not carry out an exhaustive presentation of the theory of complexity; readers will be able to deepen their knowledge of this theory by consulting a book such as Garey and Johnson (1990).

Exact algorithms are algorithms capable of answering decision problems or of providing an optimal solution to optimization problems. The membership of a problem to a complexity class taking into consideration exact algorithms will take as a criterion the time complexity of the exact algorithms leading to the solution of this problem.

Approximation algorithms are algorithms that lead to a solution which is not necessarily optimal but that hopefully will be close to an optimal solution. The term "approximation algorithm" tends to be reserved for algorithms for which there is a guarantee of the performance on the solution score. For algorithms that do not have such guarantees, *heuristics* will rather be employed. It is usually required that most approximation algorithms exhibit polynomial time complexity. The membership of a problem to a complexity class considering such approximation algorithms will depend on the performance guarantee on the approximation solutions returned by these algorithms.

It should be noted that there are complexity classes that take into account other criteria, such as memory space complexity. In the following, the term "complexity" used on its own will always refer to time complexity. The rest of this section is devoted to the presentation of a few complexity classes. To this end, general definitions that may imply abstract Π problems will be employed. The Σ_Π notation designates the set of instances for the Π problem and for an instance $I \in \Sigma_\Pi$, $|I|$ denotes the size of I.

1.7.1. *Generality*

Complexity classes group problems according to the difficulty of solving them while satisfying a certain property τ. This property can correspond to the minimum number of operations required, the minimum memory space required or the distance of the solutions provided from an optimal solution and so on. *Reductions* are functions that enable demonstrating that a problem is more difficult than another according to this property. In a very general way, they usually take the following form:

Let Π_1 and Π_2 be two problems and a property τ. Π_1 is reducible to Π_2 while preserving the property τ if there exists a function $f : \Sigma_{\Pi_1} \mapsto \Sigma_{\Pi_2}$ such that for any instance $I \in \Sigma_{Pi_1}$, if $f(I)$ is solvable while satisfying the property τ, then I is solvable satisfying τ.

The principle of a reduction is thus to build an instance of Π_2 for each instance of Π_1. If it is possible to manage the computation of a solution in the instance of Π_2 created by preserving the property τ, then we also manage to do it in the instance of Π_1. The underlying idea is that, if we know (or suspect) that Π_1 cannot be solved satisfying τ, then the solution of the instances of Π_2 cannot be achieved satisfying τ either.

For example, the notation can be used to indicate that Π_1 is reduced to Π_2 while preserving the property τ. A reduction can be seen as a relation between problems. This relation is *reflexive*, that is, for a problem Π, we have $\Pi \preccurlyeq_\tau \Pi$. This relation is also *transitive*: if there are three problems Π_1, Π_2 and Π_3 such that $\Pi_1 \preccurlyeq_\tau \Pi_2 \wedge \Pi_2 \preccurlyeq_\tau \Pi_3$ then we have $\Pi_1 \preccurlyeq_\tau \Pi_3$. This makes it possible to establish a *partial preorder* between the problems. This is a preorder and not an order because for two problems Π_1 and Π_2, it is possible to have $\Pi_1 \preccurlyeq_\tau \Pi_2 \wedge \Pi_2 \preccurlyeq_\tau \Pi_1$. In other words, the two problems are equally difficult according to the property τ. This preorder is "partial" because two problems are not always comparable according to this relation.

By taking this partial preorder, for a class of complexity C, we can designate the set of problems of C which are the most difficult according to the property τ.

Let C be a complexity class. A problem Π is C-*complete* (for the reduction $\preccurlyeq_\tau$) if

  – $\Pi \in C$;
  – for any problem $\Pi' \in C$, $\Pi' \preccurlyeq_\tau \Pi$.

To show that a problem is C-complete, it is not necessary to construct a reduction from all problems of C. Since a reduction is a transitive relation, it is actually sufficient to construct a reduction from a single C-complete problem.

PROPERTY 1.1.– *Let C be a complexity class. A problem Π is C*-complete *(for the reduction $\preccurlyeq_\tau$) if*

  – $\Pi \in C$;

  – *there exists a C-complete problem Π' such that $\Pi' \preccurlyeq_\tau \Pi$.*

However, we must know a C-complete problem before using this property. The set of C-problems that are at least as hard as any C-problem can also be referred to.

Let C be a complexity class. A problem Π is a C-*hard* (for the reduction $\preccurlyeq_\tau$) if for any problem $\Pi' \in C, \Pi' \preccurlyeq_\tau \Pi$.

The difference with C-complete problems is that membership to the C-class is not mandatory. Similarly as for C-complete problems, in order to show that a problem is C-hard, we simply have to make a reduction from a single C-hard problem.

PROPERTY 1.2.– *Let C be a complexity class. A problem Π is C-hard (for the reduction $\preccurlyeq_\tau$) if there exists a C-hard problem Π' such that $\Pi' \preccurlyeq_\tau \Pi$.*

The notions of completeness and hardness are interesting when they are defined around a set of classes called *hierarchy*. A hierarchy is a set of classes of complexity $C_1, \ldots, C_n$ such that

$$C_1 \subseteq C_2 \subseteq \cdots \subseteq C_n.$$

For a class C_i of this hierarchy, the reduction used to define C_i-complete and C_i-hard problems preserves the membership to the complexity class C_{i-1}. In other words, such a reduction ensures that if a problem Π_1 is reduced to a problem Π_2, then if Π_2 belongs to C_{i-1}, Π_1 also belongs to C_{i-1}. Thereby, if the classes C_{i-1} and C_i are different, no C_i-complete problem belongs to C_{i-1}.

In the following sections, we now address concrete examples of complexity class hierarchies that involve the concepts we have just defined.

1.7.2. *Exact algorithms*

For exact algorithms, the problems will be grouped into classes according to the minimum complexity needed to solve them.

1.7.2.1. *Classes P and NP*

Complexity classes P (for *polynomial*) and NP (for *non-deterministic polynomial*) are classes of problems containing decision problems. For the complexity class P, the definition is the following: The decision problem Π belongs to the class P if and only if there exists a polynomial algorithm that can address Π.

Typically P contains problems that can be solved with an algorithm having complexity $\mathcal{O}(n^k)$, where n is the input size and k is a constant. More specifically, we will refer to a constant complexity if $k = 0$, with a linear complexity if $k = 1$ and a quadratic complexity if $k = 2$. We should note that the complexity can also involve a logarithmic function of the input size. From a practical point of view, these are the problems that are solvable in human time. For this reason, these problems will be considered as being "easy". To show that a problem belongs to this class, it is simply enough to exhibit an algorithm. Therefore, Problem 1.1 (BRIDGE STROLL) belongs to P if only realistic bridge graphs are taken into account. Sorting algorithms capable of ordering a list of n elements and which present a complexity of $\mathcal{O}(n \log n)$ should also be introduced.

To define the class NP, we ought to first revisit the notion of certificate. Let us recall that a certificate is a string used to prove that an instance is positive. For a problem Π and an instance $I \in \Sigma_\Pi$, $sol_\Pi(I)$ denotes the set of certificates for I ($sol_\Pi = \emptyset$ if I is a negative instance). The definition of the class NP involves the notion of certificate. The decision problem Π belongs to the class NP if and only if there exists a polynomial algorithm that leads to determining for any instance $I \in \Sigma_\Pi$ and for any input E if $E \in sol_\Pi(I)$.

For example, SATISFIABILITY problems (Problem 1.8) belong to NP: a certificate is simply an assignment of the variables composing the Boolean formula. To verify that the assignment satisfies this Boolean formula, we have simply to check each clause and to verify if at least one of its literals is satisfied by β. This verification is done in linear time and thus SATISFIABILITY indeed belongs to NP. Another definition of the class NP is that the problems included in it can be solved in polynomial time using a non-deterministic Turing machine. In other words, a problem can be solved in NP by making a polynomial number of random choices.

In an obvious way, it can be seen that all the problems belonging to P also belong to NP, and thus P $\subseteq$ NP. On the other hand, it is not known if all the problems belonging to NP belong to P. This hypothesis formulated by Stephen Cook (1971) remains an open question today.

HYPOTHESIS 1.1.– $P \neq NP$

This is a fundamental question in computer science. If Hypothesis 1.1 does not hold, it implies that verifying a solution is as easy as producing a solution which satisfies a problem. The scientific consensus centered on this question admits that this hypothesis is true.

1.7.2.2. *Completeness and hardness of the class NP*

Regarding the completeness and hardness of the class NP, the possibility of solving in polynomial time will be taken into account. Therefore, a problem Π_2 is harder than another problem Π_1 if the existence of a polynomial algorithm for Π_2 implies the existence of a polynomial algorithm for Π_1. If it is suspected that the hypothesis P $\neq$ NP is true, it is because there are a certain number of problems in NP for which no polynomial algorithms able to solve them has be found, and for which it seems that there are none (although this is not proven, otherwise the question would no longer be open). Under this assumption, NP-hard problems cannot be solved in polynomial time. To show that a problem is at least as hard as another one, a *polynomial reduction* is used, also called Karp reduction: Let Π_1 and Π_2 be two decision problems. Problem i_1 is polynomially *reducible* to Π_2 if there exists a function $f : \Sigma_{\Pi_1} \mapsto \Sigma_{\Pi_2}$ such that for any instance $I \in \Sigma_{\Pi_1}$:

– $f(I)$ is computable in polynomial time;

– $f(I)$ is a positive instance of Π_2 if and only if I is a positive instance of Π_1.

To indicate that Π_1 is polynomially reducible to Π_2, the notation $\Pi_1 \preccurlyeq \Pi_2$ will be used.

Based on this reduction, the classes of NP-complete and NP-hard problems can be defined. Historically, the first problem to have been shown to be NP-complete is the SATISFIABILITY problem (Cook 1971).

For NP-hard problems, optimization problems can also be added. It will be first necessary to adapt the previous definition: therefore Π_1 and Π_2 can designate optimization problems and polynomial reduction will be achieved by taking into account their associated decision problems.

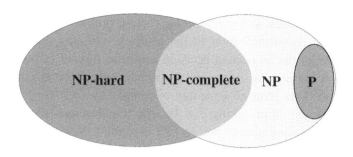

Figure 1.6. *Venn diagram illustrating inclusions of complexity classes. For a color version of this figure, see www.iste.co.uk/chateau/graphs.zip*

Just for informational purposes, it is worth noting that there are problems which are a priori neither in P, nor NP-complete. This has been shown by Ladner (1975) under the hypothesis P $\neq$ NP. Such problems are called NP-*intermediate* problems. Figure 1.6 shows the inclusions of the different classes presented so far if considering that P $\neq$ NP.

1.7.2.3. *Parameterized complexity*

When a problem does not belong to the class P, it is necessary to use an algorithm of at least exponential complexity to solve it exactly. However, as seen previously in Table 1.1, if the complexity of an algorithm is exponential or factorial in the size of the instance given as input, it will not be possible to make use of this algorithm with large instances. Other methods must therefore be found to solve NP-hard problems.

One of them is *parameterized complexity*. With this type of approach, an attempt is made to build an algorithm for which the exponential factor will not depend on the size of the instance but on a parameter that hopefully will be small. A *parameterized problem* (Π, κ) is a pair composed of a problem Π and a computable function $\kappa : \Sigma_\Pi \mapsto \mathbb{N}$ called *parameter* of Π. The complexity class FPT (for *fixed-parameter tractable*) is a class defined on parametrized problems. The parameterized problem (Π, κ) belongs to the class FPT if and only if there exists a function $f : \mathbb{N} \mapsto \mathbb{N}$ such that Π can be solved by an algorithm of complexity $\mathcal{O}(f(\kappa(I)) \cdot |I|^{o(c)})$, where $I \in \Sigma_\Pi$ is the instance given as input to the problem. Such an algorithm is called an FPT algorithm. It can be noted that if the parameter is constant, then the problem can be solved in polynomial time. This parameter can be either structural to the problem or structural to the given input instance.

Let us illustrate this with the VERTEX COVER problem. If we are looking for a structural parameterization to the problem, we may look at the size k of the cover in the associated decision problem. Instead of looking at all the subsets of vertices as in the raw algorithm, only those of cardinality k are considered. This gives an algorithm of complexity $\mathcal{O}(|V(G)|^k)$, which is indeed an FPT algorithm (taking $c = 0$). The tree decomposition is a rather conventional technique used to find an FPT algorithm. Nevertheless, it should be noted that computing a minimum width tree decomposition is an NP-hard problem.

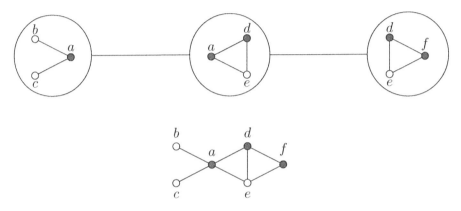

Figure 1.7. *Illustration of the solution of* VERTEX COVER *based on a tree decomposition. The covers (not necessarily minima) can be computed in the induced graphs for each of the decomposition bags and then we can consider all possible unions and select the minimum cover among these unions*

1.7.3. *Approximation algorithms*

1.7.3.1. *Classes PTAS and APX*

Another approach to solve NP-hard problems is to build approximation algorithms. As mentioned previously, an approximation algorithm is an algorithm which returns a good solution but which is not necessarily optimal. For an instance I of a problem Π and a solution x for the instance I, $val(x)$ denotes the value of the criterion to be optimized in the solution x and $OPT(I)$ the value of this criterion in an optimal solution for the instance I. It is assumed that for any solution x, $val(x) \geq 0$. To measure the performance of an approximation algorithm, the distance between the value of the solution that the latter returns and an optimal worst-case solution is examined. Let A

be an algorithm designed to compute a solution for an optimization problem Π. The application $\rho : \Sigma_\Pi \to [1; +\infty[$ is an approximation factor of A if

$$\forall I \in \Sigma_\Pi, max \left\{ \frac{OPT(I)}{val(A(I))}; \frac{val(A(I))}{OPT(I)} \right\} \leq \rho(I) \cdot OPT(I).$$

In this case, it is said that A is a ρ-*approximation* algorithm.

The underlying idea behind this approximation factor is that the closer this factor is to one, the better the quality of the solution produced by the approximation algorithm. Approximation algorithms allow building in human time solutions for NP-hard problems. The approximation classes PTAS (for *polynomial-time approximation scheme*) and APX (for *approximation*) group problems according to the criterion of the possible approximation factors for these problems. Formally, the following definitions are used. Let Π be an optimization problem:

– Π belongs to the class PTAS if and only if for all $\epsilon > 0$, Π admits a polynomial approximation algorithm having a constant approximation factor equal to $1 + \epsilon$;

– Π belongs to the class APX if and only if Π admits a polynomial approximation algorithm having a polynomial approximation factor;

– Π belongs to the class log-APX if and only if Π admits a polynomial approximation algorithm having a logarithmic approximation factor;

– Π belongs to the class *poly*-APX if and only if Π admits a polynomial approximation algorithm having a polynomial approximation factor.

If a problem can be approximated with a certain approximation factor, then it can necessarily be approximated by a "worse" approximation algorithm. Consequently, the previous definition makes it possible to outline a hierarchy among these classes, namely PTAS $\subseteq$ APX $\subseteq$ log-APX $\subseteq$ *poly*-APX.

As an example, consider the following algorithm for Problem 1.4 (VERTEX COVER). It can be shown that this algorithm has a constant approximation factor.

THEOREM 1.1.– *Algorithm 1.3 is a 2-approximation algorithm for* VERTEX COVER.

ALGORITHM 1.3. Approximation algorithm for VERTEX COVER

Input: A graph G
Output: A cover $V' \subseteq V(G)$ of the vertices

1 $V' \leftarrow \emptyset$
2 **While** *there exists an edge uv such that $uv \cap V' = \emptyset$* **do**
3 $\quad \lfloor \quad V' \leftarrow V' \cup \{u, v\}$
4 **return** V'

PROOF.– Let V_{opt} be an optimal cover of the graph G. Let $u_i v_i$ be the edge considered at step i of the loop **While** of the algorithm. We necessarily have either $u_i \in V_{opt}$ or $v_i \in V_{opt}$, otherwise the edge $u_i v_i$ would not be covered by V_{opt}. Therefore, we can establish a correspondence between each pair of vertices added to V' at line 3 with a single vertex of V_{opt} and thus $|V'| \leq 2|V_{opt}|$. $\qquad \square$

This theorem suffices to show that VERTEX COVER belongs to the approximation class APX.

1.7.4. *Solvers*

This section is dedicated to the use of solvers. It consists of a method widely employed in the operations research community and its main objective is to solve NP-hard problems exactly. *Solvers* are programs designed to solve abstract problems. A large number of solvers are used to solve a mathematical problem called *integer linear programming* (ILP). This type of problem involves a set of integer variables, a set of constraints and a function (or several functions) to be optimized. These solvers have been optimized for several years in order to reduce their solving time as much as possible. For this purpose, they can use a number of strategies or even various heuristics in order to speed up the resolution of the instances. Thereby, these solvers can be used to try to solve instances of rather large sizes. It is relatively easy to build a reduction from a large number of problems into an ILP formulation. Therefore, one strategy for solving a new problem may be to create an ILP formulation for that problem and then to use a solver to solve that formulation and thus take advantage of all the optimization work done with the solver in question. SATISFIABILITY problems can be seen as special cases of ILP, and there are powerful existing SAT solvers used to solve decision problems.

For example, for the problem INDEPENDENT SET, the following formulation can be established. Let G be the graph given as input. For each vertex $v_i \in V(G)$, a binary variable x_i is introduced which takes the value 1 if the vertex v_i belongs to the independent set and the value 0 otherwise. For every edge $v_i v_j$, it is not possible by definition to have both vertices in the independent set and so as to prevent this the following constraint is introduced:

$$x_i + x_j \leq 1 \qquad\qquad [1.1]$$

Since it is desirable that the number of vertices in the independent set be maximized, the sum of the values of the variables x_i has to be maximized and thus the objective function to be optimized is the following one:

$$max \sum_{i \leq |V(G)|} x_i \qquad\qquad [1.2]$$

Not every modeling technique is the same in terms of runtime, and this may also depend on the solver employed.

1.8. Some algorithmic techniques

1.8.1. *Dynamic programming*

In this section, we present an algorithmic technique that is very often found in problem solving. It is called dynamic programming. This is a well-known technique to reduce the complexity of algorithms, particularly where it is assumed that the data that is computed in an iterative process depends only on the computations that are performed from the sub-problems input. The philosophy behind this technique is therefore to split the general problem into sub-problems and, by storing the result of the computations on the sub-problems in dynamic programming tables, to reuse this stored information instead of restarting the computation, when a more complex piece of data comes up.

Let us revisit the TRAVELING SALESMAN problem previously seen, in which its modeling is in the form of a search for a minimum cost Hamiltonian cycle in a complete graph. We saw that this problem is NP-complete, and that it is therefore illusory, under the hypothesis that $N \neq NP$, to look for an exact algorithm of polynomial complexity to solve it. A naive, but exact, algorithm would consist of enumerating all possible Hamiltonian cycles and searching among them for a cycle of minimum cost. Since there are $\frac{(n-1)!}{2}$ possible cycles within a complete graph of order n, the time complexity of this algorithm is $\Theta(n!)$.

By using dynamic programming, this complexity can be significantly reduced, to $O(n^2 2^n)$. Consider a complete graph G of order n, with a cost function $c : E(G) \to \mathbb{N}$. The vertices are numbered from 0 to $n-1$. A Hamiltonian cycle can be considered as starting with vertex 0.

The idea of the dynamic programming algorithm, due to Held and Karp (1962), is based on the decomposition of the problem into sub-problems. It is indeed observed that:

– a Hamiltonian cycle is composed of an edge $0i$, followed by a path going from i to 0 passing through each vertex of $V \setminus \{0, i\}$ exactly once. If this cycle is optimal, then it is the shortest path from i to 0 passing through every vertex of $V \setminus \{0, i\}$;

– given a vertex $i \in V$ and a set of vertices $S \subseteq V \setminus \{0, i\}$, we denote $d(i, S)$ the length of the shortest path going from i to 0 passing through every vertex of S exactly once;

– the subpath optimality property allows us to define $d(i, S)$ recursively:
   - if $S = \emptyset$, then $d(i, S) = c(i0)$,
   - if $S \neq \emptyset$, then $d(i, S) = \min_{j \in S}(c(ij) + d(j, S \setminus \{j\}))$;

– the length of the shortest Hamiltonian cycle is $d(0, V \setminus \{0\})$.

The solution of the TRAVELING SALESMAN problem is thus reduced to the computation of the function d, which involves many redundant recursive calls. To avoid calculating the value of d several times with the same parameters, these values are stored in a table, which is called *memoization*. In a more general way, the latter will then be referred to as a dynamic programming table. If D denotes the dynamic programming table storing the values of d, an algorithm can be defined, which answers the TRAVELING SALESMAN problem, by progressively filling this table D. We should note that the table has double entries: one entry for vertices, and one entry for the subsets of V. There are 2^n subsets of V, if V is of size n. The size of the table is thus exponential here.

ALGORITHM 1.4. Dynamic programming algorithm computing the minimum cost of a Hamiltonian path

---

Input: A complete graph $G = (V, E)$ of order n and its cost function c
Output: The minimum cost of a Hamiltonian cycle

1 **For all** $i \in V \setminus \{0\}$ **do**
2   **For** *every subset S of $V \setminus \{0, i\}$* **do**
3   **If** $S = \emptyset$ **then**
4              $D[i][S] \leftarrow c(i0)$
5   **otherwise**
6              $D[i][S] \leftarrow \infty$
7   **For** *every vertex $j \in S$* **do**
8   **If** $c(ij) + D[j][S \setminus \{j\}] < D[i][S]$ **then**
9                  $D[i][S] \leftarrow c(ij) + D[j][S \setminus \{j\}]$

10 **return** $D[0][V \setminus \{0\}]$

Algorithm 1.4 leads to computing the optimal cost, but does not give a Hamiltonian cycle having this cost. To extract the information that we are interested in here, the path that allowed us to reach this cost has to be found in the table. This is the *backtracking* procedure. This procedure takes on input the table filled by the dynamic programming algorithm, and will search for the entry $D[0][V \setminus \{0\}]$, for which vertex j the minimum cost has been reached. This will be the first vertex of the optimal cycle following vertex 0. The search will carry on for which vertex k has allowed reaching the value $D[j][V \setminus \{0, j\}]$ and so on. The table is thus scanned by "backtracking" computations. Algorithm 1.5 thus finds the sought for cycle.

We now study the time complexity of these algorithms: Algorithm 1.4 proposes three nested loops: the first one in $O(n)$ (enumeration of the vertices of the graph), the second one in $O(2^n)$ (enumeration of the subsets of vertices) and the third one in $O(n)$ (enumeration of the vertices of the graph). The internal operations of these loops are in constant time (comparison and assignment). The complexity of Algorithm 1.4 is therefore $O(n^2 2^n)$. For Algorithm 1.5, the table D is scanned row-wise, each cell being examined at most once. Its worst-case complexity is therefore identical to the construction of the table D, that is, $O(n 2^n)$.

If need be, we can confirm that a lot has been achieved through the use of this procedure, by merely recalling the orders of magnitude obtained in the last two lines of Table 1.1.

ALGORITHM 1.5. Backtracking algorithm for the TRAVELING
SALESMAN

Input: A complete graph $G = (V, E)$ of order n and its cost function c, the dynamic
programming matrix D computed by Algorithm 1.4.
Output: A Hamiltonian cycle $\mathcal{C}$ of minimum cost

1   $\mathcal{C} \leftarrow \{0\}$
2   $S \leftarrow V \backslash \{0\}$
3   $i \leftarrow 0$
4   **While** $S \neq \emptyset$ **do**
5 | **For** *every vertex* $j \in S$ **do**
6 | | **If** $c(ij) + D[j][S \backslash \{j\}] = D[i][S]$ **then**
7 | | | $\mathcal{C} \leftarrow \mathcal{C} \cup \{j\}$
8 | | | $S \leftarrow S \backslash \{j\}$
9 | | | $i \leftarrow j$
10 | | | **break**

11 **return** $\mathcal{C}$

Dynamic programming is a technique that is not only applicable to
NP-complete problems; it is also widely used in many polynomial problems
for which it is possible to define optimal subproblems. They then serve the
purpose of reducing the algorithmic complexity of the proposed solution
methods, because they allow that redundant computations be avoided, at the
cost of storing intermediate computations in tables. This is the case, for
example, for sequence alignment (see Chapter 3) or the computation for
optimal folding in RNA (see Chapter 6).

1.8.2. *Tree traversal*

In this section, we address some classical algorithms that are very often
used for manipulating trees. We do not discuss evolutionary trees in this book,
but it is quite common that the organization of data be modeled in the form
of trees. In particular, this will be the case when referring to suffix trees for
indexing (see Chapter 2), as well as to taxonomic trees (see Chapter 5), or
even in the chapter on RNA folding (Chapter 6).

A *binary tree* is a tree (therefore a connected graph without cycle) whose
degree of the internal nodes (therefore those which are not leaves) is at most
equal to three. If it is rooted, it means that each internal node possesses two
children.

The tree data structure we propose to consider is a generalist data structure, not only applicable to binary trees. It concerns rooted trees. A tree is represented by a structure defined in a *recursive* way, and in a quite natural way, manipulations on trees can also be done in a recursive way:

– let $\emptyset$ denote the empty tree;

– let (e, L) be a pair consisting of a label e (which itself can be a complex structure), and a finite collection of trees L, possibly empty. This collection can be ordered or not.

Figure 1.8 gives an example of representation of this data structure using lists, for a tree with labels from the classical alphabet.

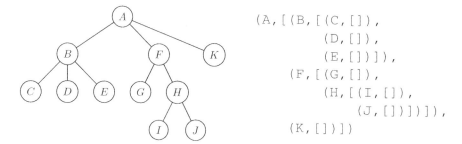

Figure 1.8. *List-based tree representation. Left: the original tree, rooted in A. Right: its representation in the form of lists (shown with square brackets)*

The manipulation of the trees is done through paths, which can either start from the leaves and continue towards the root or start from the root and continue towards the leaves, or still, consider each level of the tree successively.

1.8.2.1. *Depth-first search*

Depth-first search (DFS) is a tree traversal algorithm that gives priority to the exploration of the children first, until a leaf is reached, and which then restarts from the lowest level where there are still branches to explore. There are several existing types of depth-first searches, depending on the order in which node processing is placed in relation to the recursive calls:

– *in-order* traversal (in the binary case only): the first recursive call is performed with the left subtree, then the root is processed, and finally the recursive call is performed with the right subtree;

– *pre-order* (or *top-down*) traversal: processing first takes place with the root, then recursive calls are performed with the children;

– *post-order* (or *bottom-up*) traversal: recursive calls are performed with the children, then processing is performed with the root.

Therefore, in the example of Figure 1.8, a DFS that would result in writing the labels of the nodes traversed would produce the following sequence via a pre-order DFS:

ABCDEFGHIJK

(the labeling in this case was achieved following a pre-order DFS), and the following sequence according to a post-order DFS:

CDEBGIJHFKA.

Algorithm 1.6 indicates how such a traversal (pre-ordering here) is performed with generic processing.

ALGORITHM 1.6. DFS (depth-first search) algorithm

Input: A tree $T = (r, L)$
Output: The tree has been processed following a depth-first search

1 **If** $T \neq \emptyset$ **then**
2   **If** $L = \emptyset$ **then**
3   Process_leaf(r)
4   **otherwise**
5   Process_node(r)
6   **For** *every child* $u \in L$ **do**
7   DFS(u)

An iterative version can also be implemented, using a stack data structure (LIFO: Last In, First Out).

The time complexity of this algorithm is $O(n.f(n))$, where n is the number of vertices in the tree and $f(n)$ is the processing complexity for each node. It should also be noted that by marking the nodes already processed, this algorithm can also be applied to any graph, and the subgraph thus traversed defines a spanning tree of the graph.

1.8.2.2. *Breadth-first search*

Analogously, a search that would be based on processing the siblings can be defined. This is known as the breadth-first search (BFS). Algorithm 1.7 gives the sequence of operations for generic processing. In the example of Figure 1.8, a BFS would give the following output:

```
ABFKCDEGHIJ.
```

The implementation of this traversal can be done quite simply using a queue data structure (FIFO: First In, First Out). The general idea is to process the root, then to place its children in the queue and then to restart the processing with each element of the queue, as long as the latter is not empty. Algorithm 1.7 formalizes this principle.

ALGORITHM 1.7. BFS (breadth-first search) algorithm

Input: A tree $T = (r, L)$
Output: The tree has been processed following a breadth-first search
1    $F = \emptyset$
2    $node = r$
3   **While** *node is defined* **do**
4   Process_node(*node*)
5   **For** *every child u of node* **do**
6   Insert u into F
7        $node = $ first element of F (which is removed);

The time complexity of this algorithm is also in $O(n.f(n))$, each node being seen twice: once when it is inserted in the queue, and once when it is removed from the queue.

1.9. Validation

In this last section, we address an essential point when it comes to proposing algorithms and methods for solving problems related to practical applications. We have seen that it is not always possible to solve these problems exactly, and even when the solution is theoretically exact, implementations often experience the unforgiving reality of imperfect input data. For instance, in high-throughput sequencing data, the error rate from reads is an intrinsic parameter of the data. The errors in this case may be of different natures; they can either be point errors of the *substitution* type (one nucleotide is read instead of another), or more structural errors, such as stutters when short *tandem repeats*, those consecutive on the genome, are sequenced. Finally, larger-scale errors (large portions of genomes repeated in reverse complement) can occur, primarily with long reads. These errors can, at different scales, influence the efficiency of an assembly method (see Chapter 4), and we have to compare the behavior of methods with respect to these different types of errors. It is therefore important, when proposing a method, to determine to what extent what it proposes is close to the expected result.

The observation is	what is expected in reality	what is not expected in reality
detected by the method	TRUE POSITIVE (TP)	FALSE POSITIVE (FP)
not detected by the method	FALSE NEGATIVE (FN)	TRUE NEGATIVE (FN)

Table 1.2. *Different possible cases during a binary-type validation. The green boxes are classified as "correct", and the red boxes are classified as "incorrect". For a color version of this figure, see www.iste.co.uk/chateau/graphs.zip*

1.9.1. *The different types of errors*

When verifying whether a method produces the correct result, a binary point of view is often adopted, that is, the result is qualified as either "correct" or "incorrect". Table 1.2 indicates the terminologies of the various possible cases within this framework. A *true positive* is an observation that corresponds to what is actually expected. Therefore, in a situation where a gene is looked for in a genome, a true positive will be a gene that has been detected in the genome, and that is actually present in reality. A *false positive* is an observation that the method detects but which should not be detected in reality. For example, a gene that the method declares as belonging to the genome, but it does not. A *true negative* is an observation that is not detected and which actually should not be detected. For example, a gene that is declared as not belonging to the genome, and which is actually not present in there. Finally, a *false negative* is a "missing" observation, in our example a gene that is not detected by the method when it is actually present in the genome. True positives and true negatives are correct observations, and false positives and false negatives are incorrect observations made by the method.

When there is the possibility of comparing the result of each of the observations, between the expected and what is indicated by the method, the number of each of the cases can be counted, and a contingency table as in the example of Figure 1.9 obtained.

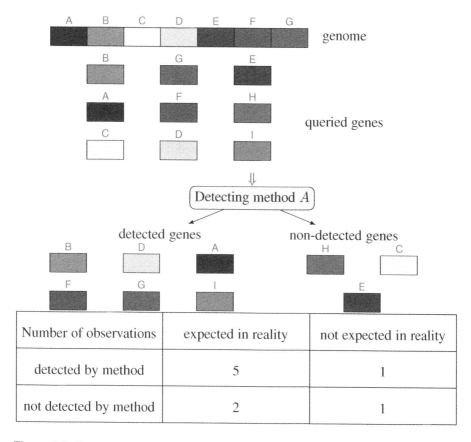

Number of observations	expected in reality	not expected in reality
detected by method	5	1
not detected by method	2	1

Figure 1.9. *Example of a contingency table for validation. On top: the problem consists of detecting genes in a genome with a method A that classifies genes into "found" and "not found". The gray gene (I) is a false positive because it is detected when it is not in the genome. The yellow gene (C) and the purple gene (E) are false negatives because they are present on the genome but are not detected by the method. The other observations are correct. Bottom: contingency table of the method with this example. For a color version of this figure, see www.iste.co.uk/chateau/graphs.zip*

1.9.2. *Quality measures*

The previous table provides indications on the validity of the results of the method, through different measures that are interdependent. In particular, the measures of intrinsic validation (with respect to the expected) can be clearly observed:

– **sensitivity**, defined by the formula $\frac{VP}{VP+FN}$, indicates the rate of observations correctly detected by the method with respect to the total number of positive observations expected. For the example of Figure 1.9, sensitivity has a value of 5/7;

– **specificity**, defined by the formula $\frac{VN}{VN+FP}$, indicates the rate of observations correctly rejected by the method with respect to the total number of expected negative observations. For the example in Figure 1.9, specificity has a value of 1/2.

These two concepts are fundamentally related. For instance, if the method has been defined on the basis of a detection *threshold*, by fiddling with this threshold sensitivity can be increased, but then specificity may decrease accordingly.

Two complementary notions are also widely used in classification; these are the *predictive values*:

– **precision** (or positive predictive value), defined by the formula $\frac{VP}{VP+FP}$, indicates the rate of observations correctly detected by the method among all those it has classified as correct. For the example of Figure 1.9, precision has a value of 5/6;

– **recall** (or negative predictive value), defined by the formula $\frac{VN}{VN+FN}$, indicates the rate of observations correctly rejected by the method among all those it has classified as incorrect. For the example of Figure 1.9, recall has a value of 1/3.

Figure 1.10 summarizes the various measures as the ratios of what is correct to everything that is reported by the method under evaluation, either by column or row, in the contingency table.

Depending on what is important to measure, we can more directly focus on specificity and sensitivity on the one hand, or precision and recall on the other.

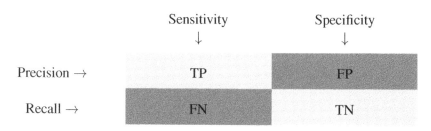

Figure 1.10. *Sensitivity, specificity, precision and recall. Each measure is defined as the rate of what is correctly classified by the method (in light green) over the total of the row (respectively column). For a color version of this figure, see www.iste.co.uk/chateau/graphs.zip*

1.9.2.1. *ROC curve*

An ROC (*receiver operating characteristic*) curve is a means of representing the interaction between sensitivity and specificity, in the case where a threshold is adjusted to perform detection. If we reconsider the example of Figure 1.9, the detection of genes can depend on a threshold corresponding, for example, to a minimal alignment score. This threshold can be set arbitrarily, or calibrated precisely according to the sensitivity and specificity it produces, for example, by trying to reach the point furthest from the coordinate point (1,0). An ROC curve is presented in Figure 1.11.

1.9.2.2. *F-measure*

Predictive values can also be combined to obtain an overall measure of tool quality, especially when it comes to comparing different tools with one another. The *F-measure* is then defined as the harmonic mean between precision and recall:

$$F = 2 \frac{\text{precision} \cdot \text{recall}}{\text{precision} + \text{recall}}.$$

For the example in Figure 1.9, the F-measure has a value of 10/21. The F-measure is widely used in the field of data mining, and more specifically with textual data, and in machine learning. A weighted variant with a β coefficient is found:

$$F_\beta = \frac{(1 + \beta^2) \cdot \text{precision} \cdot \text{recall}}{(\beta^2 \cdot \text{precision}) + \text{recall}}$$

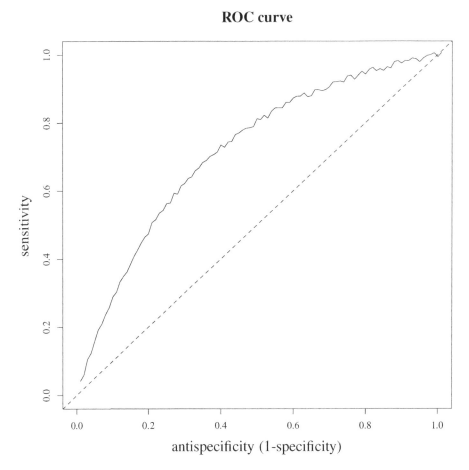

Figure 1.11. *ROC curve. Instead of representing sensitivity versus specificity, anti-specificity (1-specificity) is employed. The point of coordinates (0,1) represents the ideal to be reached. The area under the curve is sometimes used as a measure of quality. The diagonal corresponds to detection results that would be randomly obtained*

1.9.3. *And in the non-binary case?*

It is not always easy to classify observations into "correct" and "incorrect" ones in some cases. We can generalize the notions of sensitivity, specificity, precision and recall in a model with more than two classes and define a general measure of each of these parameters by averaging over all classes. However, we are still faced with a discrete model where the classes will be defined arbitrarily. In the example of the search for genes in a genome, for example, different classes could be defined according to the alignment score that is found, with successive score intervals.

But this does not necessarily apply to all cases. It is then necessary to define a metric, or a set of metrics, that will allow the proximity between the observation and the expected result to be characterized. The definition of these metrics is generally guided by usage and by how easily these metrics are computed.

1.10. Conclusion

We have seen through this very general introduction that problems in bioinformatics present many aspects that require knowledge both in biology, concerning the structure and behavior of organisms and objects of study (for instance, the genome), and in fundamental computer science, to model and formalize not only the data but also the problems themselves, in order to provide algorithmic answers to these problems raised. In the following chapters, we will see some of the fundamental questions in bioinformatics, how they are modeled, how they are analyzed, how difficult they are and what answers can be provided thereto.

1.11. References

Alberts, B. (2004). *Biologie moléculaire de la cellule*. Flammarion.

Bondy, J.A. and Murty, U.S.R. (1985). *Graph Theory with Applications*. North Holland.

Cook, S.A. (1971). The complexity of theorem-proving procedures. *Proceedings of the 3rd Annual ACM Symposium on Theory of Computing*, Shaker Heights, Ohio, May 3–5, 151–158.

Cori, R. and Lascar, D. (2003). *Logique mathématique 1 – Calcul propositionnel ; algèbre de Boole ; calcul des prédicats*. Dunod.

Crochemore, M., Hancart, C., Lecroq, T. (2001). *Algorithmique du texte*. Vuibert.

Diestel, R. (2017). *Graph Theory, Graduate Texts in Mathematics*, 5th edition. Springer.

Euler, L. (1736). Solutio problematis ad geometriam situs pertinentis. *Commentarii Academiae Scientiarum Imperialis Petropolitanae*, 8, 128–140.

Garey, M.R. and Johnson, D.S. (1990). *Computers and Intractability; A Guide to the Theory of NP-Completeness*. W.H. Freeman & Co.

Heather, J.M. and Chain, B. (2016). The sequence of sequencers: The history of sequencing DNA. *Genomics*, 107(1), 1–8.

Held, M. and Karp, R.M. (1962). A dynamic programming approach to sequencing problems. *Journal of the Society for Industrial and Applied Mathematics*, 10(1), 196–210.

Ladner, R.E. (1975). On the structure of polynomial time reducibility. *Journal of the ACM*, 22(1), 155–171.

Letunic, I. and Bork, P. (2017). 20 years of the SMART protein domain annotation resource. *Nucleic Acids Research*, 46(D1), D493–D496.

Lewis, H.R. and Papadimitriou, C.H. (1981). *Elements of the Theory of Computation*. Prentice-Hall.

Petsko, G.A., Ringe, D., Sanlaville, C. (2009). *Structure et fonction des protéines*. De Boeck.

Planck Collaboration et al. (2018). Planck 2018 results VI. cosmological parameters. Cosmology and Nongalactic Astrophysics, arXiv:1807.06209.

Robertson, N. and Seymour, P.D. (1986). Graph minors II. Algorithmic aspects of tree-width. *Journal of Algorithms*, 7(3), 309–322.

2

Sequence Indexing

Thierry LECROQ[1] and Mikaël SALSON[2]

[1]*University of Normandy, UNIROUEN, LITIS, Rouen, France*
[2]*University of Lille, CNRS, UMR 9189 – CRIStAL, France*

2.1. Introduction

The development of computer science and its computational capacities have caused for decades an exponential growth in the amount of data produced on a daily basis by fields ranging from climatology to geography and including medicine and sociology (Mayer-Schönberger and Cukier 2013). The expression data deluge is often heard. This is also the case in molecular biology where second- and now third-generation sequencers are capable of obtaining genomic and transcriptomic sequences at high throughput and at relatively small costs (Schatz and Langmead 2013; Goodwin et al. 2016). The sequences thus produced do not provide any information in themselves if they are not put into context and, in this case, compared to each other or to already known sequences. Knowing, from the sequences obtained, whether a gene is over-expressed in some individuals compared to others requires a comparison of sequences to identify those corresponding to the gene of interest. Rather than focusing on a particular gene, research is most often being carried out without too many a priori, which requires comparing each sequence with

From Sequences to Graphs,
coordinated by Annie CHATEAU and Mikaël SALSON.
© ISTE Ltd 2022.

the whole of one or more genomes. Such comparisons between sequences are not restricted to the given example but are necessary in many other situations (study of the phylogenetic evolution, genome assembly, comparison of metagenomes, etc.).

If such comparisons were made in a naive manner, it would be necessary to compare billions of sequences produced by the high-throughput sequencer to the billions of positions of a single genome. To avoid such an explosion in the number of comparisons, it is essential that the processing carried out makes it possible to accelerate this research. This optimization is based on the use of an index.

2.1.1. *What is indexing?*

In our daily life, we can use an index to locate words in a book, like in this one, for example (see, for instance, the Index at the end of this book). This index contains only predefined terms and refers to only part of the occurrences of these terms. For biological sequences, indexes are also used which, unlike the indexes at the end of the books, generally allow access to all the sequences and to all their occurrences. Due to the size of the biological sequences to be indexed (e.g. genomes), these indexes must be sufficiently cost efficient to be used on computing machines. While in the 2010s, comparisons were made most of the time based on a single reference sequence, with the diversity of the sequences that we now have access to, it becomes necessary to index several reference sequences (potentially thousands or even millions).

In a more general way, indexing a data set consists of building a data structure that speeds up the search for information in this set. Once built, the data structure will avoid the need of a sequential search for data in the set during each search for information. Therefore, the time taken by the search can be, in the best of cases, proportional to the size of the information sought for and not to the size of the indexed data set. Due to the time required to build a structure indexing the data, such an approach is only cost-effective when this time is largely compensated by the time saved during the search. In other words, indexing is possible, and even desirable, when the indexed data set rarely or never changes.

2.1.2. *When to index?*

Genomic sequences available in public databases, such as the human genome sequence, are data that vary quite rarely. For example, the reference version of the human genome available in databases in 2019 was GRCh38 (NCBI 2019). The previous version, GRCh37, was from 2013 (NCBI 2013). Despite taking into account the modifications introduced on GRCh38 (the *patches*), only 12 such modifications were achieved between 2013 and 2019. In such a situation, the creation of an indexing structure from a human genome will be made largely profitable by the billions of searches that will be carried out in this structure, before it has to be recreated with a new version of the genome.

The indexing structures presented in this chapter can easily be used to search for exact occurrences of patterns. They also constitute fundamental structures for the search for approximate patterns, allowing for differences between the searched sequence and the found occurrences. In the latter case, they require additional methods, some of which will be detailed in the next chapter on sequence alignment.

2.1.3. *What to index?*

Indexing is of interest in many fields based on large quantities of data. Databases and Internet search engines are based on indexing structures in order to propose fast results. Nevertheless, the data indexed in biology are not necessarily comparable to those of these domains, and therefore, the indexing techniques may differ.

In bioinformatics, the specificity consists of indexing very large texts with little or no structure, contrary to texts in natural language in which words, paragraphs, titles, etc., can be distinguished.

Two main types of bioinformatics problems have historically resorted to indexing: mapping read on a reference genome and the assembly of reads to reconstitute the sequence of a genome.

In the problem of locating the reads from a reference genome, a few million reads must generally be located on a genome containing a few million to a few billion bases. It would therefore be particularly inefficient to go through the reference genome for processing each read. Complete indexing of the genome makes it possible to greatly accelerate locating the reads.

To allow the read assembly, many methods rely on indexing reads to compare reads with one another and effectively find the relevant overlaps between these reads.

The use of indexing is naturally not restricted to these problems, nor in this form. The positioning of genome reads can also be achieved by indexing the reads rather than the genome, in order to take advantage of the redundancy of the reads. The indexing of the read data set facilitates their comparison in order to determine which data sets are most common. Some examples of using indexing can be seen in the chapters dedicated to alignment (see Chapter 3), to assembly (see Chapter 4) or to metagenomics (see Chapter 5).

2.1.4. *Indexing structures and queries considered*

Conventionally, an indexing structure will enable obtaining a response to certain types of queries. Conventional queries, from the simplest to the most complex, are existence, counting and locating which can be synthesized in the following three problems.

Problem 2.1. Existence of an element in indexed data

Input: An element and indexed data
Question: Is the element present in the indexed data?

Problem 2.2. Counting an element in indexed data

Input: An element and indexed data
Output: Number of occurrences of the element in the indexed data

---

Problem 2.3. Locating an element in indexed data

Input: An element and indexed data
Output: List of locations of the searched element in the indexed data

---

The purpose of this chapter is to present the methods commonly used to address these problems with biological sequences. Since the biological sequences to be indexed can be of different natures (a genome, a set of genomes, one or more sequencing data sets, etc.), we generalize the subject by considering a set of *sequences* to be indexed from a four-letter alphabet. In a first step, we present structures to be used for indexing the factors, of a fixed length, of the words of a set: Bloom filters, inverted lists, lookup tables, hash tables and de Bruijn graphs. In a second step, we present structures for full-text indexing, which are not restricted to words of fixed length: suffix trees, suffix tables and Burrows–Wheeler transforms. Next, we set out criteria for choosing an indexing solution according to the available data and the search to be done.

2.1.5. *Basic notions and vocabulary*

Indexing structures make use of specific concepts that we start by defining. We also introduce some notations (the first three are also presented in detail in Chapter 1). These elements will be used in the rest of the chapter.

– **Sequence:** a *sequence* (also called text) is a sequence of symbols from an alphabet, which is a finite set of symbols. A sequence x of length n is denoted by $x = x[1 .. n]$. Symbols are indexed from position 1. The length of the sequence x is denoted $|x|$. A fragment of a sequence is also called a *factor*. The factor of the sequence x starting at position i and ending at position j is denoted $x[i .. j]$ for $1 \leq i \leq j \leq n$. A factor starting at the beginning of the sequence and therefore of the form $x[1 .. j]$ is called a *prefix* and a factor ending at the end of the sequence and therefore of the form $x[i .. n]$ is called a *suffix*.

– **Graph:** a *graph* $G = (V, E)$ is composed of a finite set V of *vertices* and a set of *edges* E connecting these vertices. These edges are called *arcs* in the case of a directed graph. These edges can be labeled.

– **Tree:** a (rooted) *tree* is a directed acyclic graph. The vertices are called *nodes* and the arcs are called *branches*. A non-empty tree possesses a single node without predecessor called *root*. The nodes without successors are called *leaves*.

– **Rank and select:** Let T be an array of n bits with the two following operations, where $b \in \{0, 1\}$:

- $rank_b(T, i)$, which returns the number of bits b in T up to position i, that is, $rank_b(T, i) = |\{j \mid T[j] = b \text{ and } j \leq i\}|$;

- $select_b(T, i)$, which returns the position of the ith bit b in T, that is, $select_b(T, i) = \min\{j \mid rank_b(T, j) = i\}$.

For example, in the bit array $T = \overset{1\ 2\ 3\ 4\ 5\ 6\ 7}{0\ 1\ 1\ 0\ 1\ 1\ 0}$, there are two 0's up to position 5, so $rank_0(T, 5) = 2$, and three 1's up to position 5, so $rank_1(T, 5) = 3$. On the contrary, the third 0 is at position 7 ($select_0(T, 3) = 7$), while the third 1 is at position 5 ($select_1(T, 3) = 5$).

These operations can be computed in constant time using $o(m)$ bits, in addition to T which can eventually be compressed (Navarro and Mäkinen 2007).

It should be noted that such a data structure is an indexing structure which, here, indexes an array of bits. The *rank* operation is a *counting* operation while *select* is a *localization* operation.

2.2. Word indexing

We start by studying the structures indexing only words of a fixed length. The origin of these fixed-length words can be diverse: they can also originate from genomes, transcriptomes and sequencing reads. In order to generalize these different cases, we consider indexing all of the elements of a set E of n words of fixed length and possibly storing the information related to each word. The fixed length of each of these words will be denoted by k and we call these words k-mers.

Throughout this section, we will take as an example the indexing of four sequences of different lengths, namely, $S = \{\text{ACTCGA}, \text{TCGAT}, \text{CGATC}, \text{TCGC}\}$. When decomposed in the form of 3-mers, the sequences of S give us a set of seven elements:

$$E = \{\text{ACT}, \text{ATC}, \text{CGA}, \text{CGC}, \text{CTC}, \text{GAT}, \text{TCG}\}.$$

2.2.1. Bloom filters

A Bloom filter (Bloom 1970) is a probabilistic data structure that facilitates addressing the existence of k-mers in the set E (Problem 2.1). The structure is said to be *probabilistic* because there is a certain probability that a query will return a false response (a false positive, see section 1.9.1). A Bloom filter consists of a bit vector only. An element is actually stored by inserting 1's at the positions indicated by the result of several hash functions on this element. More formally, the filter is composed of an array T of p bits and of a set of h

hash functions $f_i : E \mapsto [1, p]$ for $1 \leq i \leq h$. To indicate that an element e belongs to E, the h bits at positions $f_i(e)$ in T are set to 1.

To test if an element e belongs to E, the h bits at positions $f_i(e)$ just have to be accessed: if one of them is 0, then e is not in E, and if they are all 1, then it is *probable* that e is in E.

Consider an example with 10 bits and 2 hash functions (hence, $p = 10$ and $h = 2$) (see Figure 2.1). Let us define a function *dnarank* that associates an integer between 0 and 3 to each nucleotide in alphabetical order: $dnarank(\texttt{A}) = 0$, $dnarank(\texttt{C}) = 1$, $dnarank(\texttt{G}) = 2$ and $dnarank(\texttt{T}) = 3$. Let f_1 and f_2 be our two hash functions. The hash function f_1 consists of summing the *dnarank* of each nucleotide of a k-mer, modulo 10, and f_2 corresponds to the value of the k-mer in base 4, modulo 10. More formally, $f_1 : A^3 \mapsto \{1, \dots, 10\}$ defines as follows $f_1(x) = (dnarank(x[1]) + dnarank(x[2]) + dnarank(x[3])) \bmod 10 + 1$ and $f_2 : A^3 \mapsto \{1, \dots, 10\}$ defines as follows $f_2(x) = (dnarank(x[1]) \times 16 + rang(x[2]) \times 4 + dnarank(x[3])) \bmod 10 + 1$.

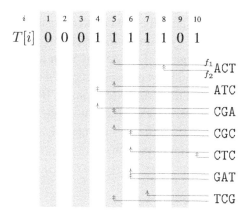

Figure 2.1. *Storage of 3-mers with a Bloom filter T of 10 bits and 2 hash functions (f_1 and f_2). The application of the functions f_1 (↑) and f_2 (↖) on each of the k-mers will indicate the positions to store a 1 in T*

In the Bloom filter defined in Figure 2.1, it is known that $\texttt{CAC}$ does not belong to E because $f_1(\texttt{CAC}) = 3$ and $T[3] = 0$. On the contrary, for $\texttt{TCC}$, $f_1(\texttt{TCC}) = 6$ and $f_2(\texttt{TCC}) = 4$ and $T[4] = T[6] = 1$. It is concluded that $\texttt{TCC}$

probably belongs to E. However, this is not the case. This is an example of false positives due to the insertion of some k-mers who added 1's at positions 4 and 6.

The hash functions used in this example are a bad choice in the general case. It is preferable to use functions distributing uniformly the indexed words at the p positions of T, regardless of the lexicographic order (Marçais et al. 2017).

The false positive rate of a Bloom filter depends on three parameters $|E|$, $n = |T|$ and h. To conclude, wrongly, that an element $e \notin E$ belongs to E, all bits at $f_i(e)$ must be equal to 1. The probability that any bit of T is 1 is $1 - (1 - \frac{1}{n})^{h|E|}$, because there is a probability $(1 - \frac{1}{n})^{h|E|}$ that a bit of T is 0 after inserting $|E|$ elements with h hash functions. Then, the probability of having h bits set to 1 at the positions $f_i(e)$ – in other words, the false positive rate – is $\left(1 - \left(1 - \frac{1}{n}\right)^{h|E|}\right)^h$ (Broder and Mitzenmacher 2004).

The false positive rate is therefore determined by the choice of the number of hash functions and the size of the filter. This makes these filters particularly flexible and space-saving. Naturally, the counterpart is to have a certain false positive rate. On the contrary, Bloom filters allow only responding (in a probabilistic way) to the request of existence. With a simple Bloom filter, it is impossible to count the number of occurrences and, a fortiori, to localize the occurrences even though there are extensions of Bloom filters that remove some of these limitations (see, for example, Luo et al. (2019)). Other methods exist to store exactly the set E of k-mers of interest, which makes it possible to query them with these different requests.

2.2.2. *Inverted list*

An inverted list consists of associating with a word of E a list of the positions at which this word appears in S. Word indexing through an inverted list is the most common method, including for natural language texts. For example, indexes that can be present at the end of the books are inverted lists.

Inverted lists can be stored in various ways. Two are mainly used in bioinformatics: lookup tables, for small k-mers, and hash tables.

2.2.2.1. *Lookup table*

A lookup table for k-mers of a set E is a table containing σ^k cells, where σ is the size of the alphabet (i.e. four classically for DNA or RNA). The k-mers are transformed by a bijective function into an integer comprised between 1 and σ^k. This integer is the index in the lookup table where the information about the k-mer will be stored. The transformation of the k-mers into an integer is most often done by considering the k-mer as being expressed in the form of a number in base σ (where each letter of the k-mer is therefore associated with a number), as for the function $dnarank$ used for Bloom filters (see section 2.2.1).

Lookup tables are used to store the presence or absence of a k-mer in E, which allow us to address Problem 2.1. It is therefore enough to have one bit of information per k-mer. Otherwise, lookup tables can also store the number of occurrences of each k-mer in S, which allow us to address Problem 2.2. Generally, these tables do not serve to store all the positions at which the k-mers appear in S. In this case, hash tables are preferred.

For example, to store the seven 3-mers of our set E, the lookup table would be composed of $4^3 = 64$ bits (see Figure 2.2).

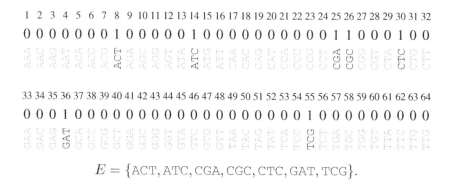

$$E = \{\text{ACT}, \text{ATC}, \text{CGA}, \text{CGC}, \text{CTC}, \text{GAT}, \text{TCG}\}.$$

Figure 2.2. *Storage of 3-mers in a lookup table. For informational purposes, we show the k-mers corresponding to each of the positions in the lookup table, but they are not really stored. The k-mers for which a 1 is stored in the lookup table are indicated in bold*

2.2.2.2. *Hash table*

A hash table can be used to store the elements of the set E in a table T of N cells by way of a hash function $f : E \mapsto [1, N]$. An element $e \in E$ is stored in $T[f(e)]$. The function f is in general non-injective. If two distinct elements e and e' of E are such that $f(e) = f(e')$, then it is said that there is a *collision*. In a lookup table, it was not possible to have a collision since each element potentially in E had its own cell.

There are several methods for handling collisions in hash tables (Cormen et al. 2022). *Open hashing*, or *closed addressing*, consists of using chained lists to store the values in the cells of table T. Chained lists are data structures in which each "cell" storing a value also points to the next cell (if it exists). This results in having a list that can arbitrarily grow without having any limit as fixed as with a table. Therefore, a closed-addressing hash table does not have a size limit set at the construction (hence the name open hashing), and the address of an element is always the same (closed addressing).

Figure 2.3 shows an example of how E is stored in a hash table with the function f_1 previously introduced (see section 2.2.1). To find out if CGC is present in the hash table, we start by calculating $f_1(\text{CGC})$ which is 5. We then scan the different k-mers present at this position in order to verify that CGC is there, which is the case.

If we search for TCC, we have $f_1(\text{TCC}) = 5$. By scanning through the list of the k-mers stored at this position, we realize that TCC is not in there. It is concluded that $\text{TCC} \notin E$.

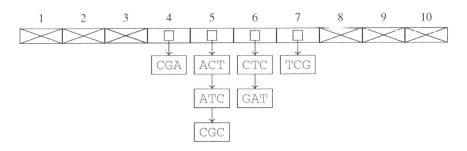

Figure 2.3. *Storage of 3-mers in a hash table with closed addressing. The hash function used f is f_1, as defined in section 2.2.1 to store E in a hash table T of 10 cells*

Unlike the lookup table, the space required for such a hash table is not proportional to the number of k-mers of a given size but mainly to the number of distinct k-mers existing in a data set, here in E. Nonetheless, such a hash table has two disadvantages: it is necessary to store the k-mer itself, and on the other hand, to verify whether a k-mer is present at a given position, it is necessary to search for it in the list at this position.

Another solution is *closed hashing*, or *open addressing*. In this case, the size of the data structure is set at the time of construction: we will be able to store a fixed number of elements. In the case of a collision, it will be necessary to find deterministically another free location in the data structure. This search for a free space can be done in a linear way (the locations directly after the original location are tested, see Figure 2.4) or, more generally, depending on a function g that gives the position to be tested. With such a structure, a given element can be inserted at very different positions depending on the elements that have been inserted beforehand. With an open-addressed hash table, the table must necessarily be of a size strictly larger than the number of elements to be inserted, in order to avoid too many collisions and having to search for the location of an element. A table with closed addressing does not have this disadvantage.

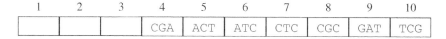

Figure 2.4. *Storage of the 3-mers [ACT, ATC, CGA, CTC, CGC, GAT, TCG], in order, in a hash table with open addressing. The hash function used f is f_1, as defined in section 2.2.1 to store E in a hash table of 10 cells. For example, $f_1(\text{ATC}) = 5$ yet ATC is stored at position 6 because ACT was previously stored at position 5. The next position that is free is then looked for (this is position 6)*

2.2.2.2.1. Perfect minimal hash function

A perfect minimal hash function f can be used for storing the n elements of the set E in a table with n locations with no collisions. The function f is therefore such that $1 \leq f(e) \leq n$ and $f(e) = f(e') \Leftrightarrow e = e'$.

It is possible to avoid having to manage collisions through the use of a perfect minimal hash function, as in a lookup table, yet the necessary number of memory locations has to be previously reserved, in contrast to a lookup table.

The computation and use of a perfect minimal hash function requires memory space. Such a function actually relies on a pre-computation performed on the data set which must therefore be previously known. A minimum bound of about 1.44 bits per element is established (Belazzougui et al. 2009).

A perfect minimal hash function is thus a means, in a way, to get the best of both worlds at a low cost. On the contrary, the set E must be known at the outset. It is not possible, in the current state of knowledge, for example, to add new elements to a perfect minimal hash function.

2.2.3. *De Bruijn graphs*

De Bruijn graphs have been introduced in a theoretical framework in Sainte-Marie (1894), Good (1946) and de Bruijn (1950). They represent k-mers, as well as their overlaps of length $k - 1$. In such a graph, the vertices of the graph are the k-mers.

Given a set of n words $S = \{w_1, \ldots, w_n\}$ and an integer k, the de Bruijn graph of order k of S is a directed graph whose vertices are therefore the k-mers of the words of S. There is an arc between a vertex u and a vertex v when the suffix of length $k - 1$ of u is equal to the prefix of length $k - 1$ of v, namely, when there is an overlap of length $k - 1$ between the end of u and the beginning of v.

It is possible to restrict this definition so that the existence of an arc is conditional on the fact that the word $u \cdot v[k]$, of length $k + 1$, is a factor of a word of the starting set from which the k-mers are derived. In this case, it is also possible to weight the arcs by the number of occurrences of $u \cdot v[k]$ in the words of the starting set.

Such a graph gives access to information that was difficult to obtain with the previous structures. By following a path in the graph, it is possible to enumerate the overlapping k-mers. This structure is particularly used for the assembly of sequences (see Chapter 4) and also to detect biological events, such as point mutations or alternative splicing events, directly from the structure of the graph (Sacomoto et al. 2012; Iqbal et al. 2012).

As an example, the third-order de Bruijn graph of S is given in Figure 2.5.

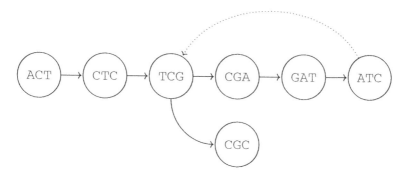

Figure 2.5. *Third-order de Bruijn graph of* $S = \{$ACTCGA, TCGAT, CGATC, TCGC$\}$. *Each vertex of the graph corresponds to an element of* S. *Each solid edge corresponds to a 4-mer that is present in* S. *For example, there is an edge from* TCG *to* CGA *because the suffix of* TCG *of length 2 is equal to the prefix of the same length of* CGA, *that is, to* CG, *and that* TCGA *appears in the first word of* S. *The dotted edge corresponds to a 4-mer that does not exist in* S (ATCG), *but for which the suffix of size 2 of the origin vertex is identical to the prefix of size 2 of the ending vertex* (TC). *According to the definition of the de Bruijn graph used, this edge might exist or not*

De Bruijn graphs are a way to represent overlaps between k-mers, and are therefore a way to keep a little more complete information on the indexed sequences.

This representation in graph form is an abstract data structure, which can be stored with the structures presented in this chapter. An effective solution is to use a Bloom filter. The filter stores the k-mers; the overlaps do not necessarily need to be stored but can be determined by performing a query for each possible overlap (there are only four possibilities with DNA). Since Bloom filters have false positives, they can be avoided by explicitly storing the false positive k-mers accessible from a vertex of the graph (Chikhi and Rizk 2013). Other solutions are detailed in a synthesis by Chikhi et al. (2019).

2.2.4. Efficient structures for targeted queries

The previous structures are efficient in terms of space required and can be used to query words whose length is chosen in advance. Querying a word of another length is not possible unless a structure dedicated to that length is rebuilt. These structures are therefore adapted to targeted requests, whose length is fixed. In case the length of the requests cannot be fixed in advance, we should consider structures indexing the whole text.

2.3. Full-text indexing

Unlike the previous section, we are now going to consider the text as a whole and not broken down into k-mers. This opens up new possibilities in terms of queries: sequences of arbitrary length can be searched. However, such a benefit is not without its drawbacks and such structures are generally more memory-intensive. We will see in this section how such structures are defined and how to use them.

Full-text indexing is based, at least for the structures presented here, on the indexing of all the *suffixes* of a text. These structures are actually based on this principle: accessing the prefixes of these suffixes gives access to all the factors in the text. Nonetheless, searching for a string in a text is tantamount to searching whether it is a factor of the text. These full-text indexing structures therefore enable easy access to the prefixes of all the suffixes of a text.

2.3.1. *Suffix tree*

An intuitive solution to access all the suffixes of a text consists of storing each one of them in a tree, more precisely in a *trie*. This is a tree in which any path from the root to a leaf represents a stored sequence, in this case, a suffix. Therefore, with such a *trie*, any path starting from the root corresponds to a prefix of one or more suffixes, and thus to any factor. From the root, it is therefore possible to access any text factor.

The suffix tree $\mathcal{S}(y)$ of a sequence y of length n is a *compact trie* representing all suffixes of y. It is defined by the following properties:

– The branches of $\mathcal{S}(y)$ are labeled by sequences.

– The outgoing branches of an internal node are labeled by sequences beginning with different letters.

– Any path in $\mathcal{S}(y)$ from the root to a leaf is labeled with a suffix of y.

– The internal nodes of $\mathcal{S}(y)$ have at least two descendants, which makes it a compact trie.

– The sequences that label the branches are represented by pairs (start position in y, length), which makes it possible to store each label in a constant space.

Moreover, if we add an ending symbol $ which appears only at the end of y, the suffixes of y correspond to the leaves of $\mathcal{S}(y)$. This implies that $\mathcal{S}(y)$

has exactly $n + 1$ leaves, thereby $O(n)$ nodes and $O(n)$ branches. Since each branch label occupies a constant space, the suffix tree of y thus occupies a linear space. Figure 2.6 shows an example of a suffix tree.

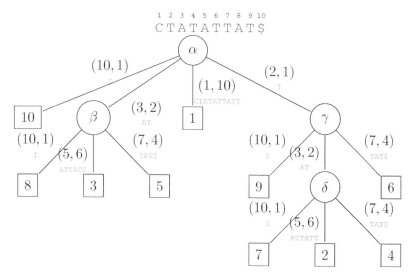

Figure 2.6. *The suffix tree of* CTATATTAT$. *The internal nodes are represented by circles (the Greek letters therein merely serve to identify them), whereas the leaves are represented by squares and contain the starting position of the suffixes which they are associated with. Any path from the root to a leaf corresponds to a text suffix. For example, the path from the root to leaf 5 corresponds to the suffix that starts at position 5, that is* ATTAT$ *that can be read on the tree with the label (3,2) =* AT *followed by the label (7, 4) =* TAT$

There are several algorithms for building the suffix tree of a sequence in linear time and space with an alphabet of constant size (McCreight 1976; Ukkonen 1995; Farach 1997). This structure can be extended to a finite set of sequences and is then called the generalized suffix tree.

Knowing whether a sequence x appears in a sequence y indexed with a suffix tree $\mathcal{S}(y)$ is tantamount to using $\mathcal{S}(y)$ as a deterministic finite automaton, and thus to accessing the characters of x one by one and to moving downwards in $\mathcal{S}(y)$ starting from the root. This means accessing the prefixes of the text suffixes, which are stored in $\mathcal{S}(y)$. If x can be scanned in its entirety, then it appears in y and the positions of all its occurrences can be found in the leaves of the subtree rooted on the first node (or first leaf) at the end of the branch where the path of x has ended.

For example, let us search for TA in the suffix tree of CTATATTAT$ in Figure 2.6. Reading T starting from the root leads to the node γ, then reading A leads to the branch between the node γ and the node δ. As such, TA appears in CTATATTAT$ at positions 2, 4 and 7 contained in the leaves of the subtree rooted at the node δ.

The search for a sequence x of length m in a sequence y can therefore be done in a time $O(m)$ from the suffix tree of y. Although linear in memory, such a structure is nevertheless greedy, making it not very useful in practice: the indexes presented hereafter, more compact, are preferred.

2.3.2. *(Extended) suffix array*

Instead of storing a whole tree, it is possible to simply consider the information stored in the leaves (the starting positions of the suffixes) provided that they are in a relevant order. The suffix array of a sequence y corresponds to the start positions of the suffixes of y sorted in lexicographical order. This suffix array was introduced independently by two groups of researchers (Manber and Myers 1990; Baeza-Yates and Gonnet 1992).

Formally, the suffix array of y, SA, is defined as follows:

$$y[SA[1] \mathinner{.\,.} n] < y[SA[2] \mathinner{.\,.} n] < \cdots < y[SA[n] \mathinner{.\,.} n].$$

The information stored in the suffix array, although more restricted than in the suffix tree, is nevertheless sufficient to search for the occurrences of any sequence.

Figure 2.7 shows an example of a suffix array.

There are several algorithms that can be used to build the suffix array of a sequence in linear time and space (Kärkkäinen and Sanders 2003; Kim et al. 2003; Ko and Aluru 2003). Nevertheless, in practice, these linear and recursive algorithms are not the most effective. Algorithms with supra-linear theoretical complexities are far superior to them, among others on genomic sequences (Puglisi et al. 2007; Bahne et al. 2019). In particular, the DivSufSort algorithm remains the best algorithm for constructing a suffix array in practice since 2006; however, the author has only published the source code, and he did not publish any scientific paper to describe the method (Mori 2015).

$$1 \; 2 \; 3 \; 4 \; 5 \; 6 \; 7 \; 8 \; 9 \; 10$$
$$\text{C T A T A T T A T \$}$$

i	$SA[i]$	$LCP[i]$	$y[SA[i]\,..\,n]$
1	10		$
2	8	0	AT$
3	3	2	ATATTAT$
4	5	2	ATTAT$
5	1	0	CTATATTAT$
6	9	0	T$
7	7	1	TAT$
8	2	3	TATATTAT$
9	4	3	TATTAT$
10	6	1	TTAT$

Figure 2.7. *The suffix array of* CTATATTAT$ *(column* $SA[i]$*). The column* $LCP[i]$ *gives the length of the longest prefixes common to two consecutive suffixes. For example,* $LCP[4] = 2$ *because the suffixes at positions 3 and 5 have an identifying prefix of length 2. The suffixes in the last column are not really stored. The longest common prefixes between two consecutive suffixes in the array are underlined*

The search for occurrences of a sequence x of length m in a sequence y of length n can be done based on a binary search in the suffix array of y. Since the comparison between x and each of the suffixes of the array may require $O(m)$ symbol comparisons, this search is carried out in $O(m \times \log n)$ time.

For example, let us search for TA in the suffix array of CTATATTAT$ of Figure 2.7. The binary search starts by considering the whole suffix array. To represent this, we will take two variables ℓ and r which represent, respectively, the start and end position of the interval considered in the suffix array. In this example, we start with the bounds $\ell = 1$ and $r = 10$. The middle position of the interval being equal to 5, TA is compared to $y[SA[5]\,..\,n] = y[1\,..\,10] =$ CTATATTAT$. TA is larger, so the bounds become $\ell = 5$ and $r = 11$. The middle position of the interval is equal to 8 and TA is a prefix of $y[SA[8]\,..\,n] = y[2\,..\,9] =$ TATATTAT$. Thereby, TA appears in y at position 2.

It is possible to reduce the complexity of the search to $O(m + \log n)$ using the array of longest common prefixes. This array consists of two parts. The first n elements correspond to the lengths of the longest prefixes shared by two consecutive suffixes in the suffix array. The following elements are the lengths of the longer prefixes common to pairs of suffixes that can be considered during the binary search in the suffix array. These pairs of positions do not depend on the word searched for. Formally, $LCP[i] = lcp(y[SA[i-1]..n], y[SA[i]..n])$ for $1 < i \leq n$, where $lcp(u,v)$ is the length of the longest common prefix of the sequences u and v. And $LCP[n + (i+j)/2] = lcp(y[SA[i]..n], y[SA[j]..n])$ for $1 \leq i, j \leq n$ and (i, j) is a pair that appears in the binary search.

The first part of the LCP array can be computed in linear time and space (Kasai et al. 2001) and the second part can be deduced by a simple depth-first traversal of the tree (see section 1.8.2.1) of the binary search using the following observation:

$$|lcp(y[SA[d]..n], y[SA[f]..n])|$$

$$=$$

$$\min\{|lcp(y[SA[d]..n], y[SA[i]..n])|, |lcp(y[SA[i]..n], y[SA[f]..n])|\}$$

for $1 \leq d < i < f \leq n$.

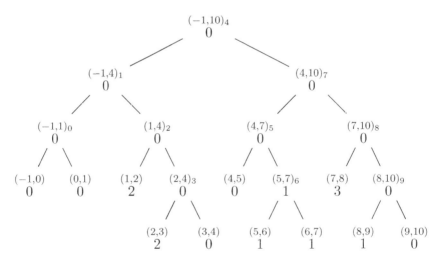

Figure 2.8. *The binary search tree for* CTATATTAT$. *The leaves* $(i-1, i)$ *correspond to the first values of the table* $LCP[i]$ *for* $1 \leq i \leq n-1$. *The internal nodes* $(i, j)_{\lfloor (i+j)/2 \rfloor}$ *correspond to the second part and the lengths of the longest common prefixes are stored in* $LCP[n + \lfloor (i+j)/2 \rfloor]$

Figure 2.8 shows an example of a binary search tree. This latter does not need to be stored as such: the LCP array is used to represent it. The leaves of the tree correspond to the first n elements of the LCP array. As for the nodes, they are deduced from the two children: these correspond to the minimum of the two children nodes.

The complete LCP array can be used in the binary search to keep the length of the longest common prefix between $y[\ell \mathinner{..} n]$ and $y[r \mathinner{..} n]$ (where ℓ and r are the starting and ending positions of the interval in which the binary search is performed) in order to obtain a search with a time complexity $O(m + \log n)$ (for details, see Crochemore et al. (2007)).

Adding the LCP array to the suffix array makes it possible to regain information that had been lost when we shifted from the suffix tree to the suffix array. Nevertheless, this makes the structure more memory consuming; the advantage compared to a suffix tree is therefore more moderate. The need to build these indexing structures on sequences of billions of nucleotides makes the use of more compact structures necessary.

2.3.3. *Burrows–Wheeler transform*

The suffix tree and the suffix array have the advantage of indexing the text in its whole, which enables searching for sequences of any length therein. Nonetheless, a major drawback is the space occupied by these structures. They require about 10 times more space than data structures indexing k-mers only. When it comes to indexing eukaryotic genomic sequences, this can become prohibitive.

However, researchers have observed the close conceptual proximity between the suffix array and the Burrows–Wheeler transform (BWT). This transform is a permutation of a sequence that enables gathering identical letters in order to better compress them. It was initially used in text compression in particular in the utility `bzip2`. Ferragina and Manzini have shown how we could benefit from these two advantages of the BWT by obtaining a compressed index (Ferragina and Manzini 2000).

To introduce the BWT, we are first going to present the notion of cyclic rotation of a word y of length n. A *cyclic rotation* of y is a word $v = y[i \mathinner{..} n]y[1 \mathinner{..} i - 1]$ with $1 \leq i \leq n$.

Let us assume a matrix M_y formed by the n cyclic rotations of y sorted in lexicographical order. The first and last columns of M_y are denoted F_y and L_y. Then, the BWT (Burrows and Wheeler 1994) of y corresponds to the pair (L_y, j), where $M_y[j] = y$. In other words, the BWT of y is the last column of M_y and the index of the row in M_y corresponding to y. In practice, a termination symbol \$ is added at the end of the text, smaller than all the letters of the alphabet. This results in reducing the BWT to the last column of M_y: the first row of M_y necessarily corresponding to \$$y$. M_y is never really computed or stored. It is just used to introduce the concept of the BWT. It should be noted that M_y corresponds to the sorting of cyclic rotations where the suffix array is obtained by sorting the suffixes, which illustrates the proximity between the two concepts.

Figure 2.9 shows an example of the BWT.

$$
\begin{array}{c}
1\ \ 2\ \ 3\ \ 4\ \ 5\ \ 6\ \ 7\ \ 8\ \ 9\ \ 10 \\
C\ T\ A\ T\ A\ T\ T\ A\ T\ \$
\end{array}
$$

	F_y	L_y
C T A T A T T A T \$	\$	T
T A T A T T A T \$ C	A	T
A T A T T A T \$ C T	A	T
T A T T A T \$ C T A	A	T
A T T A T \$ C T A T	C	\$
T T A T \$ C T A T A	T	A
T A T \$ C T A T A T	T	T
A T \$ C T A T A T T	T	C
T \$ C T A T A T T A	T	A
\$ C T A T A T T A T	T	A
(a)		(b)

Figure 2.9. *BWT of* $y = CTATATTAT\$$*: (a) cyclic rotations and (b) sorted cyclic rotations. The BWT of* y *corresponds to the last column* L_y *of sorted rotations*

The BWT of y is, in general, more compressible than y because it tends to group identical letters in chunks. Moreover, it is invertible; in other words, it is possible to find y based on its BWT. To this end, we use the fact that the BWT preserves the respective position of a letter in the first and last columns.

First, it can be noted that F_y can be deduced from L_y since F_y consists of the sorted sequence of the letters of y and therefore of L_y. Consequently, F_y can be represented by an array C defined by $C[c]$ equal to the number of letters strictly smaller than c in y for $c \in A$.

A function is then defined, called LF (for *Last-First*), which is capable of shifting from a letter in the last column (L_y) to this same letter in the first column (F_y). For example, if $L_y[i] = c$ and it is the jth c in L_y up to the position i, then $LF(i)$ will give the position of the jth c in F_y. The function is calculated as follows:

$LF(i) = C[c] + rank_c(L_y, i)$, where $rank_c(L_y, i)$ is the total number of c in L_y up to position i.

Figure 2.10 shows an example of BWT inversion using the function LF.

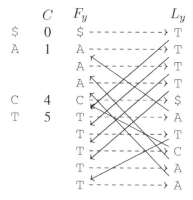

Figure 2.10. *Inversion of the BWT of $y = CTATATTAT\$$. The function LF is indicated by the solid arrows. $F_y[1] = \$$ since the terminator is the smallest letter; it is therefore preceded by $L_y[1] = T$ which is the last letter of y. The function LF can locate the position of this T in the first column. The process just has to be iterated to reconstruct y from right to left*

It is also possible to search for the number of occurrences of a sequence x of length m in a sequence y, given the BWT L_y of y, by means of a technique known as *backward search*. The general principle of this technique is to identify the interval M_y containing all cyclic rotations starting with x.

This search is achieved by reading the letters of x from right to left, hence the name *backward search* (see Algorithm 2.1).

ALGORITHM 2.1. Backward search algorithm in a Burrows–Wheeler transform

---

Input   : L – Burrows–Wheeler transform

  C – table giving for every letter the number of letters lexicographically smaller than the given letter.

  x – the sequence of length m to search for

Output : ℓ, r – the start and end positions corresponding to the occurrences of x in M_y

1 **Function** BackwardSearch(L, C, x):

  ▶ Initialize the size of the interval to the entirety of L

2   $\ell \leftarrow 1$

3   $r \leftarrow |L|$

4   **for** $i \leftarrow |x|$ **to** 1 **do**

5     $c \leftarrow x[i]$

6     $\ell \leftarrow C[c] + rank_c(L, \ell - 1) + 1$

7     $r \leftarrow C[c] + rank_c(L, r)$

8   **return** ℓ, r

The general principle of the algorithm is, starting from an interval of positions ℓ to r of M_y, containing all occurrences of $x[i .. |x|]$, to deduce the interval that contains all occurrences of $x[i - 1 .. |x|]$. For this purpose, it is necessary to consider, among the rotations of the first interval, those which are preceded by $c = x[i - 1]$. It is then necessary to count the number of occurrences of c in L_y between the positions ℓ and r and to update the values of ℓ and r (see lines 6 and 7 of the algorithm).

The process simply has to be repeated considering the letters of x in descending order of positions. It is possible to stop before the examination of all the letters of y if the interval is reduced to an empty one, in which case it means that x does not appear in y. The number of occurrences of x in y corresponds to the length of the final interval. To obtain the positions of these occurrences, the suffix array of y has to be available. In practice, this array is too large. It is possible to keep only a sample of it and to easily find the non-sampled positions, by way of the function LF. This is the principle of FM-index (Ferragina and Manzini 2000).

Figure 2.11 shows an example of a search based on the BWT.

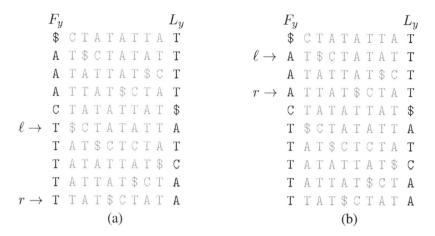

Figure 2.11. *Search for* AT *in the BWT of* $y = $ CTATATTAT$: (a) the bounds of the interval are initialized with the interval of the* T*; (b) among the five* T *(in the first column), three are preceded by* A *(in the last column). These three* A *are the first, second and third of the last column and thus correspond to the first, second and third* A *of the first column.* AT *therefore appears three times in* y

2.3.3.1. *Representation of a de Bruijn graph with a Burrows–Wheeler transform*

In section 2.2.3 on de Bruijn graphs, we have indicated that this is an abstract data structure that can be represented and stored in memory in several different ways: with Bloom filters, hash tables, etc. It can also be represented using a Burrows–Wheeler transform as shown by Bowe et al. (2012).

Let us assume that we want to construct a de Bruijn graph with a set S of m sequences. We start by transforming this set into a sequence. All sequences are concatenated and separated by a symbol different from all the others[1]. This sequence is itself preceded by a sequence of k symbols distinct from all the others. We then obtain a word $T = \$_1 \cdots \$_1 S_1 \cdot \$_2 \cdot S_2 \cdot \$_3 \cdots S_m \cdot \$_{m+1}$. The de Bruijn graph of order k is constructed on T and possesses a vertex per distinct k-mer of T; let E be this set of k-mers, and n be the number of arcs in the graph.

Figure 2.12 shows an example of such a graph.

---

1. It should be noted that in practice, some tricks allow avoiding the use of a different separator for each sequence.

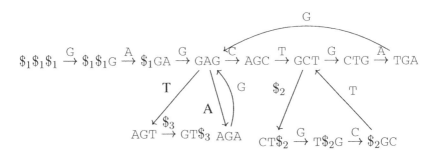

Figure 2.12. *Third-order de Bruijn graph of E, the set of the 3-mers of*
$\$_1\$_1\$_1 GAGAGCT\$_2 GCTGAGT\$_3$. *Only the arcs corresponding to k-mers present
in the data set have been drawn, and not the theoretically possible arcs*

In this section, we will see how concepts of the Burrows–Wheeler
transform, in particular the principle of its function LF, are used to represent
such a graph. The essential operations should enable us to identify the vertex
corresponding to a given k-mer, if it exists, and then to navigate in the graph
identifying the predecessors or successors of a vertex.

A de Bruijn graph is not a linear structure, so the fact of building a
Burrows–Wheeler transform on T is not enough. Nevertheless, as for the
Burrows–Wheeler transform, let us figure a matrix. This latter is composed
of n rows and $k + 1$ columns. Each row consists of a k-mer of T and the letter
that follows it in T. In other words, each row consists of a graph vertex and an
outgoing arc. We call K the first k columns of this matrix ($K[1]$ corresponds
to the first k-mer in the matrix) and W the last column. The rows are then
sorted by reading the first k columns from right to left, followed by the last
column W. This is the equivalent of the Burrows–Wheeler transform applied
to a de Bruijn graph (see columns K and W in Figure 2.13).

Nevertheless, before using this W transform, we still need to proceed to
some modifications to search through the de Bruijn graph.

First, in K, several entries (necessarily consecutive) can be identical, that
is, they correspond to the same k-mer. This happens when a vertex has several
outgoing arcs. We want to identify each separate k-mer only once. For this, we
will use *last*, an n-bit vector. It is defined such that $last[i] = 0$ if and only if
$K[i] = K[i + 1]$, with $1 \leq i < n$ (see column *last* in Figure 2.13).

	last	K	W	C	
1	1	$\$_1\$_1\$_1$	G	0	$\$_1$
2	1	$CT\$_2$	G	1	$\$_2$
3	1	$\$_1GA$	G	2	A
4	1	AGA	G^-		
5	1	TGA	G^-		
6	1	$\$_2GC$	T	5	C
7	1	AGC	T^-		
8	1	$\$_1\$_1G$	A	7	G
9	1	$T\$_2G$	C		
10	0	GAG	A		
11	0	GAG	C		
12	1	GAG	T		
13	1	CTG	A		
14	0	GCT	$\$_2$	13	T
15	1	GCT	G		
16	1	AGT	$\$_3$		

Figure 2.13. *Third-order de Bruijn graph of E represented with W. It should be noted that the k-mer GAG is present three times (positions 10 to 12), but in $last$, a 1 is stored only in the last of these positions. On the contrary, at these positions, each of the letters is different in W since they all correspond to a distinct arc coming out of the vertex GAG, and they are sorted in alphabetical order. Three k-mers end in GA (positions 3 to 5). The three corresponding vertices have a single arc exiting through G. Nevertheless, a G is stored in W only at the first position, the others store a modified version: G^-. As a reminder, K does not need to be actually stored. The function fwd at position 6 results in position 15*

In a similar way, we mark in W the letters which represent outgoing arcs, depending on whether it is the first one to be brought to a given vertex or not. If it is the first one, nothing is changed, otherwise we change the character of W, for example, by adding a $^-$ thereto. In other words, if $K[i] = s_1 s_2 \cdots s_k$ and $W[i] = c$, then $W[i] \leftarrow c^-$ if and only if there exists a position $j < i$ such that $K[j] = s'_1 s_2 \cdots s_k$ (the last $k - 1$ letters are the same as for $K[i]$) and $W[j] = c$. In this case, the positions j and i correspond to two vertices leading to the same vertex representing the k-mer $s_2 \cdots s_k c$. The size of the alphabet of W is therefore potentially doubled compared to its original size.

In a similar way to the Burrows–Wheeler transform, we also have a table C that will be used to know the interval of the positions of k-mers ending with a given letter. More concretely, $C[c]$ indicates for any letter of the alphabet the position of the first occurrence of a k-mer ending in c in the matrix.

An example is given in Figure 2.13.

Only C, W and *last* are stored and are sufficient to navigate in the de Bruijn graph. K is not stored.

2.3.3.1.1. Graph traversal

The LF function introduced for the Burrows–Wheeler transform is applied in a similar way from the table C and W and also adding the information of the bit vector *last* in order to take into account the letters modified. We will call *fwd* this function to differentiate it with LF. The function *fwd* is applied to a given position, corresponding to a vertex s and an outgoing arc, and makes it possible to find one of the positions of the vertex s' reached from this vertex s by following this arc. The function *fwd* can only be applied to positions where W does not contain a modified letter c^-. Otherwise, we must return to the closest previous position containing the same unmodified letter c. Then, the operation $rank_c$ on W will give us the number of occurrences *occ* of c up to the position considered. It remains then to use the table C to find out where is located the interval of k-mers ending with a c and to take into account only the positions where *last* is 1. The *occ*th 1 of this interval is at the position of one of the lines corresponding to the vertex s'. More formally, $fwd(i) = C[c] + select_1(last[C[c] + 1 \ldots], rank_c(W, i))$, with $c = W[i]$ and $fwd(i)$ is defined if and only if c is not a modified letter.

For example, in Figure 2.13, if we are at the position 7, $W[7] = \text{T}^-$, we have to backtrack to the previous position which contained a T; this is position 6. This T is the first one in W; it is now necessary to go to the position of the first k-mer that ends with a T and that is identified by a 1 in *last*. To this end, the table C allows us to find that the interval of interest, corresponding to the k-mers ending with a T, goes from position 14 to 16. The operations *rank* and *select* on *last* allow us to identify that the position corresponding to our criterion is 15.

This function *fwd* can, in particular, be used to identify the position of a vertex corresponding to a given k-mer. To this end, the function *fwd* must be applied k times starting from the interval containing all rows, in a similar manner to the pattern search with a Burrows–Wheeler transform (see Algorithm 2.2). For example, the search for GCT will give, respectively, the intervals $[\ell, r]$: $[1, 16]$, then $[8, 13]$, then $[6, 7]$ and then $[15, 15]$, indicating that the vertex corresponding to the k-mer GCT is at position 15.

ALGORITHM 2.2. Backward search algorithm in a de Bruijn graph represented with W

Input	: W
	C
	$last$
	x – k-mer to search for
Output	: position of a vertex corresponding to x in K

1   **Function** KmerSearch($W, C, last, x$):
     ▶ Initialization of the size of the interval to the whole of W
2      $\ell \leftarrow 1$
3      $r \leftarrow |W|$
4   **for** $i \leftarrow 1$ **to** $|x|$ **do**
5          $c \leftarrow x[i]$
6          $\ell \leftarrow C[c] + select_1(last[C[c] + 1 \ldots], rank_c(W, \ell - 1) + 1)$
7          $r \leftarrow C[c] + select_1(last[C[c] + 1 \ldots], rank_c(W, r))$
8   **if** $\ell > r$ **then**
9   **return** -1
10   **return** ℓ

2.3.3.1.2. Identifying the successor of a vertex by the letter c

Let us assume that we want to go from one vertex to another by following the arc labeled with the letter c. We take as a starting point the line i of the matrix. This line does not represent a vertex but a vertex and one of its outgoing arcs. To identify all the lines that correspond to the same vertex, the bit vector $last$ must be used. The position following the first 1 before $last[i]$ will give the first position of the top. Similarly, identifying the position of the first 1 from $last[i]$ (inclusive) will give the last position of this vertex. We then obtain an interval of all positions corresponding to the same vertex as the one at position i. This computation can be done in constant time with the help of the operations $rank$ and $select$. In this interval, assume that W does not contain c but only c^-. It is then necessary to backtrack to the position j of the previous occurrence of c in W. By definition, this position corresponds to a k-mer ending with the same $k - 1$ letters as the original vertex. The destination vertex will therefore be the one expected. From position j (where $W[j] = c$), the function has to be applied to obtain a position of the successor of the current vertex by the letter c.

In the following, we briefly describe the identification of a k-mer associated with a vertex as well as the identification of a vertex that precedes another one.

2.3.3.1.3. Identifying the k-mer associated with a vertex

At a given position, only the last letter of the k-mer is accessible (based on the table C). To reconstruct the complete sequence of the k-mer, it is therefore necessary to go back to the previous $k - 1$ vertices in order to extract each time the last letter of their associated k-mers. The inverse of the function fwd is used for this purpose.

2.3.3.1.4. Identifying the predecessor of a vertex beginning with the letter c

Assume that we want to move from a vertex to a previous vertex whose associated k-mer begins with the letter c. We start from row i of the matrix and call c' the last letter of the k-mer corresponding to this row. We can backtrack to a predecessor, for which c' is stored in W and identify all other possible predecessors: these are all the occurrences of c'^- that precede the next occurrence of c'. Among these potential occurrences of predecessors, we simply have to identify using binary search the k-mer that begins with the chosen c.

2.3.3.1.5. Time and space complexities

Only W, $last$ and C are actually stored. Assuming that the alphabet is constant, the structure with the most important space complexity is W. The table W can be represented in $n \log \sigma + o(n \log \sigma)$ bits, so as to have the operation $rank$ that runs in contant time on the table, with n being the number of arcs in the graph. C can be stored with $\sigma \log n$ bits and $last$ with $n + o(n)$ bits. The total space used is then in $n \log \sigma + o(n \log \sigma)$ bits.

The access to a successor is achieved in constant time; the identification of the k-mer of a vertex is performed in $O(k)$ similarly to the operation that accesses its predecessor.

2.4. Indexing choice criteria

We will now try to give some indications on the choice of an indexing structure according to the needs. Or why should we choose a Bloom filter, which can give inaccurate results, when there are methods for indexing, in an exact way, the whole text?

2.4.1. *Based on the type of the necessary query*

Depending on the application being considered, it is sufficient to perform queries from k-mers or, conversely, it is essential to query sequences of arbitrary length. In the first case, the indexing structures presented in section 2.2 will be sufficient, especially since they are more memory efficient, while in the second case, it will be necessary to resort to the structures of section 2.3.

Apart from the simple query on a sequence of fixed size or not, the type of response that the structure can provide is important. Some structures can only be used to find out if a given sequence exists (*existence*), whereas others make it possible to know the number of occurrences (*counting*) as well as the position of each of them (*location*). Knowing the location then allows access to information about the context of the occurrence. Table 2.1 summarizes the different features of the structures presented.

Structure	Existence	Counting	Locating	Exact
Bloom filter	Y	N	N	N
Hash table	Y	Y	Y	Y
De Bruijn graphs	Y	P	N	P
Suffix tree	Y	Y	Y	Y
Suffix table	Y	Y	Y	Y
Burrows–Wheeler transform	Y	Y	Y	Y

Table 2.1. *Features of the presented indexing structures. The structures allow (Y) or do not (N) or, sometimes, can allow (P) certain functionalities*

Various indexing structures provide the same functionality: for example, hash tables and Burrows–Wheeler transform enable locating the occurrences of a sequence searched for. Besides the functionalities, one remaining issue concerns the necessary resources to build and use such data structures.

2.4.2. *Based on the space-time and data quantity trade-off*

If we make a comparison in terms of memory space, the most efficient structure will obviously be the Bloom filter which is only composed of a bit vector, whose size depends specifically on the chosen false positive rate. Then, follows the de Bruijn graph, which can be constructed with Bloom filters or with a Burrows–Wheeler transform. The FM-index, using a Burrows–Wheeler transform, is the most inexpensive full-text indexing structure among those presented: it is compressed. Next follows the suffix arrays and the suffix tree. In order to get an idea of the space required by these structures, we can consider indexing a human genome (or its k-mers). A human genome is composed of about 3 billion nucleotides and, therefore, about as many k-mers. Table 2.2 gives an idea of the space needed for each of the indexing structures.

Indexing structure	Occupied memory (GB)
Bloom filter	1 [a]
De Bruijn graph	1
Burrows–Wheeler transform	2
Hash table	8 [b]
Suffix array	15
Suffix tree	$\simeq 30$

[a] 10^{10}-bit vector, with 2 hash functions, 20 % false positives.
[b] For counting only.

Table 2.2. *Space occupied by each indexing structure for indexing a human genome (about 3 billion nucleotides), rounded to the nearest gigabyte. The space can fluctuate depending on the selected parameters (especially for the most inexpensive structures)*

From a more formal point of view, the space occupied for indexing a text (or its k-mers) can also be expressed according to its size n. We give these space complexities in Table 2.3.

In fact, some of these structures offer a space-time trade-off. It is possible to reduce the space used by the structure provided that the time of queries be increased, or vice versa.

The query time is more difficult to estimate. Theoretical time complexities provide less direct information than space complexities on practical effectiveness. For example, counting the number of occurrences of a word of length m with only a suffix array is done in $O(m \log n)$ time while in a Burrows–Wheeler transform; it is in optimal $O(m)$ time. However, in practice, the search in the suffix array is faster by several orders of magnitude. This difference is due to the numerous memory accesses required to query a Burrows–Wheeler transform as well as the accompanying structures in an

FM-index and to the fact that these memory accesses are not contiguous. Moreover, the use of an extended suffix array improves the time complexity of the search to $O(m + \log n)$.

Indexing structure	Space complexity
Bloom filter	$2n$ to $3n$ bits
De Bruijn graph	$3.24n$ bits (Chikhi et al. 2015)
Burrows–Wheeler transform	$nH_k(y) + o(n)$ bits
Hash table	$O(n)$
Suffix array	$n \log n$ bits
Suffix tree	$O(n)$

Table 2.3. *Space complexity of the indexing structures according to n, the size of the indexed text. $H_k(y)$ is the empirical entropy of order k of the text: it measures the average number of bits needed to represent a letter of the sequence y, knowing the previous k letters. For DNA, this value is necessarily lower or equal to 2*

2.4.3. *Based on the need to add or modify indexed data*

Sequencing data used in bioinformatics are far from being immutable. New data sets as well as new species are regularly sequenced. It is then necessary to update the index that stores the sequences of interest in order to stay up to date.

For k-mer indexing structures, adding new data does not raise any particular problem. On the contrary, deleting data in a Bloom filter is not possible. A 1 cannot be inverted into a 0 because several k-mers could have led to the storage of a 1 at the same position. To enable deletions, a counter would thus be needed, rather than a bit, to know how many times an insertion has been made at a given position (Fan et al. 2000). Such a change obviously has consequences on the memory footprint of the structure.

Updates of full-text indexes are less obvious: these structures index text suffixes. However, a single modification can impact, depending on its position in the text, a large part of the suffixes. Nevertheless, using the LF function of the Burrows–Wheeler transform (see section 2.3.3), it is possible to update a Burrows–Wheeler transform, and thus an FM-index, provided that dynamic data structures that are slower by a factor $\log n$ are used (Salson et al. 2010).

2.4.4. *Indexing choices according to applications*

Not all sequencing data sets are comparable. Based on what is indexed:

– collections of thousands of individual genomes from the same species or in raw high-throughput sequencing data, consisting of millions or even billions of relatively short sequences;

– solutions will not necessarily be the same. Since this is a very active area of research at the moment, our choice is not to present specific methods, which might become quickly outdated, but the underlying ideas.

2.4.4.1. *Indexing genome collections*

Indexing numerous individual genomes of the same species is characterized by very strong data redundancy, unless we are considering highly heterozygous species, which is not the most common case.

Full-text indexes do not take advantage of such redundancy, including the FM-index which is nonetheless a compressed indexing structure. An FM-index can compress short repetitions, but is not suitable for the compression of long repetitions. In order to best manage data redundancy, it is necessary to either eliminate this redundancy upstream or downstream (Gagie and Navarro 2019). Upstream, it is possible to compress redundant sequences using grammars (such as LZ-77 compression) or by indexing aligned sequences, rather than raw sequences. Downstream, after having indexed redundant sequences in an FM-index, it is necessary to remove some of the remaining redundancy by using other compression techniques. Upstream solutions seem to be the most effective at the present time.

Another approach consists of merely indexing k-mers. In this case, redundancy is managed almost effortlessly since a large part of the k-mers will be shared by most genomes. Such approaches will therefore be very efficient in terms of memory space consumed, but will allow less fine-grained queries than full-text indexes.

2.4.4.2. *Indexing collections of sequencing sets*

Indexing collections of sequencing sets, such as the indexing of collections of genomes, is equivalent to indexing large amounts of genomic data. However, the difference resides in the nature of the data indexed. Indexing sequencing data sets means indexing billions of short sequences, possibly noisy. Because of the commonly encountered sequencing depths, in a single sequencing set, the same region can be sequenced a hundred times. We therefore have much higher levels of redundancy than those encountered when indexing genomes. However, this redundancy is also less perfect, due to sequencing errors. Although with the second generation of sequencers, sequencing errors are relatively rare, they can nevertheless constitute the majority of the distinct k-mers of a sequencing set. In this case, redundancy is more difficult to exploit, because of the small differences between the different k-mers.

At the moment, there is no real solution for full-text indexing of thousands of sequencing data sets. It turns out that taking advantage of the redundancy of thousands of highly similar genomes is already a complex task, and an even more difficult one on much shorter sequences, much more numerous, but with more differences.

On the contrary, many solutions allow indexing the k-mers of thousands of sequencing data sets; see the synthesis by Marchet et al. (2021). Either each data set is independently indexed (e.g. with a Bloom filter) and an additional structure is employed to efficiently query all the data sets, or all data sets are indexed together (e.g. with a de Bruijn graph) and a *color* is associated with each k-mer, corresponding to the data sets where this k-mer appears; this data structure is known as colored de Bruijn graphs. In all cases, a filtering is operated on the least abundant k-mers in order to remove some of the sequencing errors, which might occupy a disproportionate amount of space.

2.5. Conclusion and perspectives

2.5.1. *Efficient methods for indexing a few genomes or sequencing sets*

Genome assembly as well as genome sequence alignment are fundamental tasks in sequence bioinformatics (see Chapters 3 and 4). Yet, it would not be possible to efficiently solve alignment as well as assembly without the use of indexing structures. The indexing methods employed are based on the structures that are already known (de Bruijn graphs, suffix arrays, FM-indexes, etc.) by adapting them to the problem and scaling them up. Consequently, these indexing structures prove to be satisfactory for alignment and assembly, when restricted to the study of a genome or a data set, offering good trade-offs between the space consumed by the structure and query times (space-time trade-off).

2.5.2. *Methods that struggle to take advantage of data redundancy*

Nevertheless, indexing is not restricted to a single data set and current solutions still present significant limitations when it comes to indexing large numbers of data sets (for instance, thousands of genomes or thousands of sequencing sets).

In such a situation, the difficulty lies in the fact that the same information can be found several thousand times. Merely, compressing it efficiently is not only sufficient (there are solutions for this) but also being able to quickly retrieve all the occurrences of any sequence after such compression is important.

To a certain extent, de Bruijn graphs make it possible, but by way of removing information: indexing is only done for k-mers with a predefined value for k.

Regarding full-text indexing, by the end of the 2010s, various research studies have tried to improve their efficiency in order to better take advantage of the very high data redundancy (Gagie et al. 2018; Na et al. 2018; Sirén et al. 2020). In particular, some approaches would seek to represent, compress and index a graph rather than thousands of linear sequences, by applying the Burrows–Wheeler transform to such a graph.

Notably, it has been proposed that these different approaches are grouped under the common notion of Wheeler graphs, which more specifically correspond to non-deterministic automata capable of solving pattern search problems. These graphs can be indexed using little space while presenting faster graph traversal. More formally, a directed graph $G = (V, E)$ must verify certain properties to be a Wheeler graph. An order on the vertices must be present such that for any pair of arcs (u, k, v) and (u', k', v'), with $u, v, u', v' \in V$ and with k and k' the labels of the arcs from u to v and from u' to v', respectively, the following two properties are verified:

- $k < k' \rightarrow v < v'$;
- $k = k'$ and $u < u' \rightarrow v \leq v'$.

Besides these approaches that generalize the notion of Burrows–Wheeler, further research studies aim to develop indexing structure on top of compression methods already known for their high efficiency to strongly reduce high data redundancy. In 2019, researchers have proposed a theoretical index gathering all these compression methods under the same notion, that of *attractors*, and proposed a method to index them, regardless of the underlying compression method (Navarro and Prezza 2019). The *attractors* of a sequence constitute the set (the smallest possible) of the text positions such that any text factor can be found again overlapping one of these positions.

The different approaches presented in this section are, in 2020, still in the early stages of research prototypes and are not yet in use in bioinformatics tools for indexing thousands of data sets. Nevertheless, these approaches illustrate the need for increasingly less expensive indexing structures and perhaps foreshadow the methods that will soon be used for larger scale indexing.

2.6. References

Baeza-Yates, R. and Gonnet, G. (1992). A new approach to text searching. *Communications of the ACM*, 35(10), 74–82.

Bahne, J., Bertram, N., Böcker, M., Bode, J., Fischer, J., Foot, H., Grieskamp, F., Kurpicz, F., Löbel, M., Magiera, O. et al. (2019). SACABench: Benchmarking suffix array construction. *26th International Symposium on String Processing and Information Retrieval*, Segovia, October 7–9, 407–416.

Belazzougui, D., Botelho, F.C., Dietzfelbinger, M. (2009). Hash, displace, and compress. *European Symposium on Algorithms*, 682–693.

Bloom, B.H. (1970). Space/time trade-offs in hash coding with allowable errors. *Communications of the ACM*, 13(7), 422–426.

Bowe, A., Onodera, T., Sadakane, K., Shibuya, T. (2012). Succinct de Bruijn graphs. In *Algorithms in Bioinformatics – 12th International Workshop, WABI 2012, Ljubljana, Slovenia, September 10–12, 2012 Proceedings*, Raphael, B.J. and Tang, J. (eds). Springer.

Broder, A. and Mitzenmacher, M. (2004). Network applications of Bloom filters: A survey, *Internet Mathematics*, 1(4), 485–509.

de Bruijn, N. (1950). On bases for the set of integers. *Publicationes Mathematicae Debrecen*, 1, 232–242.

Burrows, M. and Wheeler, D.J. (1994). A block sorting lossless data compression algorithm. Technical Report 124, Digital Equipment Corporation.

Chikhi, R. and Rizk, G. (2013). Space-efficient and exact de Bruijn graph representation based on a Bloom filter. *Algorithms for Molecular Biology*, 8(1), 22.

Chikhi, R., Limasset, A., Jackman, S., Simpson, J.T., Medvedev, P. (2015). On the representation of de Bruijn graphs. *Journal of Computational Biology*, 22(5), 336–352.

Chikhi, R., Holub, J., Medvedev, P. (2019). Data structures to represent sets of k-long DNA sequences. arXiv:1903.12312.

Cormen, T.H., Leiserson, C.E., Rivest, R.L., Stein, C. (2022). *Introduction to Algorithms*. MIT Press.

Crochemore, M., Hancart, C., Lecroq, T. (2007). *Algorithms on Strings*. Cambridge University Press.

Fan, L., Cao, P., Almeida, J., Broder, A.Z. (2000). Summary cache: A scalable wide-area web cache sharing protocol. *IEEE/ACM Transactions on Networking (TON)*, 8(3), 281–293.

Farach, M. (1997). Optimal suffix tree construction with large alphabets. *Proceedings of the 38th IEEE Annual Symposium on Foundations of Computer Science*, Miami Beach, 137–143.

Ferragina, P. and Manzini, G. (2000). Opportunistic data structures with applications. *41st Annual Symposium on Foundations of Computer Science, FOCS 2000, 12–14 November 2000*, IEEE Computer Society, 390–398.

Gagie, T. and Navarro, G. (2019). Compressed indexes for repetitive textual datasets. In *Encyclopedia of Big Data Technologies*, Sakr, S. and Zomaya, A.Y. (eds). Springer.

Gagie, T., Navarro, G., Prezza, N. (2018). Optimal-time text indexing in BWT-runs bounded space. *Proceedings of the 19th Symposium on Discrete Algorithms (SODA)*, SIAM, 1459–1477.

Good, I.J. (1946). Normal recurring decimals. *Journal of the London Mathematical Society*, 21(3), 167–169.

Goodwin, S., McPherson, J.D., McCombie, W.R. (2016). Coming of age: Ten years of next-generation sequencing technologies. *Nature Reviews Genetics*, 17(6), 333–351.

Iqbal, Z., Caccamo, M., Turner, I., Flicek, P., McVean, G. (2012). De novo assembly and genotyping of variants using colored de Bruijn graphs. *Nature Genetics*, 44(2), 226.

Kärkkäinen, J. and Sanders, P. (2003). Simple linear work suffix array construction. In *Proceedings of the Automata, Languages and Programming, 30th International Colloquium, ICALP 2003, Eindhoven, The Netherlands, June 30–July 4 2003*, Baeten, J.C.M., Lenstra, J.K., Parrow, J., Woeginger, G.J. (eds). Springer.

Kasai, T., Lee, G., Arimura, H., Arikawa, S., Park, K. (2001). Linear-time longest-common-prefix computation in suffix arrays and its applications. In *Proceedings of the Combinatorial Pattern Matching, 12th Annual Symposium, CPM 2001 Jerusalem, Israel, July 1–4, 2001*, Amir, A. and Landau, G.M. (eds). Springer.

Kim, D.K., Sim, J.S., Park, H., Park, K. (2003). Linear-time construction of suffix arrays. In *Proceedings of the Combinatorial Pattern Matching, 14th Annual Symposium, CPM 2003, Morelia, Michocán, Mexico, June 25–27, 2003*, Baeza-Yates, R.A., Chávez, E., Crochemore, M. (eds). Springer.

Ko, P. and Aluru, S. (2003). Space efficient linear time construction of suffix arrays. In *Proceedings of the Combinatorial Pattern Matching, 14th Annual Symposium, CPM 2003, Morelia, Michocán, Mexico, June 25–27, 2003*, Baeza-Yates, R.A., Chávez, E., Crochemore, M. (eds). Springer.

Luo, L., Guo, D., Ma, R.T.B., Rottenstreich, O., Luo, X. (2019). Optimizing bloom filter: challenges, solutions, and comparisons. *IEEE Communications Surveys Tutorials*, 21(2), 1912–1949.

Manber, U. and Myers, G. (1990). Suffix arrays: A new method for on-line string searches. *SODA '90: Proceedings of the First Annual ACM-SIAM Symposium on Discrete Algorithms*, Industrial and Applied Mathematics, Philadelphia, PA, 319–327.

Marçais, G., Pellow, D., Bork, D., Orenstein, Y., Shamir, R., Kingsford, C. (2017). Improving the performance of minimizers and winnowing schemes. *Bioinformatics*, 33(14), i110–i117.

Marchet, C., Boucher, C., Puglisi, S.J., Medvedev, P., Salson, M., Chikhi, R. (2021). Data structures based on k-mers for querying large collections of sequencing datasets. *Genome Research*, 31, 1–12.

Mayer-Schönberger, V. and Cukier, K. (2013). *Big Data: A Revolution that Will Transform How We Live, Work, and Think*. Houghton Mifflin Harcourt.

McCreight, E.M. (1976). A space-economical suffix tree construction algorithm. *Journal of Algorithms*, 23(2), 262–272.

Mori, Y. (2015). LibDivSufSort: A lightweight suffix-sorting library [Online]. Available at: https://github.com/y-256/libdivsufsort.

Na, J.C., Kim, H., Min, S., Park, H., Lecroq, T., Léonard, M., Mouchard, L., Park, K. (2018). FM-index of alignment with gaps. *Theoretical Computer Science*, 710, 148–157.

Navarro, G. and Mäkinen, V. (2007). Compressed full-text indexes. *ACM Computing Surveys*, 39(1), 2–es.

Navarro, G. and Prezza, N. (2019). Universal compressed text indexing. *Theoretical Computer Science*, 762, 41–50.

NCBI (2013). Grch37.p13-genome-assembly-ncbi [Online]. Available at: https://www.ncbi.nlm.nih.gov/assembly/GCF_000001405.25.

NCBI (2019). Grch38.p13-genome-assembly-ncbi [Online]. Available at: https://www.ncbi.nlm.nih.gov/assembly/GCF_000001405.39.

Puglisi, S.J., Smyth, W.F., Turpin, A.H. (2007). A taxonomy of suffix array construction algorithms. *ACM Computing Surveys*, 39(2), 4–es.

Sacomoto, G.A., Kielbassa, J., Chikhi, R., Uricaru, R., Antoniou, P., Sagot, M.-F., Peterlongo, P., Lacroix, V. (2012). KIS SPLICE: De-novo calling alternative splicing events from RNA-seq data. *BMC Bioinformatics*, 13(S6).

Sainte-Marie, C.F. (1894). Question 48. *L'Intermédiaire des Mathématiciens*, 1, 107–110.

Salson, M., Lecroq, T., Léonard, M., Mouchard, L. (2010). Dynamic extended suffix arrays. *Journal of Discrete Algorithms*, 8, 241–257.

Schatz, M.C. and Langmead, B. (2013). The DNA data deluge. *IEEE Spectrum*, 50(7), 28–33.

Sirén, J., Garrison, E., Novak, A.M., Paten, B., Durbin, R. (2020). Haplotype-aware graph indexes. *Bioinformatics*, 36(2), 400–407.

Ukkonen, E. (1995). On-line construction of suffix trees. *Algorithmica*, 14(3), 249–260.

3

Sequence Alignment

Laurent Noé

University of Lille, CNRS, UMR 9189 – CRIStAL, France

3.1. Introduction

In this chapter, we focus on comparing sequences using *alignment*. Sequence alignment is the operation that consists of matching two or more sequences, in order to highlight their similarity, whether it is local or global. This is a generally unavoidable step in a number of bioinformatics problems. On the contrary, it is often considered as a costly step that must be implemented wisely, and the methods adopted should be as optimized as possible.

3.1.1. *What is pairwise alignment?*

It mainly consists of matching *two* a priori similar sequences, either in their entirety or at least for each one in a subpart. This mapping is carried out by a set of unitary operations, which we will call **edit operations**.

We take two sequences for the following examples:

$$u = \text{GCGATGTGCA and } v = \text{GCATGATGGA}.$$

According to certain constraints that we will discuss later, it is possible to find an alignment from the whole of u and v. This alignment, as well as the edit operations involved in it, can be visually represented in the following form:

From Sequences to Graphs,
coordinated by Annie CHATEAU and Mikaël SALSON.
© ISTE Ltd 2022.

GCGATG-TGCA
|| ||| || |
GC-ATGATGGA

First, we will focus on how the majority of the nucleotides *match* (represented by the central symbol |). However, some *mismatches* are highlighted: these are *edit operations* that are due to a mismatch of some portions of the two sequences. After the (arbitrary) orientation of the two sequences, three of them can be distinguished:

G → − the deletion of the third nucleotide G of the first sequence.
We will also denote it by $\left(\begin{smallmatrix} G \\ \_ \end{smallmatrix}\right)$.

− → A the insertion of the nucleotide A at the seventh position of the alignment or at the sixth position in the second sequence.
We will also denote it by $\left(\begin{smallmatrix} \_ \\ A \end{smallmatrix}\right)$.

C → G the substitution of the 10th nucleotide of the alignment C with G.
We will also denote it by $\left(\begin{smallmatrix} C \\ G \end{smallmatrix}\right)$.

Therefore, the alignment is obtained by a succession of match or edit operations with its nucleotides.

$$
\begin{matrix} \text{GCGATG-TGCA} \\ \text{|| ||| || |} \\ \text{GC-ATGATGGA} \end{matrix} = \left(\begin{smallmatrix} G \\ G \end{smallmatrix}\right) \cdot \left(\begin{smallmatrix} C \\ C \end{smallmatrix}\right) \cdot \left(\begin{smallmatrix} G \\ \_ \end{smallmatrix}\right) \cdots
$$

The two insertion or deletion operations are often grouped under a single term *indel* in the literature, which is short for *insertion/deletion*.

3.1.2. *How to evaluate an alignment?*

Given two sequences u and v, it is quite natural to try to minimize the number of edit operations applied to shift from one to another, or from a subpart of the first to a subpart of the second. It is possible to calculate a *cost* by seeking to minimize edit operations. Nevertheless, in bioinformatics, it is much more common to compute a *score* and try to maximize it, rather than minimizing a *cost*.

The basic idea consists of giving each operation (matching, substitution, *indel*) what will be called a *unit score*. Each *unit score* is a generally *positive* numerical value (reward) in the case of matching identical (or possibly close) elements or negative (and therefore penalizing) in the case of *substitutions* or *indels*.

If an alignment is already provided, then the *sum of the unit scores* is evaluated to obtain the *score of this alignment*. Otherwise, the objective of this chapter will be, among the possible alignments, to obtain the one (or the ones) that maximize this objective function *alignment score*, and thus to find the best alignment(s) according to *a scoring scheme*.

Enumerating all the existing alignments to extract an optimal alignment is a possible strategy, but it is obviously not usable in practice. The strategy commonly used in this case is inspired by the principle of dynamic programming (see section 1.8). It is indeed possible, as we will see, to make use of partial alignment scores to deduce an optimal score alignment.

Substitution matrix

First, the *match/substitution* score between two nucleotides (or two amino acids) is often given by a two-entry function $Subs(a, b)$, which itself is provided by a *substitution matrix*: this is a table, which, given a pair of nucleotides each originating from a sequence, makes it possible to associate a score with each event (matching or substitution operation) involved by this pair.

$Subs(a,b)$	A	C	G	T
A	+5	−4	−3	−4
C	−4	+5	−4	−3
G	−3	−4	+5	−4
T	−4	−4	−4	+5

The previous matrix gives a positive score of $+5$ for all *matches* and a negative score of -3 or -4, depending on which the *type of substitution* is implemented.

If we reconsider the alignment given as an example in section 3.1.1, the score associated with the set of *eight matches* and the *substitution* of the alignment is $8 \times Subs_{x \in [A,C,G,T]}(x, x) + 1 \times Subs(C, G) = 8 \times (+5) + 1 \times (-4) = 36$. By arbitrarily applying a score of -8 for any *indel*, it is then possible to compute the final score of the so-called *global* alignment (i.e. performed from end to end on both sequences) at $36 + 2 \times (-8) = 20$.

It is interesting to note that the substitution matrices make use of *log-odd ratio* computational functions in the case of proteins (Dayhoff et al. 1978; Henikoff and Henikoff 1992; Gonnet et al. 1992), and in some cases also for DNA (Chiaromonte et al. 2002). Therefore, when a **sum** of scores is computed from an alignment, a **multiplication** is carried out in the absolute of probabilities (of successive and independent events on the alignment), since $log(a) + log(b) = log(a \times b)$; more exactly, this method calculates a ratio between the probability that the alignment to be evaluated is obtained by descent according to a given model and the probability that it is obtained by pure chance.

3.2. Exact alignment

If the alignment is given, then computing a score is a relatively simple task. However, if two sequences are given, knowing the best alignment(s) in the sense that they will maximize the score becomes more difficult. The number of possible alignments actually increases exponentially with the size of two sequences. We will illustrate this principle, and show that there is, however, a dynamic programming-based method (see Chapter 1) to compute the best alignment(s) and their associated scores.

Problem 3.1. Pairwise sequence alignment

Input: Two sequences u and v
Output: The alignment (or alignments) of maximum scores

3.2.1. *Representation in edit graph form*

The representation in edit graph form (Crochemore et al. 2001) is a means to illustrate the set of possible edit operations between two sequences u and v, and thus the set of possible alignments in the form of paths.

We consider again the two sequences used as examples in section 3.1.1, in the form of a graph, as shown in Figure 3.1. To construct this graph, each of the two sequences is placed on the vertical (u) or horizontal (v) axis. Each pair of positions (i, j) in the two respective sequences u, v forms a node. The following convention will also be followed: the position denoted by 0 will be a virtual position present **before** the first letter of the sequence (which will be used to denote the empty sequence). The graph thus constituted will have $(|u| + 1) \times (|v| + 1)$ nodes.

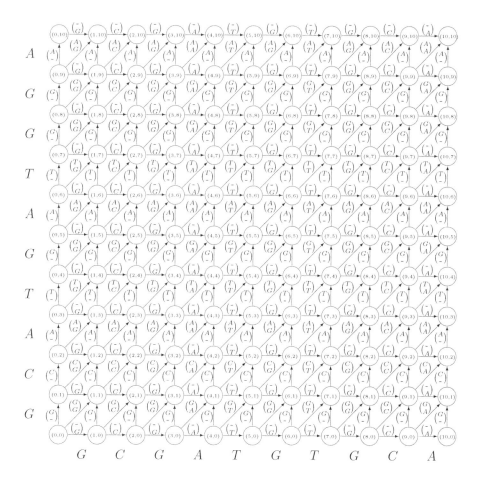

Figure 3.1. *Edit graph of two sequences*

The edges are then associated with the nodes according to a regular pattern, corresponding to edit or match operations:

1) The diagonal edges represent either matches or substitutions, depending on the nature of the pair of nucleotides involved: they make it possible to progress *at the same time* in both sequences by one nucleotide on each.

2) The vertical or horizontal edges are associated with insertion/deletion events (*indels*) because they have only one nucleotide involved in a single sequence, and therefore only progress with this single sequence.

In Figure 3.1, by following the set of paths starting from the *bottom-left* node $(0,0)$, that is, from the beginning of the two sequences, to the *top-right* node $(10,10)$, that is, to the end of the two sequences, it is then possible to *enumerate a set of so-called global alignments* between these two sequences.

It is also possible to compute for any node of coordinates (i,j), thus leading to the position i in the sequence u and to the position j in the sequence v, the best alignment score between a prefix $u[1..i]$ and a prefix $v[1..j]$. In fact, by a simple decomposition of edit or match operations, an alignment up to the position (i,j) can be achieved:

1) either by selecting the previous diagonal node $(i-1, j-1)$, and then adding the operation associated with the pair of nucleotides $u[i], v[j]$ (substitution/matching);

2) or by selecting the previous horizontal node $(i-1, j)$ (respectively the previous vertical node $(i, j-1)$), and then adding an insertion operation (respectively deletion).

The prefix scores of the maximal alignments leading to the three nodes $(i-1, j-1)$, $(i-1, j)$ and $(i, j-1)$ should simply be known to compute the score of the node (i,j), after adding the respective scores of the three operations represented on the edges. The maximum score of the node (i,j) can thus be obtained, **and the edge (operation)**, which was involved in the maximum score of the node (i,j), can also be selected.

Figure 3.2 shows the computation of the maximum scores for each node, which is applied to the edit graph of Figure 3.1, with the score being indicated inside each node. The edges represented here give the dependencies of the computation of the maximal scores of the different nodes: it is then possible to start from the *top-right* node $(10,10)$, then to retrace the origin, following the edges in their opposite direction and thus the operations involved, resulting in obtaining the score 20. Here it should be noted, for example, that it is first the *previous diagonal* cell of score 15 (coming thus from the node $(9,9)$, then associated with the operation $\binom{A}{A}$ on the edit graph of Figure 3.1) that finally leads to obtaining a score of $15 + Subs(\text{A}, \text{A}) = 15 + (+5) = 20$.

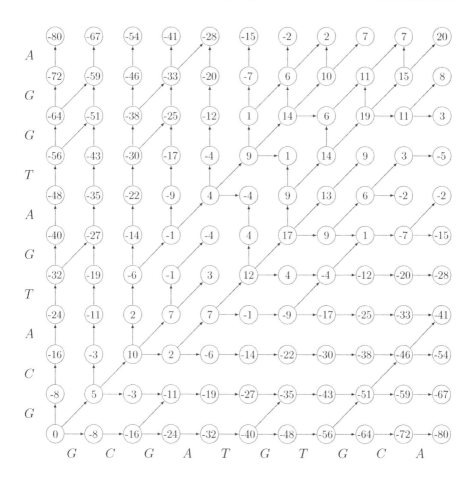

Figure 3.2. *Maximal score of prefix alignments in the edit graph*

Following the same principle of recurrence, it is possible to find the operations involved in the alignment of the section 3.1.1, which is here the optimal global alignment, according to the scoring scheme being used.

3.2.2. *Global alignment and Needleman–Wunsch algorithm*

Given two sequences u and v, as well as a score function for matches/substitutions and *indels*, the goal is to find both the best global alignment and the score achieved.

In order to compute the global alignment score, we look for a path in the edit graph whose *score is maximal*. By means of decomposition, we have previously seen that, in the graph, this *maximal* path also depends on the prefix paths of maximal score.

It is thus possible to establish a recurrence relation between the score $T(i, j)$ of a maximal path leading to the node (i, j) and the cost of the maximal paths prefixed to it: in particular, from the edit graph, the relation for $T(i, j)$ can be obtained as a function of $T(i-1, j-1)$, $T(i, j-1)$ and $T(i-1, j)$ as:

$$T(i, j) = max \begin{cases} T(i-1, j-1) + Subs(u[i], v[j]) & \text{if } 0 < i \leq |u| \text{ and } 0 < j \leq |v| \\ T(i, j-1) + Del(u[i]) & \text{if } 0 \leq i \leq |u| \text{ and } 0 < j \leq |v| \\ T(i-1, j) + Ins(v[j]) & \text{if } 0 < i \leq |u| \text{ and } 0 \leq j \leq |v| \end{cases}$$

The associated algorithm (Needleman and Wunsch 1970) computes the recurrence in two steps using a two-dimensional dynamic programming table T, which will be of size $(|u| + 1) \times (|v| + 1)$, and where $T[i, j]$ corresponds to the score of the best alignment of $u[1..i]$ and $v[1..j]$:

– The first step consists of initializing the *edges* of the table, namely assigning the values associated with the elements $T[i, 0]$ for $i \in [0..|u|]$ and with the elements $T[0, j]$ for $j \in [0..|v|]$.

– The second step (internal loop of Algorithm 3.1) computes the recurrence to finally give the global alignment score between sequences u and v (value $T[|u|, |v|]$).

3.2.3. *Local alignment and Smith–Waterman algorithm*

Global alignment provides an **end-to-end alignment between two sequences**.

There are, however, many cases where **only a portion of each sequence** presents a similarity of interest. For example, there may be a few homologous genes in two genomes, which themselves have undergone rearrangements, or for which conservation is more pronounced than for the rest of the genome: in this case, global alignment cannot be performed in absolute terms. In a much broader context where the user does not know exactly what they are looking for, local alignment is often the tool of choice, a real *Swiss army knife* for a first analysis.

ALGORITHM 3.1. Computation of the global alignment score using
the Needleman–Wunsch algorithm

Input: two sequences u and v from an alphabet Σ,
a substitution function $Subs : \Sigma^2 \to \mathbb{R}$,
two indel functions $Ins : \Sigma \to \mathbb{R}$, $Del : \Sigma \to \mathbb{R}$
Output: the global alignment score between u and v
Data: a table T of dimension $(|u| + 1) \times (|v| + 1)$

1   $T[0,0] \leftarrow 0$
2   **For** i *from* 1 *to* $|u|$ **do**
3     $T[i,0] \leftarrow T[i-1,0] + Del(u[i])$
4   **For** j *from* 1 *to* $|v|$ **do**
5     $T[0,j] \leftarrow T[0,j-1] + Ins(v[j])$
6   **For** i *from* 1 *to* $|u|$ **do**
7       $T[i,j] = max \left(\begin{array}{l} T[i-1,j-1] + Subs(u[i],v[j]), \\ T[i,j-1] + Del(u[i]), \\ T[i-1,j] + Ins(v[j]) \end{array} \right)$
8   **return** $T[|u|,|v|]$

The principle leading to the computation of the *local alignment* was published 11 years after the Needleman–Wunsch algorithm, in the article by Smith and Waterman (1981). It consists of a *minor but clever* modification. Starting from the previous Needleman–Wunsch algorithm, which computes a maximum from at most **three dependencies** from previous boxes/nodes, **a fourth dependency simply has to be added**: the start of alignment with the current cell/node (i,j). In order for any pair of positions (i,j) to initiate an alignment, the trick is to add, **when computing the maximum, the constant zero** as a fourth case.

The counterpart is, however, obvious: only the **local alignments of positive scores** can be computed. Nonetheless, since these are alignments of interest according to the *log-odd ratio*-type substitution matrices, the impact generated by this restriction is clearly negligible.

The second constraint concerns the maximal score reached: it will be necessary to locate it/them (and to keep it/them or otherwise to search for them in the a posteriori table), then from the maximal score, to backtrace to the source node that has provided the value zero. This step is not difficult if a single local alignment is searched for, but if this is desirable for obtaining *several non-overlapping local alignments* that do not make use of the same graph nodes, a principle of marking the nodes that have already been traversed then recomputing them is necessary for successive alignments.

3.2.4. *Alignment with affine indel function and the Gotoh algorithm*

In practice, it is quite common for a series of *indels* to occur consecutively: these *indels* are then grouped together in what is commonly referred to as a *gap*.

Rather than penalizing each *indel* belonging to the same *gap* with a simple unit penalty, it proves often more interesting to associate a *convex* (in absolute value) *gap* penalty function $\lambda(\ell)$, according to the length ℓ of the *gap* created. This function can serve, for example, to **strongly penalize the creation** of a *gap*, and also to **degressively** penalize its extension by the successive addition of juxtaposed *indels* of the same type.

Among the possible functions, we consider here the affine functions because they present good properties concerning dynamic programming: the Gotoh (1982) algorithm has actually made it possible to integrate quite easily this kind of functions in both previous Needleman–Wunsch and Smith–Waterman algorithms without any change of order of magnitude concerning the cost of each of the two algorithms.

Let $\lambda(\ell)$ be the affine penalty function associated with *indels*:

$$\lambda(\ell) = d + e \cdot (\ell - 1)$$

with $d, e \in \mathbb{R}^-$. It can be assumed that these two negative constants d, e will be respectively associated with the opening/extension of a *gap*. By principle, $abs(d) \geq abs(e)$.

In order to update an element (i, j) in the dynamic programming table T, we need to know the score of all upstream *insertions* and *deletions* that end in (i, j).

It is then possible to compute these quantities using two other dynamic programming matrices I and D of the same dimensions as T: the three matrices T, I, D will be mutually dependent during the whole computation. $I(i, j)$ then denotes the maximum score of an alignment whose last insertion ends in (i, j). Conversely, $D[i, j]$ designates the maximal score of an alignment whose last deletion ends in (i, j).

The completed recurrence relation (here within the framework of the Needleman–Wunsch algorithm) is then given by:

$$T(i,j) = max \begin{cases} T(i-1, j-1) + Subs(u[i], v[j]) & \text{if } 0 < i \leq |u| \text{ and } 0 < j \leq |v| \\ I(i-1, j-1) + Subs(u[i], v[j]) & \text{if } 0 < i \leq |u| \text{ and } 0 < j \leq |v| \\ D(i-1, j-1) + Subs(u[i], v[j]) & \text{if } 0 < i \leq |u| \text{ and } 0 < j \leq |v| \end{cases}$$

$$[3.1]$$

$$I(i,j) = max \begin{cases} T(i-1, j) + d & \text{if } 0 < i \leq |u| \text{ and } 0 \leq j \leq |v| \\ I(i-1, j) + e & \text{if } 0 < i \leq |u| \text{ and } 0 \leq j \leq |v| \end{cases}$$

$$[3.2]$$

$$D(i,j) = max \begin{cases} T(i, j-1) + d & \text{if } 0 \leq i \leq |u| \text{ and } 0 < j \leq |v| \\ D(i, j-1) + e & \text{if } 0 \leq i \leq |u| \text{ and } 0 < j \leq |v| \end{cases}$$

$$[3.3]$$

The point of focus here is the update of the score $I(i, j)$. If an alignment possesses, at its end, a *gap* of the *insertion* type, this can be caused by two distinct situations:

– either **the opening of this gap**: in terms of score, this is an opening penalty d, which completes a previous **gapless** alignment $T(i-1, j)$;

– or **the extension of an already open gap**: in terms of score, this is an extension penalty e, which thus continues the previous **gap** alignment of the *insertion* type $I(i-1, j)$.

A similar reasoning can be applied for $D(i, j)$. Finally, we should note that the computation of $T(i, j)$ logically includes the **gap termination** open and/or continued up to $I(i-1, j-1)$ and $D(i-1, j-1)$.

In practice, the tables D and I can be merged into a single table E having the same dimensions as T: $E(i, j)$ then logically corresponds to the score of the alignment whose last *gap* (without distinction of the *insertion* or *deletion* type) ends in i, j.

$$T(i,j) = max \begin{cases} T(i-1, j-1) + Subs(u[i], v[j]) & \text{if } 0 < i \leq |u| \text{ and } 0 < j \leq |v| \\ E(i-1, j-1) + Subs(u[i], v[j]) & \text{if } 0 < i \leq |u| \text{ and } 0 < j \leq |v| \end{cases}$$

$$[3.4]$$

$$E(i,j) = max \begin{cases} T(i-1,j)+d & \text{if } 0 < i \le |u| \text{ and } 0 \le j \le |v| \\ E(i-1,j)+e & \text{if } 0 < i \le |u| \text{ and } 0 \le j \le |v| \\ T(i,j-1)+d & \text{if } 0 \le i \le |u| \text{ and } 0 < j \le |v| \\ E(i,j-1)+e & \text{if } 0 \le i \le |u| \text{ and } 0 < j \le |v| \end{cases} \qquad [3.5]$$

This last definition is *in theory* valid only if negative values of substitutions are always less penalizing than double *gap* extensions. That is, $min_{a,b \in \Sigma^2} Subs(a,b) \ge 2 \times e$.

The definition given in the previous equations without merging [3.1]–[3.3] does not allow here any insertion operation followed by a deletion operation (or vice versa). However, the definition of equations [3.4]–[3.5] logically makes this possible (since it no longer distinguishes between the *insertion* and *suppression* types). This then implies, when $min_{a,b \in \Sigma^2} Subs(a,b) \le 2 \times e$, that the penalty of a *gap* composed of a succession of juxtaposed insertions and deletions may be less than the cost of the substitutions that should normally have taken place.

3.3. Heuristic alignment

Exact alignment algorithms are efficient for *small sequences*, but their time is unfortunately quadratic, and they are not capable of aligning too large sequences.

It is indeed quite easy to estimate the time taken by an exact dynamic programming algorithm, such as the Needleman–Wunsch algorithm or the Smith–Waterman algorithm, depending on the size of the inputs: if, for example, *one second* is spent for sequences of 10,000 nucleotides, then a time factor of 100 must be applied each time the size of the sequences is multiplied by 10. Consequently, the genome alignment of a few tens or hundreds of megabases (nucleotides) should therefore be avoided.

The choice was then made to use *heuristics*.

A *heuristic* does not guarantee to find the best or all solutions to a given problem, but achieves at best the construction of a potentially suboptimal solution, or a subset of solutions among those that can ideally be obtained.

The idea here is to speed up the search, potentially at the expense of the quality of the result or its completeness, which can only be achieved if the exact algorithm is applied without any time constraints.

3.3.1. *Seeds*

3.3.1.1. *Seed or k-mer principle*

To compensate for the computation time mentioned above, *dot-plot* software programs were among the first to use *filtering*: the idea here is to quickly detect elements that will reflect the presence of a similarity between two sequences. The most easily detectable element is at first what is called a *k-mer* (k-size word). If it is *conserved* between two sequences, it is then marked (and plotted in the case of a dot plot). Moreover, based on the indexes seen in Chapter 2, it is possible to quickly obtain the occurrences of common k-mers from two sequences.

By placing two sequences along a horizontal/vertical axis (Figure 3.3), a clear visual representation of the comparison between two sequences can thus be given by isolating the *diagonals* supported by several successive *k-mers*, or the close diagonals involving few substitutions and insertions/deletions.

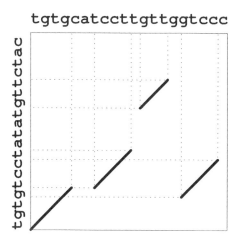

Figure 3.3. *Dot-plot principle, and the use of k-mers ($k = 3$)*

A *k-mer* constitutes a logical element that can contribute first to the acceleration of the search for similarities; however, it does not constitute a proof on its own. In fact, in the previous dot plot, random occurrences are naturally present and therefore need to be verified.

3.3.1.2. *Contiguous seeds and BLAST software*

Software programs that make use of, as a first step, the previous seed- or k-mer-based principle are numerous, which include the classic BLAST(n) (Altschul et al. 1990, 1997) as well as its predecessor FASTA (Lipman and Pearson 1985, 1988) from NCBI. It is first the agglomeration approach of k-mers on the same diagonal (or close diagonals) of the dot plot that gave rise to global alignment tools, such as FASTA. The latter then found itself supplanted by a local alignment tool (created by the same research group). BLAST is based on a single occurrence of a k-mer chosen larger for efficiency reasons. BLAST has also implemented theoretically sound statistical tools to compute the *significance of the scores* of the alignments obtained (Karlin and Altschul 1990).

Unlike FASTA, which from the location of the k-mers determines a skeleton of the alignment, BLAST knows a priori, for one alignment, only one k-mer conserved between the two sequences that must be aligned. The extension of this k-mer into a complete alignment is then done using a heuristic dynamic programming algorithm, similar to the Needleman–Wunsch algorithm (Needleman and Wunsch 1970). The main differences with the latter stem from the fact that:

– the starting positions of dynamic programming are located at the coordinates given by the left (respectively right) ends of the k-mers of two sequences;

– a heuristic is implemented to limit dynamic programming to a neighborhood when the score obtained is not considered to be satisfactory. This is the criterion known as the *X-drop*: during the step of dynamic programming, the score obtained is compared to the maximal score reached during the previous steps. If the current score decreases by a certain threshold (*X-drop* threshold) compared to the maximal score, then the extension stops.

A last important point of BLAST concerns the evaluation made on the *significance* of the alignments obtained. Therefore, this question arises: In what way can an alignment produced be exceptional? In other words, what is its expectation of appearing by chance if we had made a comparison between sequences having a priori no predefined homology, but simply similarities that are due to chance?

This question has an (asymptotic) answer according to the theory developed by Karlin and Altschul (Karlin and Ost 1987, 1988; Karlin and Altschul 1990; Karlin and Brendel 1992), in the case of alignment without *indel* (which is globally considered by the community as *valid* if *indels* are present, even if this has never been demonstrated). Under the hypothesis of a Markovian background noise $\mathcal{M}$, the distribution of alignments without *indels* follows a Gumbel distribution (Gumbel 1958). Based on this distribution, the software then gives, for a score s and according to a Markov model $\mathcal{M}$, the probability (*P-value*) of generating an alignment with a score greater than or equal to s on random sequences of the same size. The parameters K and λ originate from the chosen score system, which itself originates from the background noise model $\mathcal{M}$. The size of the two sequences that are compared is given by m and n:

$$E\text{-}value = K \cdot m \cdot n \cdot e^{-\lambda \cdot s}$$

$$P\text{-}value = 1 - e^{-E\text{-}value}$$

3.3.1.3. *Spaced seed principle*

Contiguous seeds, previously presented to define k-mers, have been regularly used. However, they exhibit limitations in terms of sensitivity to detect alignments when the mutation rate is high, and thus the number of substitutions on the alignment.

A *spaced seed* is a mask defining k-mers in which some predefined positions are ignored. Here, we make use of the notation defined by Burkhardt and Kärkkäinen (2001) and first illustrate it with an example.

With the following sequence u

ATCATGATGGA

it is possible to enumerate all of the k-mers of size 3 by using the following mask ###, composed of three symbols indicating the positions to be retained, and by making it "slide" over the sequence:

```
ATCATGATGGA
###
ATC
 ###
 TCA
  ###
  CAT
   . . .
   . . .
```

in order to extract the different k-mers of size 3. There will be a total of $|u| - k + 1$ k-mers.

On the contrary, the spaced seed-based approach consists of not considering all the consecutive positions for each k-mer, but rather of selecting only a subset of the positions with the help of a mask that we will call the *seed*. Therefore, the mask ##-#, having the same number of # as before but not the same length, will select, with a word of size 4, only the positions 1, 2 and 4, ignoring the position 3. With the previous example, this mask ##-# will define the words

```
ATCATGATGGA
##-#
AT-A that can be written as ATA
 ##-#
 TC-T that can be written as TCT
  ##-#
  CA-G that can be written as CAG
   . . .
   . . .
```

This approach was initially and independently proposed by Ma et al. (2002) and Burkhardt and Kärkkäinen (2001) in two different problems, which was derived from previous results with random hashing (Califano and Rigoutsos 1993; Buhler 2001; Buhler and Tompa 2001).

It is at first surprising to look for so-called *non-contiguous* fragments in a sequence for its indexing: their number is already lower (the previous example has one less spaced k-mer since it is longer, compared to contiguous

k-mers), and consequently a simple reasoning will show that statistically "the less numerous they are, the more likely they are to disappear" when sequencing errors or mutations appear. This statement might seem true from a quantitative point of view, but it ignores here the correlation between the different elements of the problem. Two successive contiguous k-mers actually share $k - 1$ common positions. If a mutation appears at these $k - 1$ positions, then the two k-mers will not be conserved (as well as a certain number of k-mers will overlap the mutation), and will thus be unusable for the similarity search. On the contrary, this is no longer systematically true with spaced seeds.

To illustrate the principle, we first consider a rather simple example: an alignment of size 11 with which we will place three mutations. It is possible here to distribute the mutations in this form:

```
ATCATGATGGA
||x||x||x||
ATTATCATAGA
```

so that no contiguous k-mer of size 3 is present. We denote the seed used to generate the set of k-mers only as a *mask*, represented by a sequence of symbols ###. Using the same example, it is possible to show that the seed/mask represented by a sequence of symbols ##-# is detectable at least once, for example, at the first position (as well as at the fourth and seventh positions):

```
ATCATGATGGA
||x||x||x||
ATTATCATAGA
##-#
   ##-#
      ##-#
```

What is particularly even more surprising is that, regardless of the position of the three mutations in the alignment of size 11, it is possible to show that at least one occurrence of this spaced seed ##-# will be found. This particular case is called a *lossless seed*, that is, a seed able to detect all alignments of size 11 with at most three mutations, without any risk of losses (Burkhardt and Kärkkäinen 2001). This is of course a special case illustrating the seed principle, since most alignment software programs are based on so-called *lossy seed* designs: there is no guarantee that **all alignments** will be detected with a given number of errors, but rather that the alignments generated according to a random pattern will be captured **with a high probability**.

Keich et al. (2004) propose the use of the following principle for the choice of seed: by defining an alignment model, it is possible to estimate the probability that a *spaced seed* has of detecting an alignment. More accurately, it is possible to compute the probability of obtaining, from a model alignment, at least one fragment that can be detected by the *spaced seed*.

This probability is the estimation of the sensitivity from the model. In this way, different *spaced seeds* can be compared and the best (most sensitive) ones can be selected. Naturally, this comparison must be achieved according to a set selectivity criterion, since the two characteristics' *selectivity* and *sensitivity* are linked.

To compute the sensitivity of a spaced seed, two main free parameters are involved in the problem raised:

– The class of *spaced seeds* to be selected: the choice will be carried out on a class of seeds with the same selectivity. Seeds have, for example, the same number of symbols # in their mask to get the same selectivity, since they provide the same amount of information.

– The alignment model: it is a question of giving the distribution of alignments, which can be represented in the form of words generated in a simpler alphabet than the sequences. For example, it is possible to use a simple binary alphabet {*match, mismatch*}. A choice follows to generate (or weight) the alignments, using a probabilistic model. The Bernoulli model was the first one proposed, which is still the most frequently used model for this weighting.

Finally, sensitivity is computed for a given spaced seed and from a given model. The objective is to calculate the probability that at least one seed occurrence remains on an alignment generated by the model.

This calculation can be the subject of a chapter by itself, and also remains a specific problem. Nonetheless, it is worth noting that for a given seed, the computation of its sensitivity is comparable to an NP-hard problem (Keich et al. 2004; Nicolas and Rivals 2008), the critical parameter being the number of – symbols existing in the seed. Moreover, the choice of the best seed (which can eventually benefit without the previous computation) is at least as hard (Ma and Yao 2009) as a problem known to be hard, but so far unclassified: *Golomb's rule optimal design*.

3.3.2. Min-hash *and global sampling*

The massive advent of high-throughput sequencing, and the resulting decrease in costs, have led to an explosion in the amount of data to be processed in laboratories. Furthermore, these data had to be (and still have to be) processed *as fast as possible*, and thus at least during the course of the experiments, because the simple cost of storing raw data still remains an issue.

This has led to drastic compromises in computational methods over the last decade.

The first principle was to use a *sample of the k-mers*, rather than all of them, even if this results in a logical decrease in sensitivity. We are focusing here on hash functions, knowing that Bloom filters are also another solution mentioned in Chapter 2 (see section 2.2.1).

The simplest principle concerns the concept known as *Min-hash*: the point here is to perform *a global projection* of the sequence s, selecting only a *very restricted* (and in reality *a fixed number*) of k-mers for the sequence (Narayanan and Karp 2004).

This **global sampling** of s is performed by applying, at each step i, a predefined hash function h_i, derived from a set h. This function h_i is applied on the totality of the k-mers of s, in order to then select only **the k-mer** which is considered to be **the smallest according to the order established by** h_i. The number of steps will thus depend on the number of *pseudo-random* hash functions h_i applied, and on the size of the set of initial functions $|h|$.

Since the order has been established here several times for each $h_i \in h$, several minimal k-mers are then extracted from s: the set of these k-mers will be considered as a *signature of the sequence s*, which we simply call $\mathcal{H}(s)$ once h is established.

It is worth noting that if another sequence s' shares a (single) common factor c with s, then the size of this factor $|c|$ (related to the size of both sequences by counting the common factor only once: $|s| + |s'| - |c|$) will then be *statistically proportional* to $\frac{\mathcal{H}(s) \cap \mathcal{H}(s')}{\mathcal{H}(s) \cup \mathcal{H}(s')}$, that is, *statistically proportional* to the number of common hashes found in both s and s', over the number of total hashes in the two sets $\mathcal{H}(s) \cup \mathcal{H}(s')$ according to the Jaccard rule (Narayanan and Karp 2004). A strong argument from users of these methods is the following: if false positives are present elsewhere rather than from the common retained part between s and s', they will also be proportional according to the same fraction on $\frac{\mathcal{H}(s) \cap \mathcal{H}(s')}{\mathcal{H}(s) \cup \mathcal{H}(s')}$ carried over to $\frac{\mathcal{H}(s) \cap \mathcal{H}(s')}{\mathcal{H}(s) \cup \mathcal{H}(s')}$, and will not theoretically bias the analysis.

This method is used for a **global** comparison of genomes (Jain et al. 2018), or for measuring **overlaps** between reads (Berlin et al. 2015); it is generally applied to the sequences of equivalent size (Ondov et al. 2016).

3.3.3. Minimizing *and local sampling*

In this section, we will use a simple lexicographic ordering ($A < C < G < T$) to rank the k-mers, rather than a hash function, in order to explain local sampling. For example, the lexicographic order, for $k = 2$, gives a **total order** of 16 k-mers: $AA < AC < AG < AT < CA < \cdots < TT$.

The concept of *winnowing* (Schleimer et al. 2003; Roberts et al. 2004) first consists of sliding, over the sequence s to be analyzed, a window permanently containing a fixed number w of k-mers, then of selecting in a following step, for each window, *the smallest k-mer*, and *minimizing* it, according to the chosen order.

Let us take, for example, the sequence $s = GACTGAATAGCAG$. We also take as parameters a window size $w = 3$, as well as $k = 2$ as k-mer size. We then enumerate all the windows containing w words of size k: these windows are thus themselves words of size $w + k - 1$, and factors of the initial sequence.

The first window that can be extracted from the sequence s, here $s[1 \ldots w + k - 1] = s[1 \ldots 4]$ will be $GACT$: it therefore contains $w = 3$ words of size $k = 2$ which are GA, AC, CT, respectively. From this first set, it can be deduced that *the smallest element of the set, called the minimizer*, is the k-mer AC because it is smaller than GA and CT: it is located at position 2 in the sequence s and will be selected as the *minimizer* for this window.

Next, successive windows are extracted by shifting the start and end positions one position to the right. For instance, the second window to be extracted will be $s[2 \ldots 5] = ACTG$. It has logically enough shared k-mers with the previous window: only GA has been removed and TG added from the previous set GA, AC, CT to obtain AC, CT, TG. We can also note that the minimizer that is selected here will be the **same as for the previous window** because AC is (again) the smallest element of the set AC, CT, TG. Consequently, minimizers, as opposed to conventional k-mers, perform a *sampling* of the initial sequence, remaining quite often the same during several windows.

The set of extracted minimizers **with their respective positions** will then serve as a *signature* for the original sequence s:

$$s = \qquad G \quad A \ C \ T \quad G \quad A \ A \ T \ A \quad G \quad C \ A \ G$$

$$s[i..i + w + k - 1] =$$

$(i=1)$	$G \quad \underline{A \ C} \ T \quad G$
$(i=2)$	$\underline{A \ C} \ T \quad G \quad A$
$(i=3)$	$C \ T \quad G \quad \underline{A \ A}$
$(i=4)$	$T \quad G \quad \underline{A \ A} \ T$
$(i=5)$	$G \quad \underline{A \ A} \ T \ A$
$(i=6)$	$\underline{A \ A} \ T \ A \quad G$
$(i=7)$	$A \ T \ A \quad \underline{G \quad C}$
$(i=8)$	$T \ A \quad \underline{G} \quad C \ A$
$(i=9)$	$\underline{A \quad G} \quad \underline{C \ A} \ G$

$$minimizers(s) = \quad \{([2], \underline{A \ C}\ ), ([6], \underline{A \ A}\ ), ([9, 12], \underline{A \ G}\ )\}$$

Due to the sharing of information between successive windows, the minimizer search principle is of course feasible and easily maintained over the different windows, with an algorithm whose cost **must not be permanently quadratic in** $k \times w$. For example, the approach used by the minimap (Li 2016) consists of *applying the update only between the current window and the next one* (only two k-mers separate them since one k-mer is removed and another added) only when there is a **change of minimizer**, which is verified using a simple *queue* system for the minimizers, thus without more "complex" algorithms by taking worst cases into account with ordered trees.

It is also worth noting that the lexicographical order proposed as an example in this section **is in practice not efficient and therefore rarely used**: a **different order**, giving preference, for example, to the letter G then C at the first position of the k-mer, then A or T at the second (which is only an example), or an order depending on a *hash function* as in section 3.3.2, are substitutes frequently used instead of the lexicographic order, to give a selection of the smallest k-mers, that is *guided* (Marçais et al. 2017), otherwise respectively *pseudo-random* (Li 2016, 2018).

The comparison of sequences using the minimizer principle results in, by sampling, accelerating the alignment algorithms: there is, on average, a fraction of the order of $\frac{2}{w+1}$ k-mers selected on a sequence, compared to the k-mers it contains. Regularly used tools, such as minimap2 (Li 2018), employ methods based on a pseudo-random hash principle and on taking into account the **reversed complemented** sequence with the **direct** sequence, in order to accelerate the comparison.

Of course, when mutations (or sequencing errors) appear, some minimizers can be destroyed because the word that was selected is then modified into another word: this phenomenon already existed with seed-based alignment tools (see section 3.3) but is now more deleterious when the mutation rate increases because of *sparse* sampling.

Another more subtle and less known phenomenon also occurs frequently, **specific** to methods making use of minimizers or min-hashes. When mutations and/or sequencing errors occur, they generate a new sequence to be analyzed, s' (which is supposed to look like the original sequence s). From this sequence s', new k-mers are generated because of these mutations, which can be smaller inside some windows or from the global sequence depending on the method used. They may thus destabilize the global near/min-hash minimizer(s), which are then no longer selected. Although it does not necessarily generate bias at the analysis level, but mainly a loss of additional sensitivity, this phenomenon, which I rather logically identify as the *Iznogoud* phenomenon (which is unfortunately hardly translatable in English), is much more frequent, but yet relatively little studied in 2019 concerning the loss of sensitivity generated.

Finally, the use of models related to *spaced seeds* is also possible within this sampling context, here with the help of minimizers. It should also be noted that a large number of perspectives on sampling techniques with, or even without, minimizers do exist.

3.4. References

Altschul, S., Gish, W., Miller, W., Myers, E., Lipman, D. (1990). Basic local alignment search tool. *Journal of Molecular Biology*, 215, 403–410.

Altschul, S., Madden, T., Schäffer, A., Zhang, J., Zhang, Z., Miller, W., Lipman, D. (1997). Gapped BLAST and PSI-BLAST: A new generation of protein database search programs. *Nucleic Acids Research*, 25(17), 3389–3402.

Berlin, K., Koren, S., Chin, C.-S., Drake, J.P., Landolin, J.M., Phillippy, A.M. (2015). Assembling large genomes with single-molecule sequencing and locality-sensitive hashing. *Nature Biotechnology*, 33(6), 623–630.

Buhler, J. (2001). Efficient large-scale sequence comparison by locality-sensitive hashing. *Bioinformatics*, 17(5), 419–428.

Buhler, J. and Tompa, M. (2001). Finding motifs using random projections. *Proceedings of the 5th Annual International Conference on Research in Computational Molecular Biology (RECOMB)*, ACM Press, 69–76.

Burkhardt, S. and Kärkkäinen, J. (2001). Better filtering with gapped q-grams. *Proceedings of the 12th Symposium on Combinatorial Pattern Matching (CPM)*, Amihood, A. (ed.). Springer.

Califano, A. and Rigoutsos, I. (1993). Flash: A fast look-up algorithm for string homology. *Proceedings of the 1st International Conference on Intelligent Systems for Molecular Biology (ISMB)*, 56–64.

Chiaromonte, F., Yap, V., Miller, W. (2002). Scoring pairwise genomic sequence alignments. *Pacific Symposium on Biocomputing*, 7, 115–126.

Crochemore, M., Hancart, C., Lecroq, T. (2001). *Algorithmique du texte*. Vuilbert.

Dayhoff, M., Schwartz, R., Orcutt, B. (1978). A model of evolutionary change in proteins. In *Atlas of Protein Sequence and Structure*, Vol. 5, National Biomedical Research Foundation, Chang, M.A., Dayhoff, M., Eck, R.V., Sochard, M.R. (eds). Silver Spring.

Gonnet, G., Cohen, M., Benner, S. (1992). Exhaustive matching of the entire protein sequence database. *Science*, 256(5062), 1443–1445.

Gotoh, O. (1982). An improved algorithm for matching biological sequences. *Journal of Molecular Biology*, 162(3), 705–708.

Gumbel, E. (1958). *Statistics of Extremes*. Columbia University Press.

Henikoff, S. and Henikoff, J. (1992). Amino acid substitution matrices from protein blocks. *Proceedings of the National Academy of Sciences of the USA*, 89, 10915–10919.

Jain, C., Koren, S., Dilthey, A., Phillippy, A.M., Aluru, S. (2018). A fast adaptive algorithm for computing whole-genome homology maps. *Bioinformatics (ECCB Issue)*, 34(17), i748–i756.

Karlin, S. and Altschul, S. (1990). Methods for assessing the statistical significance of molecular sequence features by using general scoring schemes. *Proceedings of the National Academy of Sciences of the USA*, 87, 2264–2268.

Karlin, S. and Brendel, V. (1992). Chance and significance in protein and DNA sequence analysis. *Science*, 257, 39–49.

Karlin, S. and Ost, F. (1987). Counts of long aligned word matches among random letter sequences. *Advances in Applied Probability*, 19, 293–351.

Karlin, S. and Ost, F. (1988). Maximal length of common words among random letter sequences. *Annals of Probability*, 16, 535–563.

Keich, U., Li, M., Ma, B., Tromp, J. (2004). On spaced seeds for similarity search. *Discrete Applied Mathematics*, 138(3), 253–263.

Li, H. (2016). Minimap and miniasm: Fast mapping and de novo assembly for noisy long sequences. *Bioinformatics*, 32(14), 2103–2110.

Li, H. (2018). Minimap2: Pairwise alignment for nucleotide sequences. *Bioinformatics*, 34(18), 3094–3100.

Lipman, D. and Pearson, W. (1985). Rapid and sensitive protein similarity searches. *Science*, 227, 1435–1441.

Lipman, D. and Pearson, W. (1988). Improved tools for biological sequence comparison. *Proceedings of the National Academy of Sciences of the USA*, 85, 2444–2448.

Ma, B. and Yao, H. (2009). Seed optimization for i.i.d. similarities is no easier than optimal Golomb ruler design. *Information Processing Letters*, 109(19), 1120–1124.

Ma, B., Tromp, J., Li, M. (2002). PatternHunter: Faster and more sensitive homology search. *Bioinformatics*, 18(3), 440–445.

Marçais, G., Pellow, D., Bork, D., Orenstein, Y., Shamir, R., Kingsford, C. (2017). Improving the performance of minimizers and winnowing schemes. *Bioinformatics*, 33(14), i110–i117.

Narayanan, M. and Karp, R.M. (2004). Gapped local similarity search with provable guarantees. *Algorithms in Bioinformatics*, 74–86.

Needleman, S.B. and Wunsch, C.D. (1970). A general method applicable to the search for similarities in the amino acid sequence of two proteins. *Journal of Molecular Biology*, 48(3), 443–553.

Nicolas, F. and Rivals, É. (2008). Hardness of optimal spaced seed design. *Journal of Computer and System Sciences*, 74(5), 831–849.

Ondov, B.D., Treangen, T.J., Melsted, P., Mallonee, A.B., Bergman, N.H., Koren, S., Phillippy, A.M. (2016). Mash: Fast genome and metagenome distance estimation using minhash. *Genome Biology*, 17(132).

Roberts, M., Hayes, W., Hunt, B.R., Mount, S.M., Yorke, J.A. (2004). Reducing storage requirements for biological sequence comparison. *Bioinformatics*, 20(18), 3363–3369.

Schleimer, S., Wilkerson, D.S., Aiken, A. (2003). Winnowing: Local algorithms for document fingerprinting. *Proceedings of the 2003 ACM SIGMOD International Conference on Management of Data*, ACM, 76–85.

Smith, T. and Waterman, M. (1981). Identification of common molecular subsequences. *Journal of Molecular Biology*, 147(1), 195–197.

4

Genome Assembly

Dominique Lavenier

IRISA / INRIA, Rennes, France

4.1. Introduction

Genome assembly consists of reconstructing its text from fragments of DNA resulting from its sequencing. We recall that these fragments are obtained by random segmentation of the genome. The reconstruction principle is based on matching portions of identical sequences between fragments. Taking into account the set of fragments and their possible overlaps, an arrangement that matches the text of the genome has to be found. Furthermore, in order for the overlap between fragments to be possible, it is necessary that the genome be available in multiple copies. Figure 4.1 illustrates the mechanism.

Although the principle seems easy, the reality is entirely different. Genome assembly is a difficult problem both for technical and theoretical reasons (Chikhi 2012). First, sequencing technologies are far from being perfect. Fragments are generated randomly and the probability of covering the whole genome shrinks as the size of the genome increases. Therefore, coverage (namely, the average number of times a nucleotide has been sequenced at a given position) along the genome is not constant, and some areas are scarcely or not covered at all. In these areas, a reliable fragment overlap is not possible.

From Sequences to Graphs,
coordinated by Annie Chateau and Mikaël Salson.
© ISTE Ltd 2022.

In general, it is estimated that a coverage of around 30X–50X is required to assemble a genome. In other words, to minimize the risk of non-sequenced regions, the equivalent of 30–50 genomes must be generated.

ATGGACAGGATATACCAGGATTTAGGGAGGGAGATTATATGGGACCAGGATGGAGCCAGATA
ATGGACAGGATATACCAGGATTTAGGGAGGGAGATTATATGGGACCAGGATGGAGCCAGATA
ATGGACAGGATATACCAGGATTTAGGGAGGGAGATTATATGGGACCAGGATGGAGCCAGATA
ATGGACAGGATATACCAGGATTTAGGGAGGGAGATTATATGGGACCAGGATGGAGCCAGATA
ATGGACAGGATATACCAGGATTTAGGGAGGGAGATTATATGGGACCAGGATGGAGCCAGATA

ATGGACAGGATATACCAGGATTTAGGGAGGGAGATTATATGGGACCAGGATGGAGCCAGATA

Figure 4.1. *Assembly principle: the text of a genome is reconstructed from the overlap of all the fragments obtained by sequencing. The fragments originate from random segmentation from several copies of the genome*

Sequencers can also make mistakes and produce erroneous fragments. Depending on the sequencing technology, the error rates are more or less important. Overlaps between fragments must then take these errors into account, which, from a computer science point of view, significantly complicates the processing. These errors must be detected and corrected.

However, the main difficulty of the assembly comes from the structure itself of the genomes. The texts of the genomes, especially those of more evolved organisms, actually contain a lot of repeated areas, either exactly or approximately (Garrido-Ramos 2012). It is easily shown that if the size of the fragments is smaller than the size of the repeats, the problem not solvable. Figure 4.2 shows, with a simple example, how the same list of fragments can lead to two different assemblies because of a subsequence repeated several times. The initial text contains the subsequence TTGATGC in triplicate. With the nine proposed fragments, of smaller size than TTGATGC, there are two overlapping arrangements between fragments that lead to two different texts.

```
                                              ATGCTT
                                         TTGAT CTTGAT
AGTTGA     TTGAT CTTGAT                    GATGCT     ATGCCC
    GATGCT     ATGCTT ATGCCC          AGTTGA GCTTG
    TGAT CTTG    GCTTG                    TGAT CTTG

AGTTGATGCTTGATGCTTGATGCCC             AGTTGATGCTTGATGCCC
```

Figure 4.2. *The repetition problem: from the same list of fragments having repeats (underlined text), two overlapping organizations are possible, leading to two different genome texts*

The assembly is also confronted with the heterozygous and/or polyploidy nature of genomes which can be seen, at the genome scale, as the duplication of very similar texts. As a reminder, a heterozygous genome is composed of pairs of chromosomes that look similar overall but which differ more or less locally. Therefore, for weakly heterozygous genomes, such as the human genome, for example, the result of the assembly is a text that merges the pairs of chromosomes. For genomes with a high rate of heterozygosity (some %), the assembly must make a distinction between the texts. The difficulty is that the heterozygosity rate is rarely uniform. Long regions can be very similar between chromosomes. It is then necessary to identify these areas so that they appear in each of the chromosomes.

For all these reasons, the result of assembly is a more or less fragmented partial text. It appears as a list of *scaffolds* that correspond to the regions of the genome that could have been reconstructed. A scaffold is defined as a succession of *contigs* separated by white areas. A contig is a sequence of characters from the alphabets A, C, G and T. The white areas are caused, as we have seen, by sequencing problems in certain regions of the genome, in places of high complexity in repeats that the methods cannot solve, at low coverage, etc. In the text, they are represented by sequences of **N**.

Problem 4.1. Genomic assembly

Input: Sequencing data
Output: Scaffold list representing the genome sequence

The quality of the assembly is measured by size and relatively to the number of scaffolds. The longer the scaffolds are, and the less numerous they are, the better the assembly. The quality of the scaffolds is also an important criterion, but difficult to evaluate since the final text is not a priori known. It must however comprise as few sequences of **N** as possible. The perfect assembly is obtained when the number of scaffolds is equal to the number of chromosomes. This is achieved for small and low complexity genomes, that is, with a reduced number of repeats, such as the bacteria genome, for example. For more complex genomes, this is still a significant challenge.

Finally, the volumes of data generated by the sequencers are considerable. Assembly requires significant sequencing coverages (of the order of 50X). The algorithms that manipulate these massive data must therefore be extremely efficient, both in terms of computing time and memory footprint. An important part of the research on this subject concerns the development of data structures that are as cost-efficient as possible in terms of memory space.

The purpose of this chapter is to present the various methodologies related to genome assembly. First, sequencing technologies are briefly recalled. In fact, they strongly condition the assembly strategies due to the nature itself of the fragments produced. The following section gives an overview of the different methodologies by specifying the different steps that lead to the final assembly of a genome. The two following sections are successively devoted to the two main steps that are almost systematically found in the various strategies implemented: the construction and the ordering of scaffolds. The penultimate section focuses on validation methods for the assemblies. The final section concludes this chapter.

4.2. Sequencing technologies

The raw material of the assembly process is a set of DNA fragments called *reads*. These reads are obtained by sequencing the DNA of the genome. Sequencing technologies are varied and produce reads of different natures (Mardis 2017). Their properties strongly condition the assembly methods. Furthermore, we think that it should be interesting to review the main categories. Sequencing technologies that produce them are not described; only the characteristics are analyzed.

4.2.1. *Short reads*

Short reads correspond to fragments of a few hundreds of base pairs. The dominant technology on the market is the *Illumina* technology capable of producing in a few hours hundreds of millions of reads. In addition, this technology produces paired reads, that is, pairs of fragments close in the genome and separated by a known distance. This latter is defined by the *insert size* (see Figure 4.3). Typically, the result of sequencing is a set of pairs of 150 bp reads, separated by a distance of 100 bp (insert size = 400 bp). The size of the insert is not constant. It is approximate and centered around a value generally greater than the sum of the sizes of the two sequences. The text of the second read, for technological reasons, is given in reverse complement.

Figure 4.3. *Paired read: it consists of two sequences of identical size, each one being sequenced in a different direction. The size of the insert is calculated in relation to the two external ends of the sequences*

The main advantage of this technology is its reliability. The error rate is extremely low, significantly lower than 1 %. The majority of errors are substitutions errors where a nucleotide is replaced by another. With sufficient coverage, these errors can be easily corrected. The resulting assembly is of excellent quality.

The cost of this technology is also very low and the data rates very high. Sequencing is not the limiting step. A large quantity of short reads of excellent quality can be produced in a short period of time. The major disadvantage, however, is the size of the reads. Most genomes contain repeats that far exceed their size. The sole use of short reads cannot solve the assembly problem.

To partially overcome this drawback, a variant of the paired reads has been developed: the *mate pair*. This alternative always combines two short reads, but the size of the insert is much larger, of the order of a few thousand base pairs. Theoretically, with this technique, the management of repeats larger than the insert is possible. In fact, the technology struggles to produce homogeneous insert sizes.

4.2.2. *Long reads*

Long reads range from a few thousand to even hundreds of thousands of base pairs. There are mainly two existing technologies: that from PacBio and the one by Oxford Nanopore Technology.

Both produce reads with a relatively high error rate, from 5% to 10%. The errors are rather insertion or deletion errors. Sequencers add or forget nucleotides, especially in areas of homopolymers (in sequences of identical characters). This type of error is more difficult to manage than substitution errors and much less easy to correct.

Sequencing costs are higher than the cost of short reads. The flow rates are lower but remain still fairly decent to produce the set of reads required for an assembly. The big advantage of these technologies is that it facilitates the management of repeats. The sizes of the reads exceed most of the repeated areas, thus eliminating many of the ambiguities that cannot be resolved by short reads.

4.2.3. *Linked reads*

This technology, based on short reads, combines the same *barcode* to reads that are topologically close in the genome. Schematically, the genome is first fragmented into long molecules of several tens of thousands of base pairs. Each molecule has a barcode and is sequenced with a low coverage, typically 0.1X. The result of the sequencing is a set of reads with additional proximity information from several tens of kilobases. The exploitation of this type of information facilitates the management of repeats.

The advantage of this approach is that the sequencing is achieved with the proven Illumina technology and benefits from both high throughput and low costs. It simply requires, upstream of the process, an additional barcoding step during the preparation of libraries.

In reality, several molecules possess the same barcode. The reads that are identically labeled are therefore originating from different regions of the genome. The molecules being randomly distributed along the genome, those with the same barcode are therefore statistically unlikely to be located at the same locations. The assembly therefore favors locally read overlaps that minimize the number of different barcodes.

4.2.4. *Hi-C reads*

The purpose of this technology is primarily for studying the 3D structure of DNA. However, it can be advantageously used to improve the assembly. The Hi-C process builds fragments composed of two DNA sequences spatially close in the genome (de Wit and de Laat 2012). But since it has at first a linear organization, the majority of the reads contain two DNA segments that are topologically close.

This proximity information is generally used during the final stages of assembly. It serves to linearly order the scaffolds. The closer the scaffolds are, the more they will share a significant number of Hi-C reads.

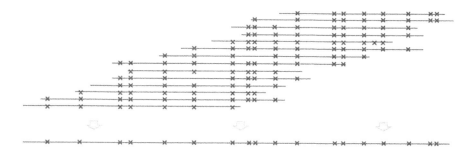

Figure 4.4. *Optical map: it is built based on the enzymatic profiles of long DNA molecules*

4.2.5. *Optical mapping*

An optical map can be obtained from enzymatic profiles of a set of DNA molecules. The profiles of the molecules are determined by the size and order of the fragments obtained after digestion and marking. Technically, a large number of large DNA molecules of several hundred thousand base pairs are selected and tagged at the restriction sites. They are then aligned by matching as many tags as possible to produce the final map, as shown in Figure 4.4. The optical map is used in the following steps of the assembly.

4.3. Assembly strategies

4.3.1. *The main steps*

There are extremely varied methods to solve the assembly problem. A considerable amount of literature can be found on the subject, just as a large range of software programs resulted from the work of numerous research teams. In addition, the methods are constantly improving and keep with the (rapid) pace of technological change. Furthermore, proceeding to an exhaustive inventory would be both tedious and become quickly obsolete.

We therefore give a overview of the solving methods for the problem of the assembly by pointing out the processes, or building blocks, which are generally common and more or less shared by different strategies. The objective is to get a global view based on understanding how these different modules are organized.

The diagram in Figure 4.5 summarizes the essential steps. The first step analyzes raw data and filters them according to quality information delivered by the sequencers. Error correction-based techniques can also be applied to increase the overall quality of the reads. The second step consists of producing longer genome segments than the reads: that is, *scaffolds*. The final step seeks to order the scaffolds to obtain the final assembly.

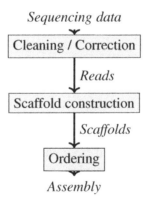

Figure 4.5. *The main assembly steps. The result is a set of large scaffolds that represent the genome text*

This is a very general layout and admits many variations according to the complexity of the genomes to be assembled and the data available. It is understood that assembling a bacterium, is infinitely easier than assembling a more developed polyploid organism. The strategies will therefore be very different, as will the quantity and the diversity of the sequencing data that will be implemented. The following three sections outline the strategies according to these elements.

4.3.2. *Cleaning and correction of reads*

This first step is very important. It conditions the quality of the final assembly. If, at the beginning, data are of bad quality, errors will inexorably propagate, or even increase, within the pipeline and yield an assembly of poor quality.

Cleaning

One of the first tasks is therefore to verify data quality and then exclude or modify the reads that do not satisfy the required level of quality. Sequencers combine quality information with each read. Software programs such as FastQC (Andrews et al. 2012) (for Illumina-type data) analyze this information and return a synthesis of the overall quality of a dataset.

In the case of short reads, the cleaning process estimates first the quality of each read based on a score associated with each nucleotide. In general, the quality at the beginning or end of the read is lower. The ends of the reads below a certain score can then be truncated, or completely eliminated.

For long reads, regions with low quality can be excluded, which consequently result in fragmenting a read into several pieces. This task is usually achieved in advance by *basecalling* software.

Correction

The correction of short reads is based on data redundancy. A coverage of 30X means that a nucleotide at a given position is sequenced on average 30 times. A read alignment around this position should, in principle, carry over 30 times the same nucleotide. If one of the reads proposes a different nucleotide, then it can reasonably be assumed that there has been a sequencing error and it can be corrected with the one indicated by the other reads. In the case of heterozygous genomes, for example, this position will indicate two possible nucleotide values in the same numbers. The reads will not be modified, because we are faced with a polymorphism and not a sequencing error. Bloocoo (Benoit et al. 2014) is an example of short read correctors developed with the GATB toolbox (Drezen et al. 2014).

Long read correction is more difficult because of the error rates and the nature of the errors (namely, large numbers of insertion or deletion errors). The general principle is based on sequence alignment followed by building a consensus. More specifically, we align all the other sequences over the sequence to be corrected. The alignment portions that overlap this sequence are set aside. A pseudo multiple alignment is obtained which is then used to build a consensus sequence.

When both short and long reads are available, these latter can be corrected by aligning the short reads over the long reads. The LoRDEC software program makes use of this principle (Salmela and Rivals 2014).

4.3.3. *Scaffold construction*

Depending on the type of sequencing data, scaffold construction follows different strategies. Several data types can also be combined to produce these elements.

With short reads

In a first step, contigs are built from the overlapping of reads. Since the number of reads is generally very important, pairwise comparison of all the reads is not possible. K-mer-based indexing techniques, such as those presented in section 4.4.3, are implemented to generate contigs whose sizes essentially depend on the complexity of the genome. In general, at this stage, contigs are small. They cannot integrate long repeats.

Taking into account the information carried by the paired reads, these contigs can then be connected. If a pair with one of the reads is similar to an end of a contig and the other similar to the end of another contig in a non-ambiguous manner, then these two contigs can be merged into one. That being said, the inter-contig space must be filled with a coherent text. If it is not feasible, by extending the contigs around the point of junction, then the space is filled by a sequence of **N** whose number is approximated by the insert size of the paired reads.

With long reads

Obtaining scaffolds from long reads starts with a comparison phase involving all of the sequences in order to determine all overlaps. An optimal combination of overlapping groups is then looked for (see section 4.4.2). Each group corresponds to a potential scaffold. The text is obtained by consensus with a procedure similar to long read correction. It is therefore not necessarily advantageous to correct reads beforehand. When it is not possible to establish consensus on certain regions, sequences of **N** are inserted.

With short and long reads

If both long and short reads are available, they can be combined to produce longer scaffolds and with better quality. The objective is to mix the best of technologies (quality for short reads, size for long reads).

One strategy, for example, consists of producing contigs based on short reads, then in merging them into scaffolds by positioning them relatively to long reads. This is a methodological extension with respect to the information of paired reads that can only merge two contigs separated by a limited distance. With this approach, several small-sized contigs can be ordered in a relatively accurate manner.

4.3.4. *Scaffold ordering*

The objective of the final step is to organize the positioning of scaffolds in relation to one another. Assembly fragmentation from the previous step has multiple causes which originate from both incomplete (some regions of the genome have not been sequenced) or erroneous sequencing data, of highly complex regions such as telomeres or centromeres, where repeats extend over very long distances, namely, methodologies that struggle in constructing long fragments, etc. Therefore, at the level of the global genome structure, short reads and long reads cannot solve the assembly in a complete manner.

Linked reads, Hi-C reads or optical cards prove to be a better solution. The information contained in these data provides more or less accurate indications on the proximity between scaffolds.

In the case of linked-reads, the number of common tags of the reads that map onto the scaffold ends is a measure of distance. Two topologically distant scaffolds will statistically unlikely contain molecules with identical tags. The closer they will be, the more the number of common molecules will increase. For Hi-C reads, in a similar way, the number of reads that map between two scaffolds is accounted for. The higher this number is, the smaller the distance. Therefore, for these two data types, a matrix of the distances between scaffolds is extracted. Therefrom, several strategies can be implemented for computing an ordering based on different criteria (see section 4.5.1, the Seriation section).

Optical cards yield different information since they are able to directly position the scaffolds against one another from enzymatic fingerprints.

4.4. Scaffold construction methods

From a purely IT point of view, the problem to be solved is the following one: from a substantial set of character strings that symbolize sequencing data (the reads), much longer chains (scaffolds) that are more likely to partially reconstruct the text of the genome have to be built. This reconstruction is based on sequence overlapping and possibly on distance information between sequences.

4.4.1. *Greedy assembly*

The method operates in two stages: first, an overlap score is calculated between all sequences. Then, the following algorithm is applied: as long as there exist overlapping pairs, the pair with the best score is merged. At each iteration, the number of sequences decreases. The process stops when it is no longer possible to merge sequences. Figure 4.6 illustrates the principle.

Computing the overlap score can be more or less complex. The number of identical characters in an overlap is considered as an immediate score. In this case, the alignment of the two sequences is simple to calculate, but only substitution errors are considered. To take insertion or omission errors into account, the alignment is calculated by way of dynamic programming to which a score is associated (see section 3.2.3 about this topic).

The advantage of this method lies in its simplicity. On the contrary, it has two major drawbacks. The first is that it requires an alignment computation from all sequences, which is extremely expensive. If N is the number of sequences and P is the size of these sequences, the complexity is N^2P^2. The term N^2 comes from the pairwise comparison of all sequences. The term P^2 is due to the complexity of dynamic programming.

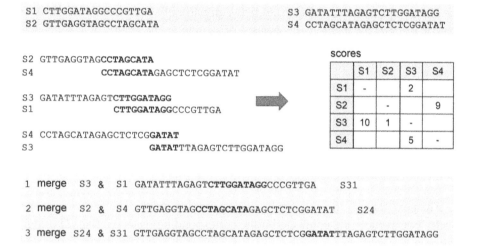

Figure 4.6. *OLC (overlap–layout–consensus) assembly. An overlap score is calculated from all of the sequences. A graph whose nodes are the reads and the overlapping edges are the scores is constructed. The search for an Hamiltonian path with a maximal score gives the optimal arrangement between reads. The consensus sequence is given by the resulting multiple alignment*

The second disadvantage is that sequence merging is never evaluated. The algorithm systematically progresses by merging two sequences on the basis of the best overlap score. When the same score is met, an arbitrary choice is made. This can lead to assembly errors, especially in the presence of repeats.

The first assemblers were built on this model (Bonfield et al. 1995; Sutton et al. 1995; Huang and Madan 1999). They quickly found their limits with the evolution of sequencing technologies, on the one hand, by the quantity of sequences to be considered and, on the other hand, by the complexity of the genomes to be processed.

4.4.2. *OLC assembly*

The OLC algorithm is structured around three stages:

– **overlap**: find all the read pairs that overlap;

– **layout**: organize these overlapping reads into a contiguous sequence;

– **consensus**: build a consensus sequence.

The computation of the overlap between pairs of sequences is identical to that of the greedy method. It consists of matching the prefix of a sequence with the suffix of another. An alignment is calculated on the basis of a dynamic programming algorithm. To avoid considering alignment computation between all the pairs of sequences, these can first be indexed based on k-mers (short sequences of k characters). If two sequences share one or more k-mers, then a computation for the alignment can be triggered. This technique avoids considering every possible pair. Nevertheless, the index must be previously calculated, a process that incurs a cost, both in terms of computation time and memory space (see Chapter 2 on sequence indexing).

The next stage is the construction of an overlap graph. The vertices are the reads. Two vertices are connected if the corresponding reads overlap. The edge between two vertices is weighted by the alignment score. In theory, once this graph is established, a Hamiltonian path has to be found in this graph, that is, a path that traverses once and only once every vertex. The sum of the weights of the edges must be maximal. This path maximizes the linear organization of the overlaps and thus corresponds to the solution. The alignment of the reads with each other based on the Hamiltonian path corresponds to a multiple alignment from which a consensus sequence can be inferred. Figure 4.7 illustrates the complete process with an example.

Finding a Hamiltonian path in a graph is an NP-complete problem. In addition, the computation of the best global overlap between reads is based on heuristics that serve for simplifying the graph. Edges are removed if their overlap score falls below a certain threshold or others are deleted by transitivity as shown in the diagram below. The resulting graph is simpler, or even broken down into several parts with which it is easier to work.

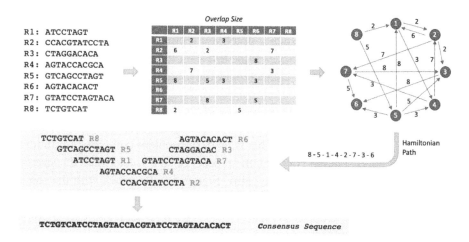

Figure 4.7. *OLC assembly. An overlap score is calculated from all of the sequences. A graph whose nodes are the reads and the overlapping edges are the scores is constructed. The search for an Hamiltonian path with a maximal score gives the optimal arrangement between reads. The consensus sequence is given by the resulting multiple alignment*

However, the main limitation of this approach remains the computation step of the overlaps between sequences, especially with large numbers of sequences. In practice, short-read sequencing datasets that contain several tens or hundreds of millions of elements cannot be employed with this method. The OLC method should rather be applied to long reads. The *Newbler* (Margulies et al. 2005), *Celera Assembler* (Kececioglu and Myers 1995), *Canu* (Koren et al. 2017) and *Arachne* (Batzoglou et al. 2002) assemblers are based on this methodology.

4.4.3. *DBG assembly*

The limitation of greedy and OLC methods mainly results from the pairwise comparison phase of all pairs of sequences for identifying overlaps. When the number of sequences reaches a few million, the computational costs become prohibitive. k-mers-based assembly addresses this disadvantage.

The basic idea is the construction of an automaton that recognizes all possible assemblies starting from a decomposition into k-mers of the fragments and noting the possible sequences (de Bruijn automaton introduced in section 2.2.3). Therefore, each read is split into k-mers (k-characters words) to build this automaton which is similar to a graph and that is called a de Bruijn graph (DBG). The nodes of such a graph are represented by the k-mers, and there is an edge between two nodes if the last $k-1$ characters of a node (suffix) are identical to the first $k-1$ characters of the other (prefix).

Based on this graph, the assembly problem is reduced to the search for Eulerian paths (Pevzner et al. 2001). An Eulerian path is a path that contains a graph edge once and only once. This is an easy problem compared to finding Hamiltonian paths. On the contrary, the repeats of size greater than the size of the k-mers limits the length of the paths. Figure 4.8 illustrates with the same example as previously, the assembly from a de Bruijn graph built with k-mers of size 5. The repeat **CCTATAC** whose nodes are represented in darker color is surrounded by two branches that indicate different path possibilities.

R1: ATCCTAGT
R2: CCACGTATCCTA
R3: CTAGGACACA
R4: AGTACCACGCA
R5: GTCAGCCTAGT
R6: AGTACACACT
R7: GTATCCTAGTACA
R8: TCTGTCAT

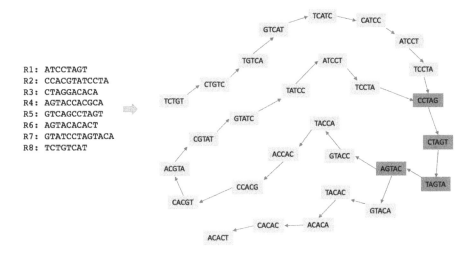

Figure 4.8. *DBG assembly. A de Bruijn graph is constructed from the k-mers of the reads (here $k = 5$). Finding Eulerian paths in the graph corresponds to an assembly of reads without repeat*

The representation of the set of reads in the form of a de Bruijn graph effectively compresses the information. All identical k-mers between reads are present only once in the graph. Compression is all the more effective when sequencing coverage is significant. That said, sequencing errors lead to artificially multiplying the number of nodes. A substitution error adds, for example, $k-1$ additional nodes. To avoid this inflation, the graph is often built on the so-called *solid* k-mers, namely k-mers that are found several times in the reads. Therefore, a sequencing error will generate a sequence of erroneous k-mers whose probability of appearing several times will be very reduced. They will be eliminated during the graph construction phase.

The k-mer size is an important parameter because it directly affects the production of contigs: repeats larger than k nucleotides make the graph more complex and lead to contig fragmentation; it proves fruitful to set k to a large value. On the contrary, the longer k is, the greater the chances a k-mer will be incorrect; therefore, for this criterion, small k-mers will tend to be preferable. Another drawback is that when two reads overlap by less than k characters, they do not share nodes in common in the de Bruijn graph, which interrupts the generation of a potential contig. The choice of k therefore represents a trade-off between these different antagonistic criteria that it is often difficult to evaluate. The *KmerGenie* software that is based on several heuristics and on the k-mer histogram gives a value of k which reflects the best trade-off.

Finally, a de Bruijn graph has the advantage that it can be supported by relatively lightweight data structures comparatively to the size of the sequencing data. As previously seen, k-mers are instantiated only once. Moreover, the links between nodes are implicit. We can be easily deduce whether two nodes are linked on the basis of their suffix and prefix. There is therefore no need to store this information. Very optimized structures can thus be employed to represent genomes of very large size in memory (Salikhov et al. 2013). The *minia* assembler (Chikhi and Rizk 2012), for example, uses a Bloom filter, and requires only a few gigabytes to store the de Bruijn graph representation of a mammalian genome (see section 2.4.2).

With the advent of NGS data, and thereby with the need to manage hundreds of millions of short reads, a large number of assemblers based on de Bruijn graphs have been developed. As examples of software programs associated with the DBG methodology, we can cite *ALLPATHS-LG* (Gnerre et al. 2011), *ABySS* (Simpson et al. 2009), *Velvet* (Zerbino and Birney 2008), *SOAP de-novo* (Luo et al. 2012), *Minia* (Chikhi and Rizk 2012) and *SPAdes* (Bankevich et al. 2012).

We mentioned earlier the difficulty of finding a size for k that is ideal for assembly. Some assembly methods get around this problem by using several sizes for k, either iteratively by progressively increasing k, as in *IDBA* (Leung et al. 2013), or simultaneously by using k of variable size depending on the complexity of the de Bruijn graph locally, as in *SPAdes* (Bankevich et al. 2012).

4.4.4. *Constrained assembly*

This method locally optimizes the contig or scaffolds ordering based on proximity information delivered by sequencing technologies and not necessarily taken into account by greedy, OLC or DBG strategies. It can be considered as an optimization step for overcoming the difficulties of the previous strategies in producing long contigs in high complexity genome regions.

These complex regions are often similar to mosaics composed of short repeated sequences, possibly palindromic, existing simultaneously in the forward or in the reverse direction. A de Bruijn graph, for example, cannot restore all this complexity. The texts of the repeated sequences are present only in one specimen and the graph traversal will therefore generate only one contig. Taking into account two types of additional information can help solve the problem: namely, the estimation of contig coverage and the estimation of the distance between contigs.

The number of times a sequence is repeated can be deduced by the sequencing coverage of the contig. This can be estimated from a count of k-mers. Proximity information is varied and depends on sequencing strategies. In the case of short *paired-end* or *mate-pair* type of reads, the distance between two contigs can be estimated by the size of the insert if the two reads of the pair overlap each end of the contigs. In the case of hybrid sequencing, that is, carried out in both short and long reads, contig mapping (obtained from assembling short reads) with long reads also makes it possible to establish a distance between contigs.

The problem can be modeled as a graph where the nodes are the contigs with which the coverage attributes are associated. The edges are the overlaps between contigs, evaluated by their size. The graph is completed by constraints of distances between contigs. The assembly can then be formulated as an integer linear optimization problem (Briot et al. 2014; François et al. 2018). It consists of finding the longest path consistent with the constraints that have been set.

Figure 4.9 illustrates the problem with a simple example. The starting data are as follows:

– the list of contigs with their size and number of occurrences;

– the overlaps between the ends of the contigs;

– the distances between some contigs obtained by proximity information related to the sequencing technology.

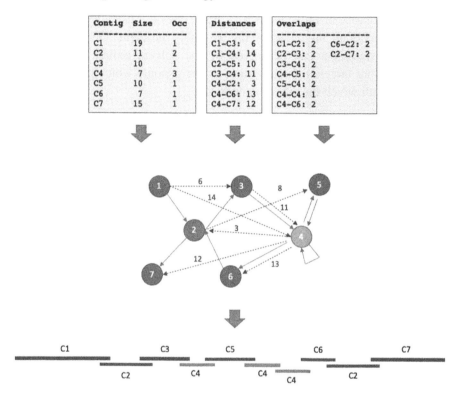

Contig	Size	Occ
C1	19	1
C2	11	2
C3	10	1
C4	7	3
C5	10	1
C6	7	1
C7	15	1

Distances
C1–C3: 6
C1–C4: 14
C2–C5: 10
C3–C4: 11
C4–C2: 3
C4–C6: 13
C4–C7: 12

Overlaps	
C1–C2: 2	C6–C2: 2
C2–C3: 2	C2–C7: 2
C3–C4: 2	
C4–C5: 2	
C5–C4: 2	
C4–C4: 1	
C4–C6: 2	

Figure 4.9. *Constrained assembly. The initial data consist of (1) the set of contigs to be ordered with, for each one, its number of occurrences; (2) inter-contig overlaps (solid arrows); (3) distances between contigs (dotted arrows) obtained by proximity information provided by the sequencing technologies. The longest path in the resulting graph is the solution of the assembly (here: C1-C2-C3-C4-C5-C4-C4-C6-C2-C7). The number of times we might loop over node 4 is limited by its coverage (here 3). For a color version of this figure, see www.iste.co.uk/chateau/graphs.zip*

From these data, a graph with seven vertices is obtained. The solid lines represent the overlaps and dotted lines indicate the distance constraints. The longest path that respects all the constraints (distances between contigs and number of occurrences of contigs) starts at contig C1 and ends with contig C7. Contigs C2 and C4 which have respectively an occurrence of 2 and 3 appear this number of times in the solution.

The formulation in the form of a mixed-integer linear program is not immediate. Our goal is not to describe it in detail here. Interested readers should refer to François et al. (2018) and to Briot et al. (2014).

The particularity of this approach is that it does not use any heuristic and provides an accurate modeling of the assembly problem. On the contrary, the problem sizes that can be solved by the solvers remain limited. The method therefore targets limited regions of the genome which present a high complexity with which the other methods fail.

4.5. Scaffold-ordering methods

This final part of the assembly process concerns the organization of scaffolds, produced in the previous steps, at the genome scale. Information that indicates relative proximities between contigs originates essentially from two main technologies. The first is based on chromosomal conformational capture with Hi-C sequencing technology. The second is based on the concept of fingerprinting obtained by enzymatic restriction.

4.5.1. *Hi-C data-based methods*

As introduced in section 4.2.4, the Hi-C technology, initially developed for studying the 3D structure of genomes, produces read pairs that are spatially close in the genome. Since genomes also exhibit a strong linear organization, it is inevitably captured by this approach to approximate the distances between scaffolds. Schematically, a distance (i, j) is obtained by counting the number of pairs whose reads align each with one of the scaffolds i and j.

The following four sections describe four different methods that employ this information exclusively for ordering scaffolds. These methods are referenced by the name of the software that implements them (except the last one).

LACHESIS

This is one of the first methods that has adopted the Hi-C technology for solving the scaffold-ordering problem (Burton et al. 2013). It consists of three main steps, as shown in Figure 4.10:

1) scaffold clustering into chromosomal groups;

2) scaffold ordering within each group;

3) scaffold orientation.

The clustering algorithm agglomerates the scaffolds hierarchically based on a metric normalizing the read density that links scaffold pairs. The number of groups is specified beforehand with respect to the expected number of chromosomes.

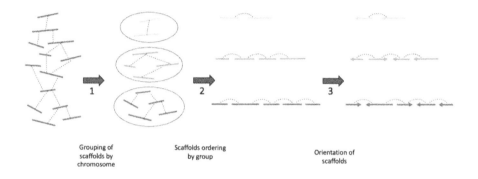

Figure 4.10. *LACHESIS. The three main steps of the method: scaffold clustering, ordering and orientation*

Then, (step 2) a graph is constructed for each group. The nodes are scaffolds and the edges between nodes are weighted by a value corresponding to the inverse of the density previously mentioned. A minimal spanning tree is then sought from which the longest path is extracted. This path represents a subset of ordered scaffolds which will be used for inserting the rest of the scaffolds on the basis of a proximity computation that maximizes the number of links between adjacent scaffolds.

The final step orients the contigs by precisely taking into account the alignment positions (*mapping*) of the Hi-C reads. An acyclic, weighted and directed graph represents all possibilities for scaffold orientation on the ordering predicted in the previous step. The weights are calculated as the logarithmic probability of Hi-C bonds observed between adjacent contigs for a given orientation, assuming that the probability of linkage between two contigs is approximated to a genomic distance of decay $\frac{1}{x}$ (for $x \geq 100\,\mathrm{Kb}$). The maximum likelihood path through this graph predicts an orientation for each scaffold.

GRAAL

The method iteratively applies virtual rearrangements to an initial set of DNA fragments in order to generate one-dimensional genomic structures compatible with the Hi-C data (Marie-Nelly et al. 2014).

A set of DNA fragments used to initialize the process are first generated by dividing the scaffolds into elementary packages of fragments. The idea is to statistically evaluate the genomic structures obtained by rearranging these packages. More precisely, at each iteration, the algorithm randomly considers a packet, without replacing it, then chooses a number N of partner packages with a probability that depends on the contact frequencies computed from the Hi-C data.

GRAAL then examines 14 different types of virtual mutations within these packages that mimic biological rearrangements such as inversions, insertions, deletions and mainly duplications. These mutations define a set of $14 \times N$ candidate genomes whose likelihoods are calculated using a very elaborate statistical model. The most probable structure is selected for the next iteration. In total, thousands of iterations are applied and the position of each package is re-examined several times.

GRAAL differs from the previous method in several ways. First, the initial scaffolds are called into question by the decomposition into elementary packages, making it thus possible to correct possible assembly errors. Next, GRAAL explicitly addresses duplications by means of the virtual mutation mechanism. New segments, not identified during scaffold assembly, can then be inserted. Finally, the algorithm generates families of structures with their associated probabilities, which leads to an objective measure of the likelihood of the assembled genome.

SALSA

A graph of scaffolds is built based on a similar approach to that of the *string graph* (Myers 2005). The graph is composed of nodes that represent the ends of the scaffolds. The edges represent the links between scaffolds computed with Hi-C paired reads. The edges are weighted by the weight of the link. This weight is normalized by the scaffold size (see Ghurye et al. (2017) for an accurate description of the weight computation). The ends of the scaffolds are arbitrarily labeled B (Begin) or E (End).

Building the graph is achieved as follows. The edges are first sorted by decreasing weight. The ones that are below a threshold are eliminated. The edges are then considered in order of decreasing weight and inserted in a greedy manner in the graph if both nodes are not present therein. The construction is completed by connecting the nodes B and E of the same scaffold. Algorithm 4.1 summarizes the construction of the graph.

ALGORITHM 4.1. BuildScaffoldGraph

Input: LE – edge list
LS – scaffold list
Output: G – scaffold graph

1 $G \leftarrow \emptyset$;
2 **While** $LE \neq \emptyset$ **do**
3      $e \leftarrow$ current edge;
4      $u, v, w \leftarrow e$.source, e.target, e.weight;
5   **If** u *and* $v \notin G$ **then**
6   G.addEdge(u,v,w);
7   LE.remove(e);
8 **For all** $s \in S$ **do**
9   G.addEdge(s.B,s.E);
10 **return** G

The resulting graph has two interesting properties. The first one is that the degree of a node is less than or equal to 2. The second is that each linked component of the graph possesses exactly two first-degree nodes.

An ordered scaffold sequence is therefore contained in every linked component of the graph. The two first-degree nodes are the beginnings (u) and ends (v) of the path that traverses every node of the linked component. The authors of the method divide the components into two groups according to their number of nodes (scaffolds). Those that exceed a certain threshold are considered as being valid orderings. The scaffolds belonging to the other linked components are separately reconsidered and inserted in the valid orderings.

Seriation

In general, the seriation problem applied to a set of elements aims at finding a latent order based on proximity information. The starting point is a matrix that indicates pairwise proximity between these elements. It is of course assumed that they possess a serial structure; in other words, they can be ordered along a chain where the proximity between elements decreases with their distance within this chain. In practice, a permutation of this matrix is available, in which the elements are not indexed according to this latent order. Seriation then seeks to find it using only the proximity information between the pairs.

More precisely, let $D_{i,j}$ be the distance between element i and j, and pi_k be the permutation of index k. The seriation problem seeks to minimize the following sum S:

$$S = \sum_{i=0}^{n} D_{i,j}(\pi_i - \pi_j)^2.$$

The result that matters to us here is the order of the permutations which minimizes this sum. Figure 4.11 shows a visual representation of the solution steps of the seriation problem. The left matrix represents the initial state: the elements are randomly ordered. The brighter a dot is, the more it indicates a proximity between elements. By minimizing S, the elements are ordered by positioning side by side those which are close. The matrix on the right-hand side is thus obtained where clearly emerges a diagonal that visualizes a linear organization of the elements.

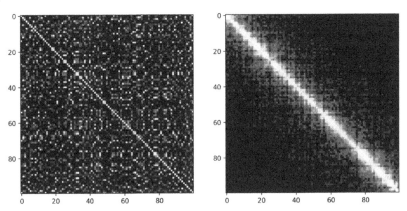

Figure 4.11. *Seriation. The left matrix represents the initial distance matrix. The one on the right is the permuted matrix. The diagonal clearly visualizes a linear structure of the data. The brighter the dots, the closer the distance between scaffolds. For a color version of this figure, see www.iste.co.uk/chateau/graphs.zip*

Applied to scaffold ordering, this technique thus requires a distance matrix to be constructed. A cell (i, j) of the matrix reflects the distance between the scaffolds i and j. This distance can be computed from the alignment of the Hi-C read pairs over the scaffolds. The thesis written by A. Recanati (2018) presents this method in an extremely detailed manner.

4.5.2. *Optical mapping-based methods*

It should be remembered that an optical map locates specific enzyme sites along a genome. In general, the map covers the whole genome sequence, or at least a good part of it. Using this map for ordering scaffolds relies on matching the restriction sites of the map with those obtained by in silico digestion of the scaffolds. Figure 4.12 illustrates the idea.

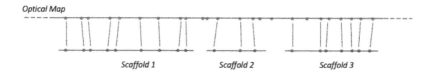

Figure 4.12. *Principle underlying the use of an optical map for scaffold ordering*

The resolution of an optical card is lower than that of a scaffold. Furthermore, the alignment between scaffolds and the map must be flexible to take into account an error interval on the distance between restriction sites. Besides, since the technologies are not perfect, insertions or deletions of restriction sites, both in terms of building the optical card and in terms of scaffold production, are possible. The alignment algorithm must consider these situations.

Ideally, a scaffold should only be matched in one place in the map and present no overlapping with its neighbors. In practice, due to the errors mentioned above and the complexity of certain genomes, several locations are possible. Again, this is tantamount to an optimization problem in which one has to choose the optimal arrangement of scaffolds.

One of the first strategies proposed by Nagarajan et al. (2008) illustrates well the way the problem is solved. It breaks down into two phases as follows:

1) find *good* matches between scaffolds and map;

2) find a coherent ordering based on these pairings.

The first phase initially requires a metric for computing a matching score. If a scaffold with $n + 1$ restriction sites is considered, it can be decomposed into n fragments, each fragment being surrounded by two restriction sites (external fragments are eliminated). The sequence $(C_1, C_2, \ldots, C_n)$ represents the sizes of these fragments. If the sizes of a sequence of n fragments of the optical map $(O_j, O_{j+2}, \ldots, O_{j+n-1})$ are also considered, established using the same method, the matching quality between these two sequences of fragments can be expressed using the following χ^2 score function:

$$\sum_{k=1}^{j} \left(\frac{C_k - O_k}{\sigma_k} \right)^2$$

where σ_k represents the standard deviation of the size of the fragment O_k given by the software that produced the optical card.

The introduction of errors significantly complicates matters. Scaffold 3 in Figure 4.12, for example, presents a deletion that should not prevent this matching to be considered. The authors of this method consider that the match is *reasonable* if the sum of the sizes is in agreement, or more formally if for $(C_s, \ldots, C_t)$ and $(O_u, \ldots, O_v)$:

$$\left| \sum_{i=s}^{t} C_i - \sum_{j=u}^{v} O_i \right| \le Z_\sigma \sqrt{\sum_{j=u}^{v} \sigma_j^2} \qquad [4.1]$$

with a value of $Z_{sigma} = 4$ obtained experimentally.

The score function described above can be easily optimized using dynamic programming (introduced in section 1.8.1). If m_r is the number of missing restriction sites and x is the matching χ^2 score, the combined score $T_r \times m_r + x$ can be used as a substitute. It is assumed that T_r is a greater constant than the score of the highest χ^2, thus giving preference to alignments that correspond to a large number of sites. If $S[i][j]$ is the score of the best alignment between the end of the ith fragment of the scaffold and the end of the jth fragment of the optical map, the recursion is given by

$$S[i][j] =$$

$$\max_{0 \le k \le i, 0 \le l \le j} \left(-T_r \times (i - k + l - j) - \frac{\left(\sum_{s=k}^{i} C_s - \sum_{t=l}^{j} O_t \right)^2}{\sum_{t=l}^{j} \sigma_t^2} + S[k-1][l-1] \right)$$

with $S[-1][j] = 0$ and $S[i][-1] = -\infty$.

The complexity of this algorithm is $O(m^2n^2)$ for an optical map composed of m fragments and a scaffold of n fragments. In practice, the constraint specified by Equation [4.1] serves to restrict the search space.

This first step therefore produces possible scaffold alignments on the optical map. However, their locations may be mutually inconsistent. Assuming that scaffolds cannot overlap, the problem in choosing a good scaffold ordering can be modeled as follows: let M_i be the set of possible alignments of the scaffold i and P be the set of selected alignments. Two conditions are set as follows:

1) $\forall i, |P| \cap |M_i| = 1$;

2) for $a, b \in P, a \cap b = \emptyset$.

The first condition indicates that the ordering contains the scaffold i only once. The second prohibits overlapping.

This optimization problem is analogous to interval ordering, widely known in operational research. Given a set of tasks and time intervals with which are associated weighted tasks according to certain criteria. A schedule has to be found that satisfies assigning tasks to time intervals and optimizes the criteria being considered.

By transposing to the scaffold ordering, the tasks become the scaffolds and the time intervals the matches between optical map and scaffolds. This optimization problem is known to be a difficult problem (NP-complete), but several approximation algorithms have been proposed (Bar-Noy et al. 2001) for solving the problem in a reasonable time.

4.6. Assembly validation

At the end of the assembly process, the question about the quality of the result arises. How can it be verified that the text built from the sequencing data indeed matches the genome text? How can a choice be made between different assemblies originating from different parametrizations of the same tool? Or, in a similar vein, how can the assemblies of various software programs be appreciated, knowing that each one of them possesses its own specificities? The problem is not an easy one and the experience of the bioinformaticians who manipulate these complex software programs is a major concern. Validation is generally based on several strategies largely complementary to one another.

4.6.1. *Metrics*

N50: the N50 metric defines the assembly quality in terms of contiguity. Given a set of scaffolds, it is defined as the length of the shortest scaffold corresponding to 50% of the total length of the assembly (see Figure 4.13).

NG50: the drawback of the preceding metric is that it does not allow several assemblies to be compared insofar as each one of them could have produced a list of scaffolds whose sum of sizes is different. On the contrary, the NG50 metric refers to the estimated genome size.

These two metrics should be used with caution. They provide synthetic and quantitative indications on scaffold sizes, but no information about their quality. If the objective is to produce the longest possible scaffolds, this criterion must not be allowed to prevail over the quality of the reconstructed text.

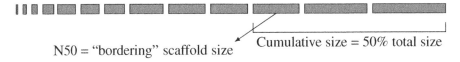

N50 = "bordering" scaffold size   Cumulative size = 50% total size

Figure 4.13. *N50 metric. In this example, a list of scaffolds with the following lengths is taken into consideration: 1 kbp, 2 kbp, 3 kbp, 5 kbp, 10 kbp, 10 kbp, 11 kbp, 18 kbp, 20 kbp, 25 kpb, 35 kbp and 40 kbp; the total size of the assembly is equal to 200 kbp. The sum of the sizes of the three longest scaffolds is equal to 100 kbp. The N50 is therefore set at 25 kbp (the shortest of the three scaffolds)*

4.6.2. *Read realignment*

One of the assembly errors lies in the construction of chimeric contigs or scaffolds. These scaffolds gather two (or more) genome parts that are not contiguous. A relatively simple manner to detect this type of error is to realign the reads over the contigs. If two distant portions are assembled by mistake, then read alignment on the connection region is not (or hardly) possible. A discontinuity in coverage is then observed at this junction point.

The analysis can be done with all types of reads: short reads, paired reads, linked or long reads. The principle remains the same: to detect coverage discontinuities that would reveal a chimerical construction.

This validation phase can also be incorporated into the general assembly process, for example, before the scaffold-ordering step. In this case, if such an event is detected, the scaffold is redivided into smaller scaffolds.

4.6.3. *Gene prediction*

Another way to appreciate the quality of the assembly is to compare it with the knowledge stored in gene databases. The idea is to search for a set of orthologous genes existing in single copy. These genes are selected on the basis of their representation in various phylogenetic clades. The hypothesis is that a high percentage of these genes can be found in all organisms of a given clade.

This method is instantiated, for example, in the BUSCO software (Benchmarking Universal Single-Copy Orthologs) (Waterhouse et al. 2017) which calculates four indicators as follows:

1) **complete:** percentage of complete genes found in scaffolds;

2) **duplicated:** percentage of duplicated genes. These are complete genes but found in multiple copies;

3) **fragmented:** percentage of fragmented genes. Only part of the gene was found;

4) **missing:** percentage of missing genes.

From these indicators, several conclusions can be drawn. For instance, if the percentage of complete genes is low, it will indicate that the assembly does not cover the whole genome; if the percentage of fragmented genes is high, it may mean that a text contains many errors, including insertion or omission errors that prevent having a stable basis for reads that allow for gene localization.

4.6.4. *Competitions*

Competitions do not verify the quality of an assembly. Their main purpose is to compare the assembly strategies and therefore, by extension, to assign them a certain degree of trust. They also position them relatively to each other according to various criteria, enabling the selection of the best suited software program to assemble a given organism. Each *assembler* actually has its own specificities inferred by its internal strategies and heuristics.

In these competitions, such as the Assemblathons (Earl et al. 2011; Bradnam et al. 2013), the genome texts to be assembled are known in advance by the organizers. Sequencing data are artificially generated and constitute the raw material for which the competitors compete. The objective, from these synthetic data, is to find the original text.

Since the genome is known, accurate qualitative measurements are possible. In this way, they bring forward the advantages and disadvantages of the different assembly methodologies. They also allow some conclusions to be drawn about the ongoing research in this area. As an example, the organizers of Assemblaton-2 concluded with the following advice:

– do not rely on the results of a single assembler. As far as possible, generate multiple assemblies with different assemblers and/or different parameters;

– do not put your trust in an assembler on a single metric;

– if the purpose of the assembly is primarily gene analysis, metrics such as N50, NG50 or the size of the assembly are not necessarily relevant;

– to assess the level of heterozygosity in the genome. Some assemblers are not suitable for this situation.

These competitions mainly show that the diversity of methodologies has a strong impact on the outcome. They also show that none is better considering the criteria evaluated. Their specificity means that according to the nature and the complexity of genomes, they will produce more or less satisfactory results.

4.7. Conclusion

De novo genome assembly is a complex computer problem. There are many reasons: first, sequencing technologies produce extremely fragmented information, often incomplete and possibly very noisy. Next, the textual structure of genomes is very complex. Genomes are not random texts. They are part of a process which, at the level of the DNA sequence, is reflected by multiple, exact or approximate repeats of any size. Heterozygosity and/or polyploidy adds another level of complexity. Finally, the volumes of data to be handled are substantial and require algorithms and data structures to solve the problem in a reasonable amount of time and on machines also with reasonable memory sizes.

It is obvious that the problem of assembly is strongly linked to sequencing data. NGS (Next Generation Sequencing) data have contributed to democratize sequencing by providing both volume and quality. On the contrary, the short size of reads remains an almost insurmountable obstacle in assembling complex genomes (namely, with a large number of repeats). The reads, however, represent an interesting step forward for overcoming this limitation. The next generation generates much longer reads capable of spanning most repeated areas. Nonetheless, they are of lower quality and still incur relatively high costs. In addition, these technologies require the extraction of long DNA fragments of the organisms to be sequenced, which is not always feasible.

The evolution of sequencing technologies is constant. It is therefore possible to reasonably predict that long reads of excellent quality will see the light of day in the more or less long term. This will facilitate the problem of genome assembly and will profoundly modify the current assembly strategies. Data structures such as de Bruijn graphs which now are capable of very efficiently structuring the large amounts of information obtained from short-read sequencing will become less relevant; decomposition into k-mers causes, in fact, a loss of information which proves to be extremely damaging to processing repeats. It will therefore be necessary to devise new ways of representing this information in a compact way while at the same time combining powerful algorithms capable of supporting high throughputs which should continue to grow at a steady pace.

4.8. References

Andrews, S., Krueger, F., Segonds-Pichon, A., Biggins, L., Krueger, C., Wingett, S. (2012). FastQC, a quality control tool for high throughput sequence data. Report, Babraham Institute.

Bankevich, A., Nurk, S., Antipov, D., Gurevich, A.A., Dvorkin, M., Kulikov, A.S., Lesin, V.M., Nikolenko, S.I., Pham, S., Prjibelski, A.D., Pyshkin, A.V., Sirotkin, A.V., Vyahhi, N., Tesler, G., Alekseyev, M.A., Pevzner, P.A. (2012). SPAdes: A new genome assembly algorithm and its applications to single-cell sequencing. *Journal of Computational Biology*, 19, 455–477.

Bar-Noy, A., Bar-Yehuda, R., Freund, A., Naor, J.S., Schieber, B. (2001). A unified approach to approximating resource allocation and scheduling. *Journal of the ACM*, 48, 1069–1090.

Batzoglou, S., Jaffe, D.B., Stanley, K., Butler, J., Gnerre, S., Mauceli, E., Berger, B., Mesirov, J.P., Lander, E.S. (2002). Arachne: A whole genome shotgun assembler. *Genome Research*, 12(1), 177–189.

Benoit, G., Lavenier, D., Lemaitre, C., Rizk, G. (2014). Bloocoo, a memory efficient read corrector. Poster, European Conference on Computational Biology (ECCB).

Bonfield, J.K., Smith, K.F., Staden, R. (1995). A new DNA sequence assembly program. *Nucleic Acids Research*, 23(24), 4992–4999.

Bradnam, K.R., Fass, J.N., Alexandrov, A., Baranay, P., Bechner, M., Birol, I., Boisvert, S., Chapman, J.A., Chapuis, G., Chikhi, R. (2013). Assemblathon 2: Evaluating de novo methods of genome assembly in three vertebrate species. *GigaScience*, 2(1).

Briot, N., Chateau, A., Coletta, R., de Givry, S., Leleux, P., Schiex, T. (2014). An integer linear programming approach for genome scaffolding. Paper, 10th Workshop on Constraint-Based Methods for Bioinformatics (WCB).

Burton, J., Adey, A., Patwardhan, R., Qiu, R., Kitzman, J., Shendure, J. (2013). Chromosome-scale scaffolding of de novo genome assemblies based on chromatin interactions. *Nature Biotechnology*, 31(12), 1119–1125.

Chikhi, R. (2012). Computational methods for de novo assembly of next-generation genome sequencing data. Thesis, École normale supérieure de Cachan – ENS Cachan.

Chikhi, R. and Medvedev, P. (2014). Informed and automated k-mer size selection for genome assembly. *Bioinformatics*, 30(1), 31–37.

Chikhi, R. and Rizk, G. (2012). Space-efficient and exact de Bruijn graph representation based on a Bloom filter. *Algorithms in Bioinformatics: 12th International Workshop, WABI 2012, Ljubljana, Slovenia, September 10-12, 2012. Proceedings.* Springer.

Drezen, E., Rizk, G., Chikhi, R., Deltel, C., Lemaitre, C., Peterlongo, P., Lavenier, D. (2014). GATB: Genome assembly & analysis tool box. *Bioinformatics (Oxford, England)*, (20), 2959–2961.

Earl, D., Bradnam, K., John, J.S., Darling, A., Lin, D., Fass, J., Yu, H.O.K., Buffalo, V., Zerbino, D.R., Diekhans, M., Nguyen, N. (2011). Assemblathon 1: A competitive assessment of de novo short read assembly methods. *Genome Research*, 21(12).

François, S., Andonov, R., Lavenier, D., Djidjev, R. (2018). Global optimization for scaffolding and completing genome assemblies. *Electronic Notes in Discrete Mathematics*, 64, 185–194.

Garrido-Ramos, M.A. (2012). *Repetitive DNA*, Vol. 7. Karger.

Ghurye, J., Pop, M., Koren, S., Bickhart, D., Chin, C. (2017). Scaffolding of long read assemblies using long range contact information. *BMC Genomics*, 18(1), 527.

Gnerre, S., Maccallum, I., Przybylski, D., Ribeiro, F.J., Burton, J.N., Walker, B.J., Sharpe, T., Hall, G., Shea, T.P., Sykes, S., Berlin, A.M., Aird, D., Costello, M., Daza, R., Williams, L., Nicol, R., Gnirke, A., Nusbaum, C., Lander, E.S., Jaffe, D.B. (2011). High-quality draft assemblies of mammalian genomes from massively parallel sequence data. *Proceedings of the National Academy of Sciences of the USA*, 108.

Huang, X. and Madan, A. (1999). CAP3: A DNA sequence assembly program. *Genome Research*, 9(9), 868–877.

Kececioglu, J. and Myers, E. (1995). Combinatorial algorithms for DNA sequence assembly. *Algorithmica*, 13, 7–51.

Koren, S., Walenz, B., Berlin, K., Miller, J., Phillippy, A. (2017). Canu: Scalable and accurate long-read assembly via adaptive k-mer weighting and repeat separation. *Genome Research*, 27(5), 772–736.

Leung, H.C., Yiu, S.-M., Parkinson, J., Chin, F.Y. (2013). IDBA-MT: De novo assembler for metatranscriptomic data generated from next-generation sequencing technology. *Journal of Computational Biology*, 20(7), 540–550.

Luo, R., Liu, B., Xie, Y., Li, Z., Huang, W., Yuan, J., He, G., Chen, Y., Pan, Q., Liu, Y. (2012). SOAPdenovo2: An empirically improved memory-efficient short-read de novo assembler. *Gigascience*, 1.

Mardis, E.R. (2017). DNA sequencing technologies: 2006–2016. *Nature Protocols*, 12, 213–218.

Margulies, M., Egholm, M., Altman, W.E., Attiya, S., Bader, J.S., Bemben, L.A., Berka, J., Braverman, M.S., Chen, Y.-J., Chen, Z. (2005). Genome sequencing in microfabricated high-density picolitre reactors. *Nature*, 437, 376–380.

Marie-Nelly, H., Marbouty, M., Cournac, A., Flot, J.-F., Liti, G., Poggi Parodi, D., Syan, S., Guillén, N., Margeot, A., Zimmer, C., Koszul, R. (2014). High-quality genome (re)assembly using chromosomal contact data. *Nature Communications*, 5(5695).

Myers, E. (2005). The fragment assembly string graph. *Bioinformatics*, 21, 79–85.

Nagarajan, N., Read, T., Pop, M. (2008). Scaffolding and validation of bacterial genome assemblies using optical restriction maps. *Bioinformatics*, 24(10), 1229–1235.

Neely, R.K., Deen, J., Hofkens, J. (2011). Optical mapping of DNA: Single-molecule-based methods for mapping genomes. *Biopolymers*, 95, 298–311.

Pan, W., Jiang, T., Lonardi, S. (2019). OMGS: Optical map-based genome scaffolding. In *Research in Computational Molecular Biology*, Cowen, L.J. (ed.). Springer International Publishing.

Pevzner, P., Tang, H., Waterman, M. (2001). An Eulerian path approach to DNA fragment assembly. *Proceedings of the National Academy of Sciences*, 98, 9748–9753.

Recanati, A. (2018). Relaxations of the Seriation problem and applications to de novo genome assembly. Thesis, PSL Research University.

Salikhov, K., Sacomoto, G., Kucherov, G. (2013). Using cascading Bloom filters to improve the memory usage for de Brujin graphs. *Algorithms in Bioinformatics*, Springer.

Salmela, L. and Rivals, E. (2014). LoRDEC: Accurate and efficient long read error correction. *Bioinformatics*, 30(24), 3506–3514.

Simpson, J.T., Wong, K., Jackman, S.D., Schein, J.E., Jones, S.J.M., Birol, I. (2009). ABySS: A parallel assembler for short read sequence data. *Genome Research*, 19, 1117–1123.

Sutton, G.G., White, O., Adams, M.D., Kerlavage, A.R. (1995). TIGR assembler: A new tool for assembling large shotgun sequencing projects. *Genome Science and Technology*, 1(1), 9–19.

Waterhouse, R.M., Seppey, M., Simão, F.A., Manni, M., Ioannidis, P., Klioutchnikov, G., Kriventseva, E.V., Zdobnov, E.M. (2017). BUSCO applications from quality assessments to gene prediction and phylogenomics. *Molecular Biology and Evolution*, 35(3), 543–548.

de Wit, E. and de Laat, W. (2012). A decade of 3C technologies: Insights into nuclear organization. *Genes & Development*, 26(1), 11–24.

Zerbino, D. and Birney, E. (2008). Velvet: Algorithms for de novo short read assembly using de Bruijn graphs. *Genome Research*, 18, 821–829.

5

Metagenomics and Metatranscriptomics

Cervin Guyomar[1] and Claire Lemaitre[2]

[1]*GenPhySE, University of Toulouse, INRAE, ENVT, France*
[2]*University of Rennes, CNRS, INRIA, IRISA-UMR 6074, France*

5.1. What is metagenomics?

5.1.1. *Motivations and historical context*

Microorganisms (bacteria, viruses and unicellular eukaryotes) represent an invisible but important percentage of biomass, either by their abundance or their diversity. Estimates indicate that bacterial biomass alone could account for nearly 15 % of the total biomass (Bar-On et al. 2018). This category of living organisms is also home to an immense diversity. Microorganisms are present in all ecosystems, including the most extreme ones, and it is estimated that the number of microbial species could reach 1 trillion (10^{12}) (Locey and Lennon 2016). They are integrated into their ecosystems, where they perform a multitude of functions. For example, all macroorganisms are associated with microorganisms involved in, among other things, their metabolism or their health. The study of microbial communities within their environments is therefore a central task.

From Sequences to Graphs,
coordinated by Annie CHATEAU and Mikaël SALSON.
© ISTE Ltd 2022.

Although existing for a long time, the study of these communities has been restricted for a long time to the use of imaging techniques that only enable the observation of morphological characters. Within this framework, only organisms that could be put into culture could be studied. Therefore, before the rise of molecular biology technologies, only a low-resolution study of a small fraction of existing microbes was possible.

Advances in molecular biology techniques have led to overcoming obstacles and have revolutionized microbiology. The advent of Sanger sequencing has provided access to the structure and function of bacterial genomes. In particular, ribosomal RNA is described as a marker used for the taxonomic classification of species. These approaches were applied to environmental data by Pace and colleagues who proposed in 1986 to sequence ribosomal RNA directly in the environment (Pace et al. 1986), without involving a bacterial culture process. This idea means that the bias of culturability is eliminated, which until then made a large fraction of the microbial diversity invisible (Rappé and Giovannoni 2003). Proposed in 1998 by Handelsman and collaborators (Handelsman et al. 1998), the term *metagenomics* refers to directly sequencing DNA in a medium, which potentially enables accessing the genomes of all members of a community.

5.1.2. *The metagenomic data*

5.1.2.1. *Targeted and whole-genome metagenomics*

There are two main types of metagenomic data. Targeted metagenomics or *metabarcoding* consists of amplifying and sequencing a particular region of the genome, called a genomic marker. A frequently used region for bacteria is 16S ribosomal DNA, which is an excellent phylogenetic marker. In contrast, whole-genome or *shotgun* metagenomics consists of sequencing the whole DNA in the sample. Rather than amplifying a specific region of the genome, the entire DNA of the genome or metagenome is randomly sheared into fragments that are sequenced with conventional high-throughput techniques. All the genomes of the members of the community can therefore be sequenced.

There is some vagueness about how targeted metagenomics should be referred to. According to many authors, the term metagenomics is not very appropriate, since it consists of a technique targeted on a small portion of the genome (Esposito and Kirschberg 2014). Therefore, in the remainder of the chapter, which focuses on *shotgun* techniques, we use the term metagenomics to refer to whole-genome metagenomics.

Targeted metagenomics is used to taxonomically characterize a sample. Because only a small fraction of the genome is sequenced, it is less expensive than whole-genome metagenomics, and results in the identification of rarer organisms for an equivalent sequencing effort. For these reasons, it has been primarily used in the early stages of metagenomics, as well as for large-scale projects for cataloguing bacterial diversity.

Compared to targeted metagenomics, the information obtained in whole-genome metagenomics is simultaneously more voluminous, more difficult to interpret and richer. Whole-genome information leads to better taxonomic resolution than markers used in targeted metagenomics. *Shotgun* metagenomics suffers less from biases derived from the amplification of targeted sequences, which makes it more capable of quantitatively representing communities. Last but not least, while targeted metagenomics provides information about the taxonomic composition of communities only, whole-genome metagenomics informs about the functional potential of communities, through the gene repertoires of its members. Therefore, the *shotgun* method is able to answer the classical questions raised in metagenomics, concerning the members of microbial communities: "Who are they?" and "What are they able to do?" In comparison, targeted metagenomics is hardly capable of answering the latter (see Figure 5.1).

On the other hand, sequencing a sample using whole-genome metagenomics is significantly more expensive, as a large amount of reads must be sequenced to achieve sufficient coverage for less abundant organisms. However, due to the continuous progress of sequencing technologies, this technique is becoming widely democratized, and major metagenomic projects have multiplied. One should mention the MetaSoil project (Delmont et al. 2011) for the study of soil microbiome or the HMP project (for *Human Microbiome Project*) for the study of the different human microbiota. *Shotgun* and targeted metagenomics can also be employed together. They are complementary, especially for addressing the most complex communities, where rare organisms can only be identified by targeted methods. One example is the TARA Oceans project (Bork et al. 2015), whose aim is to explore the microbial diversity of the oceans, and which combines these two approaches.

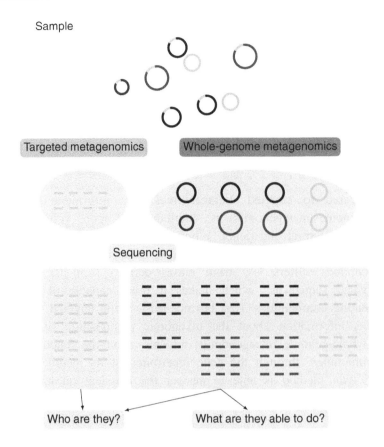

Figure 5.1. *Targeted metagenomics versus full-genome metagenomics. On top, the sample to be analyzed contains the genomes (circles) of several organisms. The 16S ribosomal DNA portion is shown in green. Depending on the type of method used, only this sequence (left) or the whole genome (right) will be sequenced. Targeted metagenomics provides answers to the question "Who are these organisms?" whereas whole-genome metagenomics also makes it possible to answer the question "What are they able to do?" For a color version of this figure, see www.iste.co.uk/chateau/graphs.zip*

5.1.2.2. *Third-generation reads*

The emergence of high-throughput sequencing technologies in the 2000s corresponds to the beginning of the rise of metagenomics. Compared to previous technologies, this new generation enables the sequencing of large data volumes at a reasonable cost. The sequencing depths thus achieved allow the exploration of almost all bacterial communities, with low error rates.

Nevertheless, these technologies remain limited for certain applications. In the case of metabarcoding, the short length of reads reduces the taxonomic resolution achieved, while biases during the amplification step prevent the correct quantification of the species present. In whole-genome metagenomics, community genome assembly is strongly limited by the length of the reads.

The main limitation of second-generation sequencing is the limited length of the reads, which makes certain assembly problems difficult or even impossible to solve. The most recent sequencing technologies can be described as "long-range" sequencing (Sedlazeck et al. 2018). For example, they enable the sequencing of longer reads, reaching up to a million bases (Pacific Biosciences or NanoPore technologies), or linking short-reads originating from the same genomic region (10X genomics and Hi-C technologies). These techniques have a high potential to address some of the problems raised by metagenomics outlined in the previous section. As such, longer reads lead to improved metagenomic assemblies. Techniques such as Hi-C can distinguish reads derived from different organisms (Burton et al. 2014). Nonetheless, the throughput offered by long-read sequencing technologies does not currently compete with second-generation sequencing. Given that this parameter is critical in metagenomic applications that require large sequencing efforts to understand the diversity of communities, the use of new methods remains conditional on their future technological progress.

5.1.3. *Bioinformatics challenges for metagenomics*

Although metagenomic data brings, in principle, a fresh perspective on communities that were previously poorly known, these new data exhibit certain particularities that justify and require the development of dedicated methods.

5.1.3.1. *Data volume*

The sequencing of metagenomic data can generate large volumes of data. In complex ecosystems such as soil or seawater, characterizing rare organisms requires major sequencing efforts (Roesch et al. 2007; Welch and Huse 2011). As an example, a sample from the TARA Oceans project can contain nearly 300 million reads. In addition, many studies require sequencing and joint analysis of several tens or hundreds of samples in order to compare different ecosystems.

This large volume of data raises issues in all stages of the analysis. There are dedicated tools and databases existing for storing, indexing and cataloging such data (IMG/MER (Chen et al. 2019), CAMERA (Seshadri et al. 2007), MG-RAST (Keegan et al. 2016) and MGnify (Mitchell et al. 2019)). From an algorithmic point of view, the search for efficient solutions capable of managing a multitude of large datasets is a priority.

5.1.3.2. *Genomic diversity*

Bacterial communities generally exhibit a continuum of diversity, broken down into several taxonomic levels. Classically, we distinguish within these communities several different microbial species, whose genomes can present homologous regions, for instance, consecutive to the horizontal transfer of a gene. Abundances of these species are measured by their coverage by metagenomic reads, and can be very unbalanced.

Furthermore, each species is represented by a variable number of individuals, which may have different genotypes, including short variants and structural variations. Unlike genomic data whose ploidy is known, metagenomic data therefore harbor a very large amount of variations. These different variants can also be quantified by measuring their coverage. Depending on the sequencing effort, some rare variants can easily be confused with sequencing errors or with regions from another species in the community.

Understanding this diversity proves therefore to be complex, especially when comparing different communities that may harbor distinct species. Classical genomics tasks, such as assembly or variant calling, are made difficult by this polymorphism (Sczyrba et al. 2017) and require the development of dedicated algorithms. Often, one way of addressing this problem consists of restricting the analysis to operational taxonomic units that can be identified by arbitrary criteria (e.g. a similarity threshold), and not considering variability within these units, which nonetheless might have functional impacts. This simplification of metagenomic diversity allows for the use of diversity metrics usually employed in ecology. Among these metrics, the Shannon index, which can be used to measure the diversity in a sample (alpha diversity), or measures such as the Jaccard distance or the Bray–Curtis dissimilarity, which are used to measure the dissimilarity between samples (beta diversity). This last category of metrics is described in section 5.4.1.

5.2. "Who are they": taxonomic characterization of microbial communities

Taxonomic characterization, or metagenomic profiling, strives to answer a question that does not usually arise when studying a single organism, by describing at the taxonomic level the organisms present in the sample. The purpose is to identify and eventually quantify the organisms present in a community based on metagenomic reads. More formally, two problems can be identified: the *identification* of the taxonomic units present and the *quantification* of each of these units in the sample. The identification problem takes as input a set of nucleic sequences and returns a list of distinct taxonomic identifiers. The quantification problem takes as input the set of sequences and the list of taxa returned by the first problem and returns a numerical value associated with each taxonomic identifier, representing the absolute (e.g. the number of reads) or relative (the percentage of reads) amount of each taxon in the sample.

Problem 5.1. Identification of taxonomic units

Input: nucleic sequences
Output: list of taxonomic identifiers

Problem 5.2. Quantification of taxonomic units

Input: nucleic sequences and list of associated taxonomic identifiers
Output: quantification of each taxonomic identifier in the sequences

---

This section aims to present the different families of methods that can be used to solve the problem of identification. These methods differ in particular by the use or not of existing databases, built from genomes already sequenced and identified. We thus distinguish between *reference-based* and *reference-free* methods. Generally, the methods that rely heavily on these databases prove to be hardly capable of identifying previously uncharacterized organisms, which is a critical problem in metagenomics. In addition, the performance of taxonomic assignment varies according to the different techniques. Some provide at best an inventory of the species present, while others enable the study of finer variations between microbial strains. Bearing these two aspects in mind, this section presents the different methods for the taxonomic characterization of metagenomic samples. We briefly look into methods dedicated to *barcoding* data, before studying in more detail those allowing for the taxonomic assignment of reads derived from whole-genome metagenomics, whether or not making use of reference databases.

5.2.1. *Methods for targeted metagenomics*

Environmental amplicon sequencing, or targeted metagenomics, is a widespread method to analyze the taxonomic composition of a microbial community. Because it is not a whole genome-based method, sequencing with a moderate sequencing effort results in a sequencing of a large majority of the organisms present. A first approach to analyze such data consists of aligning the sequences against phylogenetic marker sequence databases (mainly 16S ribosomal DNA), such as Silva (Quast et al. 2013) or GreenGenes (DeSantis et al. 2006). The reads are aligned against a reference alignment of phylogenetic markers, typically by means of a multiple alignment program such as SINA (Pruesse et al. 2012) for Silva. Considering the small size of the marker sequences used, this task remains relatively fast. On the other hand, this method does not enable the treatment of organisms that do not exist in these reference databases, and it presents a certain number of biases related in particular to the amplification steps. Another approach followed, for example, by the tools Qiime (Caporaso et al. 2010) and Mothur (Schloss et al. 2009), consists of grouping reads sharing a very high sequence similarity, in order to form OTUs (Operational Taxonomic Units). Reference databases can then be used to annotate the resulting OTUs by a taxon.

The main weakness of metabarcoding for the taxonomic characterization of communities is that very often a single marker is used to describe the sample. These markers rarely provide sufficient taxonomic resolution to determine which species are present in the sample, and a fortiori do not make it possible to reliably identify different strains. In addition, possible horizontal transfers of ribosomal RNA genes may also mislead taxonomic assignment (Schouls et al. 2003). Finally, the quantification of taxon abundance can be affected by amplification biases or variations in the number of copies of the marker under consideration (Schouls et al. 2003).

The principle of taxonomic characterization for targeted metagenomics is illustrated in Figure 5.2.

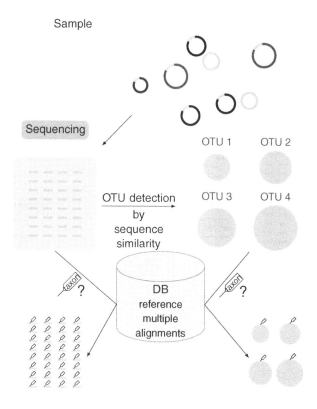

Figure 5.2. *Principle of taxonomic characterization with targeted metagenomics. Sequencing reads are aligned against a database of marker sequences, either directly (on the left) or after a similarity-based clustering into OTUs (right). The sequences are then annotated by making use of these alignments*

5.2.2. *Whole-genome methods with reference*

These methods consist of comparing metagenomic reads to reference information which is in the form of collections of genes or genomes that have already been assigned to a taxon. The most often used approach consists of aligning reads either on complete genomes or on sequences that have been designated as taxonomic markers. Alternatively, and to address the problems of scaling with large-sized datasets, other methods allow this assignment without resorting to alignment. The various methods presented in this section are illustrated in Figure 5.3.

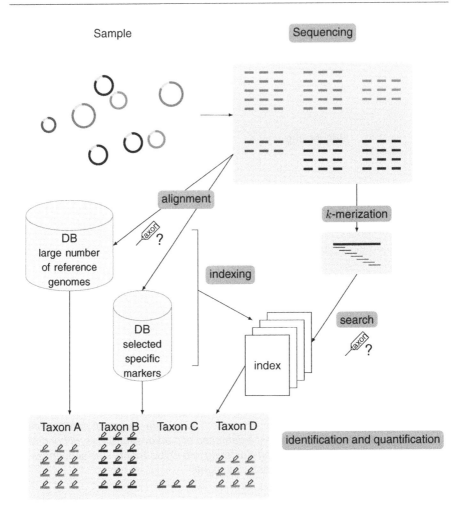

Figure 5.3. *Principle of taxonomic characterization methods in whole-genome metagenomics. On the left, alignment methods directly search for sequences in reference databases. These databases contain either complete genomes or smaller sequences of selected markers. On the right, alignment-free methods break down sequences into k-mers and query them in (often locally) optimized indexing data structures obtained from the reference databases. All these methods result in obtaining a taxonomic assignment and a quantification*

5.2.2.1. *Sequence alignment*

In the case of a community composed of organisms for which a large number of reference genomes are available, a first approach involves aligning the metagenomic reads against this collection of genomes. The Blast program (Altschul et al. 1990) was mostly used for analysis of the first metagenomic datasets, but faster aligners such as DIAMOND (Buchfink et al. 2014) have also been designed to better scale up with large datasets. The MEGAN program (Huson et al. 2016) is a reference in alignment analysis of metagenomic datasets. From a Blast result, it assigns a read to a taxon, which is the smallest common ancestor of the taxa with which this read is aligned. In addition, it also offers multiple visualization options. By correcting the number of alignments by the length of the reference genomes, tools such as GAAS (Angly 2009) or GRAMMY (Xia et al. 2011) can be used for quantifying the abundance of different taxa. The resolution achieved by these tools is highly dependent on the density of the reference database used. Moreover, the assignment of reads to reference genomes sharing a high sequence similarity (for instance, close strains) requires the use of dedicated methods, known as *strain tracking* methods. Tools such as Pathoscope (Francis et al. 2013) and Sigma (Ahn et al. 2015) can perform this task. Particularly, these software programs are based on statistical tools. Pathoscope is based on a Bayesian model, while Sigma relies on a probabilistic model for estimating the probability that a read originates from a given genome with maximum likelihood optimization.

There are two major drawbacks in aligning metagenomic reads with reference databases. The first is related to the time needed to align the sequences. As a matter of fact, scaling up to metagenomic datasets that can include hundreds of millions of reads proves to be difficult. Since it is necessary to align each read, the time spent on alignment increases rapidly with the size of the sequencing projects. Secondly, this approach is highly dependent on the quantity and quality of available reference genomes. The majority of microorganisms that can be found in metagenomic samples are not cultivable, and the number of reference genomes is limited. Therefore, with the exception of bacteria of medical interest for which numerous strains are known, these methods do not enable reaching a resolution higher than the species. Finally, apart from model communities, such approaches do not make it possible to achieve a detailed study of the diversity and the functional potential of microbiomes.

5.2.2.2. *Use of phylogenetic markers*

Methods based on aligning reads against complete genomes meet scaling difficulties due to the size of the reference sequences and the number of reads to be processed. As a result, some of the taxonomic assignment techniques that make use of references merely use a set of gene sequences instead of complete genomes. Amphora (Wang and Wu 2013) uses 31 genes present in single copy in bacterial genomes. The short length of these reference sequences makes scaling easier compared to alignment methods against whole genomes. Compared to targeted metagenomics, the use of several distinct genes reduces errors due to possible horizontal transfers. The fact that these genes are present in single copy also allows for better quantification of species abundance. Finally, the resolution obtained is higher than that employed in targeted metagenomics because these genes generally evolve more rapidly than 16S ribosomal RNA. In the best of cases, distinct bacterial strains can eventually be identified. For its part, Metaphlan (Truong et al. 2015) uses a database containing nearly 1 million taxon-specific genes. There are complementary tools that can detect the existence of different bacterial strains based on SNP profiles within marker genes, or based on the presence/absence of genes in a pangenome identified from reference genomes. One of the limitations of this approach is that it is particularly difficult to update the reference database with new genomes through the identification of new specific markers.

Tools based on phylogenetic marker sequence databases produce good results when the community under study is properly represented in the database (Sankar et al. 2015). On the other hand, characterizing bacterial strains is one of their limitations, and requires very extensive databases for this purpose, which restricts these analyses to model communities.

5.2.2.3. *Alignment-free methods*

Aligning large sets of reads against a large collection of complete genomes is a computationally expensive task. To overcome this problem without restricting the analysis to phylogenetic markers, alignment-free taxonomic assignment methods have been developed. The solution found to scale up the metagenomic taxonomic assignment is to use short sequences, called k-mers, namely sequences of size k. Because of their short length, it is possible to enumerate and index all the k-mers present in a genome collection. The first tool to use this technique is Kraken (Wood and Salzberg 2014). Kraken embeds a large database, containing the k-mers present in nearly 25,000 genomes of bacteria, archaea and viruses. For each k-mer of a given read, the index is queried to obtain the smallest common ancestor of the genomes having the same k-mer. This information for each k-mer is then used to associate a taxon with the read. A certain level of uncertainty remains, however. If no genome is close enough to the read, the read is associated with a higher taxonomic level. In order to obtain performances compatible with the volume of metagenomic data, these tools require particular data structures. Kraken is based, for example, on a hash table, built with k-mer minimizers, which results in quickly querying neighboring k-mers in the read, which are likely to share the same minimizer (see Chapter 3). In its fastest mode, Kraken can assign nearly 4 million reads per minute, which indeed makes it a very fast tool. On the other hand, it is necessary to load the entire index into memory, which requires large amounts of memory (nearly 70 GB for the whole index) and restricts the number of genomes that can be included in the database. This approach is refined in the Clark tool (Ounit et al. 2015), which builds a lighter index from genome-specific k-mers. More recently, the Kaiju (Menzel et al. 2016) and Centrifuge (Kim et al. 2016) programs have been developed using an alternative indexing structure that does not rely on a k-mer hash table, but on an FM-index, and which results in reduced memory usage and improved assignment. For example, Centrifuge is thus able to store 4,300 prokaryotic genomes in an index occupying 4 GB of memory.

5.2.2.4. *Limitations of reference-based methods*

All these methods rely heavily on databases composed of previously sequenced genomes. The main drawback of this approach resides in the low representativeness of these databases. While a large number of species have been sequenced, the number of strains available for a single species varies greatly. The RefSeq database currently contains nearly 144,000 genomes from about 11,000 species or an average of 13 genomes per species. However, this important sequencing task represents only a tiny fraction of the existing bacterial species (roughly estimated at more than 1 billion in (Dykhuizen 2005)). In addition, 60% of these species are represented by only one strain, and 14 % of the best-represented species represent 90% of the genomes in RefSeq. Among these species extensively sequenced and assembled, most present a biomedical interest. As such, the three most abundant species in RefSeq are *Escherichia coli*, *Salmonella enterica* and *Staphylococcus aureus*, with nearly 10,000 strains each. Taxonomic assignment of reads derived from poorly studied communities thus suffers from low taxonomic resolution: characterization of the community is most often limited to an inventory of the species present (see Figure 5.4). Yet, important functional differences can be explained by genomic variations at lower scales. To address this limitation, a few approaches have been developed to search for and make use of variations from reference sequences. ConStrains (Luo et al. 2015) and StrainPhlan (Truong et al. 2017) use SNP profiles, detected on marker genes in the Metaphlan database. Although it is possible to reconstruct a phylogeny of the different strains identified, this analysis is restricted to a few genes, and therefore does not enable gaining access to the complete genomic sequence of the microorganisms, which prevents the assessment of the functional impact of the different strains.

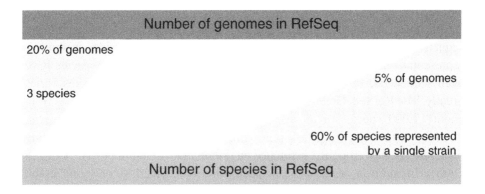

Figure 5.4. *Composition of the RefSeq database and indication of the orders of magnitude involved*

5.2.3. *Reference-free methods*

Since microbial diversity is largely unknown, methods requiring comparisons to reference databases quickly show their limitations. Methods known as de novo methods have been developed to identify new genomes from metagenomic data with little or no use of reference genomes, and are the primary means of identifying members of microbial communities. In these methods, the main objective is to aggregate reads from the same organism.

5.2.3.1. *Metagenomic assembly*

5.2.3.1.1. Assembly principle

Current limitations of sequencing methods make it impossible to sequence a whole genome in a single read. Assembly is the task that involves transforming a multitude of short reads into longer genome portions (see Chapter 4). Assembly programs usually generate a graph representing the overlaps between reads. There are two main families of assemblers, depending on the type of graph used by the assembly. Overlap graph assemblers such as Celera (Denisov et al. 2008) employ full reads as graph nodes. Assemblers based on *de Bruijn* graphs, such as Abyss (Simpson et al. 2009), resort to a *k-mer graph* (*k*-sized words) smaller than the reads, which makes it easier to detect overlaps.

In this graph, the assembler searches for paths, whose sequence will form contigs, representative of the genome of the sequenced organism. While this is possible, it is rare to assemble a genome in a single contig, as assembly graphs are often complex, forcing the assembler to interrupt contigs. In particular, it is the presence of repeats in the genome that causes an assembly to be generally split into contigs smaller than the genome. For example, when a de Bruijn graph is used for assembly, any *k*-mer repetition within the genome is reflected by an "X" structure in the graph. This structure cannot be resolved by the assembler without extrinsic information, which forces the program to interrupt contigs at these repeats.

Another cause for complexity in the structure of these graphs is the existence of alternative paths, which may be due either to sequencing errors or to true variations of the genomic sequence (for instance, the two alleles of a diploid individual). These variants generate bubble-like structures in the graph. The strategy used by most assemblers consists of removing the least abundant *k*-mers in the graph, which generally correspond to sequencing errors, and to merge the remaining bubbles due to polymorphism.

It is then necessary to evaluate the quality of an assembly. To this end, a first important criterion is the length and number of contigs. A good assembly is composed of a small number of large contigs, whose sum of lengths approaches the length of the target genome. A frequently used indicator that synthesizes these criteria is the N50, which is the minimum length for covering at least half of the genome with larger contigs (see section 4.6.1). However, although they are included in de novo methods, proper evaluation of the assemblies also requires verifying the veracity of the contig, for example, by aligning them against the expected reference genome when possible. This is made possible by tools such as Quast (Gurevich et al. 2013), which report the number of errors made during assembly.

5.2.3.1.2. Metagenomic assembly methods

The assembly methods previously mentioned were developed with the objective of assembling a single genome from a single species. When applied to metagenomic data, as in Venter et al. (2004), the main difficulties encountered in classical genomics are exacerbated due to the diversity present in bacterial communities.

First, a multitude of species may be represented in unbalanced amounts in the sequencing data. Conventional assemblers use genome coverage information to identify repeats and sequencing errors. In a metagenomic context, where the abundance of different species varies, and where genomic regions may be shared by several species, this strategy is no longer valid. Therefore, in Venter et al. (2004), the most covered genomes were considered as repeats by the Celera assembler, and a prior step was necessary to better assemble them. As mentioned before, in the case of a *de Bruijn* graph assembly, any repeated sequence of length greater than k interrupts the contigs. This situation frequently occurs in metagenomics, where related species may share common genes. Repeated regions between genomes to be assembled add up to the repeats within a genome, and make assembly more complex. Second, the polymorphism that exists within bacterial communities complicates the assembly in several ways. Many genotypes or strains of the same microbial species can be sequenced within a metagenomic sample. This polymorphism is not evenly distributed along the genomes, and it is difficult to jointly assemble conserved and specific regions of different strains. Possible structural variations within the population also complicate the task.

In order to solve these problems, dedicated algorithms have been developed for the de novo assembly of metagenomic data, such as IDBA-UD (Peng et al. 2012), MetaVelvet (Namiki et al. 2012), metaSPAdes (Nurk et al. 2017) or MegaHit (Li et al. 2015). These programs have different algorithmic features that, in principle, make it possible to both scale up with large metagenomic datasets and assemble mixtures of species (see the review by Ayling et al. (2020)). For example, MetaVelvet uses the differences in coverage and connectivity in a *de Bruijn* graph to separate it into subgraphs that are then assembled separately using the Velvet algorithm. To date, the assemblers considered to be the most efficient are those based on an approach known as *multi-k* (Vollmers et al. 2017). They successively use *de Bruijn* graphs constructed with increasing k-mer sizes, small values of k being more adapted to sparsely covered genomes, and larger ones to more abundant genomes. Among these assemblers, IDBA-UD takes into account the strong variations in coverage present in metagenomics to apply different thresholds for simplifying the graph. MetaSPAdes reuses the SPAdes algorithm that was already designed to account for coverage variations present in *single-cell* data. In addition to the multi-k approach, it incorporates information associated with paired reads into the graph, and traverses the contig graph to identify chimeric contigs, interspecies repeats and possible intraspecies variation. Finally, MegaHit stands out by the use of a *succinct de Bruijn graph*, an efficient data structure that can achieve a good trade-off between assembly quality and low computational resource usage.

5.2.3.1.3. Limitations of metagenomic assembly

Despite their development, these dedicated tools have not solved the problem of metagenomic assembly. The CAMI challenge (Sczyrba et al. 2017) has contributed to confront different tools on issues specific to metagenomics, including assembly. The results illustrate the difficulty of this task with current methods. In this competition, for the "high-complexity" dataset, which contains 596 genomes, 399 of which show more than 95% ANI, the longest assembly covers only 70% of the community, at the cost of nearly 8,000 alignment errors against the targeted reference genomes. The quality of the assemblies obtained depends first of all on genome coverage. Naturally, the least covered genomes are difficult to assemble. In a less intuitive manner, some assemblers struggle to assemble very abundant genomes. One solution employed by a number of assemblers (such as MegaHit) consists of using different k-mer sizes, adapted to different abundances. Additionally, the presence of highly related genomes in the community makes it difficult to assemble these species with any of the tools that have been considered. This seems to be a particularly problematic aspect, given the existence within most communities of a continuum of diversity among individuals.

Furthermore, the relevance of representing the assembly of a metagenome in the form of linear sequences may be questionable. Bubbles created by punctual polymorphism or branchings due to structural variations are present in the assembly graph, but absent from the contigs. Assemblers suppress these variations, crushing bubbles and stopping contigs when branchings occur. The result is a set of contigs, whose sequence is a consensus of those of the sequenced organisms, and in which structural variations are not represented. A current trend is to go beyond this linear genome representation based on sequences towards a representation using a graph of sequences. The assemblies are built based on graphs, from which linear regions are extracted to give contigs. Compared to the assembly graph, the contigs generally given as output by the assembly program therefore contain less information. Formally, these structures are bi-directed graphs, where nodes are nucleotide sequences and edges represent overlaps between sequences. Bearing in mind that DNA sequences can be read in both directions, four types of overlaps are possible (*forward–forward*, *forward–reverse*, *reverse–forward* and *reverse–reverse*). Thereby, it is proposed to replace linear reference genomes by graphs accounting for genomic variations (Paten et al. 2017), and some assemblers such as metaSPAdes (Nurk et al. 2017) include in their results a graph in the GFA format in which the structural diversity of genomes can be observed.

Finally, it is currently impossible to completely and accurately assemble the organisms of a metagenome, and to account for the genomic diversity within these communities. Assemblers return contigs as long as possible, while avoiding building chimeras by assembly of reads obtained from different organisms. Intra-specific diversity is most often ignored, in order to return a consensus of the genomes present. Consequently, assembly is not sufficient to characterize the metagenomic diversity of a sample, and complementary tools are needed to find contigs derived from the same species.

5.2.3.2. *Metagenomic sequence binning*

The purpose of binning methods is to group sequences of the same taxonomic origin. They take as input previously assembled contigs, and place them in clusters according to their supposed taxonomic origin. Since no reference information is used, these bins are not associated with a taxon, but they can then be assembled relatively easily using conventional methods, theoretically allowing the reconstruction of complete genomes of community members.

A first family of binning methods uses the nucleotide content of sequences, making the assumption that the content in nucleotides or words of a certain size is homogeneous along the genome of a species and differs between two species that are sufficiently phylogenetically distant. The first such method is TETRA (Teeling et al. 2004), which calculates for each sequence tetranucleotide profiles as well as the correlation between these profiles, which leads to grouping reads from close organisms. The major limitation of nucleotide content-based methods is that they are only applicable to large-sized genomic fragments (close to 10 kilobases), in which the nucleotide content is representative of that of the whole genome. They can therefore only be applied to previously assembled contigs of large size, thereby strongly limiting their interest. In addition to nucleotide composition, it is possible to classify contigs based on their coverage, under the assumption that contigs with similar coverage are derived from the same genomes. Some methods use *differential* coverage between datasets originating from different locations, for example. The underlying idea is that sequences from the same organism, in addition to having similar levels of coverage in one sample, will have coverage that covaries in the same way across multiple samples. Tools that involve both coverage and composition information generally achieve the best performance in contig binning. Among the main software programs, we can mention Concoct (Alneberg et al. 2014), GroopM (Imelfort et al. 2014) or MaxBin (Wu et al. 2014). These multiple alternatives sometimes return different results, which has promoted the development of tools for visual comparison of their results (VizBin (Laczny et al. 2015)), or for validating the quality of the bins (CheckM (Parks et al. 2015)).

The main limitation of these techniques is that the objects (the contigs) they group together result from prior assembly. In these contigs, the majority of the intra-specific diversity was eliminated by the assembler. It is therefore difficult or impossible for these methods to characterize fine genomic variations, such as the presence of different bacterial strains. Furthermore, binning sensitive to possible errors caused by the assembly, such as the creation of chimeric contigs. Finally, some genomic peculiarities make binning difficult: a genomic region particularly rich in variants for a particular strain may, for example, be assigned to a new cluster different from the rest of the genome.

Only a small number of tools enable binning at the read level, since they are too short to provide a reliable genomic signature, and too numerous for the tools to scale up with large datasets. LSA (Latent Strain Analysis) (Cleary et al. 2015) is an original tool for binning metagenomic reads, which allows independent assembly for each bin. The method is based on the comparison of abundance profiles of k-mers within several samples. From a matrix giving the abundance of each k-mer in each dataset, LSA performs a singular value decomposition (SVD) that provides a selection of k-mers showing the same covariance profile, and likely originating from the same genome. A clustering step then allows building sets of associated reads. The reconstructed bins can thus lead to isolating distinct strains, which correspondto a resolution rarely achieved by contig binning methods.

5.3. "What are they able to do?": functional metagenomics

One of the central questions in the study of microbial communities relates to the characterization of the functional effect of their different components. Metagenomics makes it possible to sequence all of the genomes of a community, and consequently to access their genetic content. It is therefore possible to describe novel functions that may be of great interest, in the fields of health (e.g. through antibiotic research (Garmendia et al. 2012)), as well as agri-food (De Filippis et al. 2017) or energy (Tiwari et al. 2018). As for taxonomic characterization, two functional characterization problems can be distinguished: the one involving the identification of the functions present and that related to quantifying each of these functions in the sample. The identification problem takes as input a set of nucleic sequences, most often derived from the assembly of a metagenomic sample, and returns a list of distinct functional identifiers, such as enzyme identifiers (EC number) or functions from gene ontologies. The quantification problem takes as input the set of sequences and the list of features returned by the first problem and returns a numerical value associated with each feature, representing the absolute (e.g. the number of reads) or relative (the percentage of reads) abundance of each feature in the sample. Nevertheless, both tasks are made difficult by the complexity of the metagenomic data and the non-model nature of most of the organisms studied.

5.3.1. *Gene prediction and annotation*

Once the genomes of the bacterial community are assembled, coding sequence prediction from these genomes can be performed in a manner quite similar to what is done in classical genomics, either by comparison with protein databases, or ab initio, which enables the detection of new genes. In the first case, the nucleotide sequences are converted into protein sequences according to the six possible reading frames, and then compared to known protein databases. This type of analysis is, for example, possible with the BlastX software program (Altschul et al. 1990). Given the incompleteness of reference databases, ab initio methods are preferred in metagenomics. Different tools have been developed specifically for this purpose, such as MetaGeneMark (Zhu et al. 2010) or Orphelia (Hoff et al. 2009). The difficulties deriving from metagenomics are primarily due to the generally shorter contig length with respect to single species assemblies. Noteworthy, most techniques are based on models (HMM, machine learning) trained with known genomes.

The next step consists of assigning a function to the detected genes, whether it is metabolic, structural or regulatory. This is known as functional annotation. The process is similar to that performed in classical genomics, with a generally much higher number of genes. This involves comparing the protein sequences obtained during the previous step with protein databases. Among these numerous databases, we can mention KEGG (Kanehisa 2004), PFAM (Finn et al. 2014) or Uniprot (Bateman et al. 2017). These different databases do not cover all known functions, and there are tools such as InterPro (McDowall and Hunter 2011) or MG-RAST (Keegan et al. 2016) that enable an effective use of several of them.

5.3.2. *Metatranscriptomics*

In order to answer questions about the functions performed by a microbial community, metatranscriptomics effectively complements metagenomics. As a matter of fact, the presence of a gene does not guarantee its expression. Metatranscriptomics makes it possible to obtain an overview of gene expression in a sample at a given time and under a given condition.

Metatranscriptomic data are generally dominated by ribosomal RNAs. Although they can be used to compare the activity of different taxa, they are not very informative about the functions performed by these organisms. However, different protocols can be used to filter these sequences before their sequencing (Sultan et al. 2014).

Similarly as in conventional transcriptomics, two approaches are possible to analyze such data: read alignment against known reference genomes, or de novo assembly of metatranscriptomes. Nevertheless, in metatranscriptomics, these approaches are limited either by the incompleteness of existing databases or by the difficulty of correctly assembling reads due to large coverage variations and the risk of chimerism.

In both cases, relatively few tools dedicated to metatranscriptomics have been developed (Aguiar-Pulido et al. 2016), but there are dedicated pipelines available, such as MG-Rast (Keegan et al. 2016) or HUMAnM (Abubucker et al. 2012)). De novo methods rely on transcriptomic assemblers such as *Trinity* (Celaj et al. 2014), and use, for example, RSEM (Li and Dewey 2011) for individual transcript expression quantification. Assemblers designed for metatranscriptomic assembly can also be mentioned, such as IDBA-MT (Leung et al. 2013), IDBA-MTP (Leung et al. 2014) or TAG (Ye and Tang 2016). They take into account the specificities of metatranscriptomics and lead to assembling fewer chimeric contigs. Alternatively, approaches based on reference databases also most often make use of conventional programs such as Bowtie (Langmead and Salzberg 2012) or Blast (Altschul et al. 1990) for aligning reads.

5.3.3. *Reconstruction of metabolic networks*

One purpose of gene annotation is the reconstruction of metabolic networks. If the networks can be reconstructed independently for each species of the assembled and annotated community, an interesting perspective offered by metagenomics is to reconstruct the network of the whole microbial community. The MetaPath tool (Liu and Pop 2010) aligns metagenomic reads to a generic meta-network in order to identify which components are present in a dataset. We should note that this method is based on read alignment to a metabolic network, and therefore does not require the assembly and binning techniques previously presented. Functional analysis of metagenomic sequencing data may, for example, enable the identification of novel metabolic pathways, which may be useful to the host of symbiotic communities (Cecchini et al. 2013). In the case of environmental samples, it is possible to identify the compounds for which an organism is dependent on its environment (Borenstein et al. 2008). By comparing the metabolic network topologies of several species living in the same environment, it is possible to identify cooperation (Levy et al. 2015) or competition (Kreimer et al. 2012) within a community.

Metagenomic data thus offer the possibility to access the functioning of complex communities. However, this step occurs after many other analyses, and may suffer from errors emerging during assembly, taxonomic assignment or annotation, especially in the case of poorly known organisms.

5.4. Comparative metagenomics

Comparative metagenomics consists of comparing metagenomic samples from a genomic perspective. The aim is to estimate similarity (or dissimilarity) measures between samples or communities, taken as a whole. The result is a matrix of size $N \times N$, where N is the number of samples to be compared. Each matrix cell indicates the similarity (or conversely the dissimilarity) between a pair of samples.

The sample sets compared can be time series or samples collected at different geographic locations or under different conditions. Since a metagenomic sample corresponds to the image of a community at a given time, location and under given conditions, metagenomic projects are generally composed of several samples. It is the comparison of the samples, associated with their metadata, that makes it possible to extract knowledge. Among the major metagenomic projects that possess this comparative dimension, we can cite the human microbiome project (Lloyd-Price et al. 2017) (HMP), whose ambition is to explore the human microbiome in various tissues and among various healthy individuals (more than 690 samples), or the TARA Oceans project (Bork et al. 2015), which collected about 2,000 samples of seawater at different depths and for different sizes of organisms in about a hundred geographical locations around the world.

There are two types of comparative metagenomic methods: those that rely on previously identified diversity in each sample (such as, for example, the taxonomic composition obtained through the approaches presented above), and those that do not rely on any sample pre-processing, nor use any a priori knowledge, and directly compare all the sequences of the samples. These latter methods are grouped under the de novo comparative metagenomics designation.

5.4.1. *Comparative metagenomics with diversity estimation*

A first group of comparative metagenomic methods follows the approaches described above to characterize samples, either in terms of taxonomy or in terms of functions. The samples are thus each represented by a set of elements (taxa, OTUs, bins, genes or functions). For a given pair of samples, similarity depends on the number of elements which they have in common and which are specific to them. There are many existing similarity indices used in ecology that combine these numbers differently, and that can be grouped mainly into two families: qualitative indices and quantitative indices (see Legendre and Cáceres (2013) for a more detailed classification of these indices). The first family considers elements equally whether they are rare or very abundant in the samples and uses only the information of the presence or absence of the elements. In this family, the most classical index is the Jaccard distance which is the ratio between the intersection and the union sizes of the compared sets ($J(A, B) = \frac{|A \cap B|}{|A \cup B|}$). Conversely, quantitative indices use the abundance information of the elements in each sample. If two samples share the same elements, they can still be differentiated if the elements are not present in the same proportions. A consequence is also that the most abundant elements will have more weight in the computation of the similarity index than the rare elements. The Bray–Curtis dissimilarity (Bray and Curtis 1957) is one of the most popular indices of this category. It is defined by the following formula, where N_{iA} is the abundance of element i in sample A:

$$BC(A, B) = 1 - 2\frac{\sum_{i=1}^{p} min(N_{iA}, N_{iB})}{\sum_{i=1}^{p} N_{iA} + N_{iB}}$$

These indices are implemented in some metagenomic data analysis software programs such as MEGAN (Huson et al. 2016), which also include functionalities for multidimensional data visualizations (for instance, by PCoA).

5.4.2. *De novo comparative metagenomics*

Given the difficulties in establishing a good taxonomic or functional inventory of metagenomes, there is an alternative which consists of comparing samples by their sequences directly, without attempting to assign them to OTUs or functions. This is then referred to as de novo comparative metagenomics. The objective of these methods is to estimate the shared genomic content between two sets of reads.

A naive approach consists of comparing (e.g. by sequence alignment) all the reads of the first sample to all the reads of the second sample. Pairs of reads with high sequence similarity are said to be similar and assumed to originate from the same taxon. The similarity between the two samples can then be defined by their percentage of similar reads. More formally, two sets of sequences without any annotation are given as input, and the problem consists of returning as output the number of sequences in the first set that are similar to at least one sequence in the second set and vice versa.

This naive approach faces two scaling problems. The first comes from comparing two samples. A whole-genome sample contains hundreds of millions of reads, each of which must be compared to the sequences of the other sample. The second is that $O(N^2)$ similarity measures must be computed between all pairs of the N samples under consideration.

5.4.2.1. *Alignment-free approaches*

To address this scaling problem, de novo comparative metagenomics approaches have replaced computationally expensive sequence alignment steps with exact comparisons of k-mers (k-sized words). Unlike reads, k-mers are very fast to process because their comparison is carried out in an exact way: two k-mers are identical or not. The k values used are generally large ($k > 21$), so most of the k-mers are specific to a genome and their abundances in the sample are proportional to those of the genomes from which the k-mers are obtained. These large sizes of k-mers then raise issues in indexing and storage in memory, since the number of all possible k-mers (4^k) grows exponentially with k (see Chapter 2).

Compareads (Maillet et al. 2012) and Commet (Maillet et al. 2014) methods estimate for each read of a sample whether it is similar to at least one read of the other sample by computing the number of k-mers shared between the read and the sample as a whole. To this end, the set of k-mers of a sample is indexed in a data structure with a small memory footprint, a Bloom filter (Bloom 1970) (see Figure 5.5). This data structure is a simple array of bits, associated with one or several hash functions, which allows us to query very quickly the existence of an element in a set. One of the particularities of this data structure is that it is probabilistic: since the collisions of the hash functions are not handled, false positives can appear in the querying step at a rate that can be controlled (see Chapter 2). This approach is about 30 times faster than Blast but remains too long when the number N of samples is large since the indexing and query steps must be repeated between N and N^2 times.

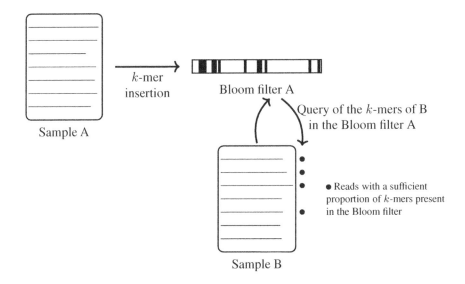

Figure 5.5. *Alignment-free comparative metagenomics example with Compareads. The k-mers of the reads of sample A are inserted in a Bloom filter. Then, to compare the reads of sample B with the reads of A, each read of sample B is simply queried with the Bloom filter of A. Next, the number of reads that share a sufficiently large number of k-mers, according to the Bloom filter, is counted*

5.4.2.2. *Comparison of k-mer spectra*

The methods that are currently the most efficient go even further and forget about the structure in reads of the datasets. With the Simka method (Benoit et al. 2016), each sample is seen as a set of k-mers, associated with their abundance, referred to as its k-mer *spectrum*. The same similarity indices seen in the previous section can then be calculated by replacing the species/OTUs/genes by the different k-mers with their abundances in the samples (see Figure 5.6). The main difficulty lies then in the counting and in the in-memory representation of these sets of elements which are much larger than when considering taxonomic or functional compositions. Typically, in a single classical whole-genome metagenomic sample, several billion distinct 21-mers can be observed. As an example, an abundance matrix, with the distinct k-mers in rows and the 690 HMP project samples in columns, would require several hundred terabytes of memory storage. To address this memory issue, the Simka method counts the k-mers using disk storage (a method inspired by DSK (Rizk et al. 2013) and KMC2 (Deorowicz et al. 2015) which use the notion of *minimizer* to partition the set of k-mers; see Chapter 3) and never stores the abundance matrix in memory but computes the similarity indices iteratively and in parallel, k-mer after k-mer. Therefore, in a few hours, the similarity indices between the 690 samples of the HMP project (32 billion reads) can be computed and they produce results about sample classification similar to taxonomic assignment-based methods (Benoit et al. 2016).

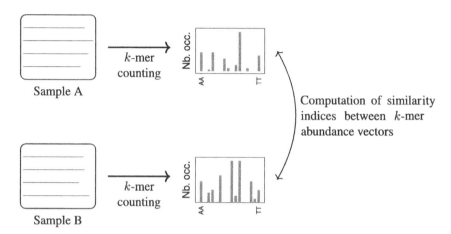

Figure 5.6. *k-mer-spectrum-based comparative metagenomics. The k-mers in each dataset are counted and their counts are compared to compute similarity indices*

5.4.2.3. *k-mer subsampling-based approaches*

While Simka uses the whole set of k-mers present to estimate similarity indices, other approaches rely on subsampling the k-mer space for solving the data dimension problem. This is the case of MetaFast (Ulyantsev et al. 2016), which performs a rather coarse de novo read assembly step before the comparison, in order to select the k-mers present in the components of the de Bruijn graph satisfying a number of topological and abundance criteria. The selected components then serve as references, and the abundance of each component is quantified in each sample through the abundances of the k-mers they contain. Assembly is a way to select k-mers in order to reduce their number. This strategy is interesting because the selection is based on criteria that are biologically meaningful: namely, the selection of k-mers shared by several samples, and the elimination of k-mers resulting from sequencing errors or from regions that are very complex to assemble. However, the major disadvantage of this approach resides in its cost in terms of computational resources (time and memory) which naturally result from the assembly step since the de Bruijn graph must be built and represented in-memory and its size is of the order of the number of distinct k-mers. For example, this method does not scale up with the data of the HMP project.

The most effective approaches in comparative metagenomics are those based on "random" subsampling of the k-mer space. The Mash (Ondov et al. 2016) method, developed primarily for genome comparison, introduced this type of method. Mash is based on the Minhash technique (Broder 1997) which is a statistical approach for estimating the Jaccard index between two sets using only a few thousand of their elements. Each sample to be compared is represented by a sorted list of n k-mers, called its *signature* or *sketch* (with n being very small with respect to the set of k-mers present). Random selection and sorting of k-mers are carried out by way of a uniform hash function which for a given k-mer returns a 64-bit integer (with a collision probability close to 0). The n distinct k-mers of the sample having the smallest hash values constitutes its signature. The Jaccard index between two samples is then computed by applying the Jaccard formula on the first n k-mers of the union of the two signatures. In terms of performance, it seems unlikely to be more efficient than Mash. In fact, to compute the signature of a set of m k-mers, only a sorted list of n elements must actually be stored in memory; the time complexity is almost linear with m (if $n \ll m$), and the signatures of the different samples can be computed in parallel. Finally, the computation of the distances is extremely fast considering the size of the signatures ($n = 1000$ in general). Its weakness lies in the results provided, which are limited to an estimate of the Jaccard index. This measure only takes into account the presence/absence of the k-mers and not their abundance. While it is well suited for comparing genomes, it proves to be much less adapted to compare metagenomic samples with highly variable species diversity profiles or simply sets of reads with sequencing errors. The SimkaMin method solved this problem by extending the Mash approach to the Bray–Curtis index and by performing a filtering of rare k-mers (Benoit et al. 2020). The k-mers are selected similarly with a hash function, independently of their abundance, but the abundances of the selected k-mers are stored in the signature and used in the calculation of the Bray–Curtis index. SimkaMin is about 10 times faster than Simka with very small memory and disk footprints, without qualitatively impacting downstream analysis results.

These k-mer-based approaches were developed for second-generation sequencing data. The low sequencing error rate and the often large sequencing depth in these data allow for using rather large values of k, generally between 20 and 30. These approaches are thus not very well adapted to third-generation sequencing data, because their higher error rate implies that most k-mers possess at least one sequencing error, which does not make possible a direct comparison without editing between several samples. For this type of noisier data, other types of seeds could be considered such as spaced seeds.

5.5. Conclusion

Metagenomics is a promising tool for the study of microbial communities. On the one hand, it eliminates the cultivability bias and thus allows the description of all the interacting organisms; on the other hand, it brings an unprecedented resolution, which leads to describing the structure, the function and the evolution of these communities at the same time. For the same reasons, metagenomics also raises many methodological challenges due to the complexity of these communities and the limited knowledge of their members. In this chapter, we have presented a set of methods that allow us to answer the main questions addressed by metagenomics.

Very often, the choice of these tools results from a trade-off between the complexity of the community, the availability of reference data and the accuracy (often taxonomic) of the results obtained. The state of the art thus allows the structure and function of reference communities to be finely described, the members of non-model communities characterized or the most complex systems to be more roughly understood. To make progress on these issues requires breakthroughs in both bioinformatics and biology.

From a bioinformatics perspective, a major topic in metagenomics remains characterizing the content of metagenomes as finely as possible. More specifically, the problem concerning the taxonomic resolution achieved by current assembly and binning tools still remains an open question. The genomes of organisms living in the same environment interact with each other, and a metagenome results from a *continuum* of diversity, which makes assembly difficult. In particular, one of the recent challenges in metagenomics is the finer description of genomes, using assembly at finer taxonomic levels

(Segata 2018). At the same time, the emergence of long-read sequencing opens new avenues for facilitating not only metagenomic assembly (Kolmogorov et al. 2019), but also taxonomic assignment (Dilthey et al. 2019).

The biological questions that metagenomics raises vary greatly depending on the communities studied. However, the increase in the quality and quantity of data and the development of methods to process them allow metagenomic studies to provide increasingly detailed answers The study of the human microbiome is at the forefront of metagenomic research and is a perfect example of the evolution of the discipline. While its first phase aimed to catalogue the species present in the different human microbiota (Turnbaugh et al. 2007), the second one, completed in 2019 (iHMP Research Network Consortium et al. 2019), proposed an integrative and longitudinal approach, allowing the evolution of microbial profiles to be monitored under different conditions. More than a simple assembly of species, a microbiota should be considered as a complex entity, in constant evolution, while taking into account the functional links between its constituents. Consequently, the study of these systems could benefit from contributions from evolutionary biology, emphasizing the determinants of the evolution of these communities (Proctor 2019).

5.6. References

Abubucker, S., Segata, N., Goll, J., Schubert, A.M., Izard, J., Cantarel, B.L., Rodriguez-Mueller, B., Zucker, J., Thiagarajan, M., Henrissat, B. (2012). Metabolic reconstruction for metagenomic data and its application to the human microbiome. *PLoS Computational Biology*, 8(6), e1002358.

Aguiar-Pulido, V., Huang, W., Suarez-Ulloa, V., Cickovski, T., Mathee, K., Narasimhan, G. (2016). Metagenomics, metatranscriptomics, and metabolomics approaches for microbiome analysis: Supplementary issue: Bioinformatics methods and applications for big metagenomics data. *Evolutionary Bioinformatics*, 12, EBO–S36436.

Ahn, T.H., Chai, J., Pan, C. (2015). Sigma: Strain-level inference of genomes from metagenomic analysis for biosurveillance. *Bioinformatics*, 31(2), 170–177.

Alneberg, J., Bjarnason, B.S., de Bruijn, I., Schirmer, M., Quick, J., Ijaz, U.Z., Lahti, L., Loman, N.J., Andersson, A.F., Quince, C. (2014). Binning metagenomic contigs by coverage and composition. *Nature Methods*, 11(11), 1144–1146.

Altschul, S.F., Gish, W., Miller, W., Myers, W.E., Lipman, D.J. (1990). Basic local alignment search tool. *Journal of Molecular Biology*, 215, 402–410.

Angly, F.E. (2009). The GAAS metagenomic tool and its estimations of viral and microbial average genome size in four major biomes. *PLoS Computational Biology*, 5(12), e1000593.

Ayling, M., Clark, M.D., Leggett, R.M. (2020). New approaches for metagenome assembly with short reads. *Briefings in Bioinformatics*, 21(2), 584–594.

Bar-On, Y.M., Phillips, R., Milo, R. (2018). The biomass distribution on earth. *Proceedings of the National Academy of Sciences*, 115(25), 6506–6511.

Bateman, A., Martin, M.J., O'Donovan, C., Magrane, M., Alpi, E., Antunes, R., Bely, B., Bingley, M., Bonilla, C., Britto, R., Bursteinas, B. (2017). UniProt: The universal protein knowledgebase. *Nucleic Acids Research*, 45(D1), D158–D169.

Benoit, G., Peterlongo, P., Mariadassou, M., Drezen, E., Schbath, S., Lavenier, D., Lemaitre, C. (2016). Multiple comparative metagenomics using multiset k-mer counting. *PeerJ Computer Science*, 2, e94.

Benoit, G., Mariadassou, M., Robin, S., Schbath, S., Peterlongo, P., Lemaitre, C. (2020). SimkaMin: Fast and resource frugal de novo comparative metagenomics. *Bioinformatics*, 36(4), 1275–1276.

Bloom, B.H. (1970). Space/time trade-offs in hash coding with allowable errors. *Communications of the ACM*, 13(7), 422–426.

Borenstein, E., Kupiec, M., Feldman, M.W., Ruppin, E. (2008). Large-scale reconstruction and phylogenetic analysis of metabolic environments. *Proceedings of the National Academy of Sciences*, 105(38), 14482–14487.

Bork, P., Bowler, C., De Vargas, C., Gorsky, G., Karsenti, E., Wincker, P. (2015). Tara Oceans studies plankton at Planetary scale. *Science*, 348(6237), 873.

Bray, J.R. and Curtis, J.T. (1957). An ordination of the upland forest communities of southern Wisconsin. *Ecological Monographs*, 27(4), 325–349.

Broder, A.Z. (1997). On the resemblance and containment of documents. *Proceedings of the Compression and Complexity of Sequences 1997*. IEEE, 21–29.

Buchfink, B., Xie, C., Huson, D.H. (2014). Fast and sensitive protein alignment using DIAMOND. *Nature Methods*, 12(1), 59–60.

Burton, J.N., Liachko, I., Dunham, M.J., Shendure, J. (2014). Species-level deconvolution of metagenome assemblies with Hi-C–based contact probability maps. *G3:Genes|Genomes|Genetics*, 4(7), 1339–1346.

Caporaso, J.G., Kuczynski, J., Stombaugh, J., Bittinger, K., Bushman, F.D., Costello, E.K., Fierer, N., Peña, A.G., Goodrich, J.K., Gordon, J.I. (2010). QIIME allows analysis of high-throughput community sequencing data. *Nature Methods*, 7(5), 335–336.

Cecchini, D.A., Laville, E., Laguerre, S., Robe, P., Leclerc, M., Doré, J., Henrissat, B., Remaud-Siméon, M., Monsan, P., Potocki-Véronèse, G. (2013). Functional metagenomics reveals novel pathways of prebiotic breakdown by human gut bacteria. *PLoS ONE*, 8(9), e72766.

Celaj, A., Markle, J., Danska, J., Parkinson, J. (2014). Comparison of assembly algorithms for improving rate of metatranscriptomic functional annotation. *Microbiome*, 2(1), 39.

Chen, I., Chu, K., Palaniappan, K., Pillay, M., Ratner, A., Huang, J., Huntemann, M. (2019). IMG/M v. 5.0: An integrated data management and comparative analysis system for microbial genomes and microbiomes. *Nucleic Acids Research*, 47(D1), D666–D677.

Cleary, B., Brito, I.L., Huang, K., Gevers, D., Shea, T., Young, S., Alm, E.J. (2015). Detection of low-abundance bacterial strains in metagenomic datasets by eigengenome partitioning. *Nature Biotechnology*, 33(10), 1053–1060.

De Filippis, F., Parente, E., Ercolini, D. (2017). Metagenomics insights into food fermentations. *Microbial Biotechnology*, 10(1), 91–102.

Delmont, T.O., Robe, P., Cecillon, S., Clark, I.M., Constancias, F., Simonet, P., Hirsch, P.R., Vogel, T.M. (2011). Accessing the soil metagenome for studies of microbial diversity. *Applied and Environmental Microbiology*, 77(4), 1315–1324.

Denisov, G., Walenz, B., Halpern, A.L., Miller, J., Axelrod, N., Levy, S., Sutton, G. (2008). Consensus generation and variant detection by Celera Assembler. *Bioinformatics*, 24(8), 1035–1040.

Deorowicz, S., Kokot, M., Grabowski, S., Debudaj-Grabysz, A. (2015). KMC 2: Fast and resource-frugal k-mer counting. *Bioinformatics*, 31(10), 1569–1576.

DeSantis, T.Z., Hugenholtz, P., Larsen, N., Rojas, M., Brodie, E.L., Keller, K., Huber, T., Dalevi, D., Hu, P., Andersen, G.L. (2006). Greengenes, a chimera-checked 16S rRNA gene database and workbench compatible with ARB. *Applied and Environmental Microbiology*, 72(7), 5069–5072.

Dilthey, A.T., Jain, C., Koren, S., Phillippy, A.M. (2019). Strain-level metagenomic assignment and compositional estimation for long reads with metamaps. *Nature Communications*, 10(1), 1–12.

Dykhuizen, D. (2005). Species numbers in bacteria. *Proceedings. California Academy of Sciences*, 56(6 Suppl. 1), 62–71.

Esposito, A. and Kirschberg, M. (2014). How many 16S-based studies should be included in a metagenomic conference? It may be a matter of etymology. *FEMS Microbiology Letters*, 351(2), 145–146.

Finn, R.D., Bateman, A., Clements, J., Coggill, P., Eberhardt, R.Y., Eddy, S.R., Heger, A., Hetherington, K., Holm, L., Mistry, J., Sonnhammer, E.L.L., Tate, J., Punta, M. (2014). Pfam: The protein families database. *Nucleic Acids Research*, 42(D1), D222–D230.

Francis, O.E., Bendall, M., Manimaran, S., Hong, C., Clement, N.L., Castro-Nallar, E., Snell, Q., Schaalje, G.B., Clement, M.J., Crandall, K.A., Johnson, W.E. (2013). Pathoscope: Species identification and strain attribution with unassembled sequencing data. *Genome Research*, 23(10), 1721–1729.

Garmendia, L., Hernandez, A., Sanchez, M., Martinez, J. (2012). Metagenomics and antibiotics. *Clinical Microbiology and Infection*, 18, 27–31.

Gurevich, A., Saveliev, V., Vyahhi, N., Tesler, G. (2013). QUAST: Quality assessment tool for genome assemblies. *Bioinformatics*, 29(8), 1072–1075.

Handelsman, J., Rondon, M.R., Brady, S.F., Clardy, J., Goodman, R.M. (1998). Molecular biological access to the chemistry of unknown soil microbes: A new frontier for natural products. *Chemistry and Biology*, 5(10), R245–R249.

Hoff, K.J., Lingner, T., Meinicke, P., Tech, M. (2009). Orphelia: Predicting genes in metagenomic sequencing reads. *Nucleic Acids Research*, 37(Suppl. 2).

Huson, D.H., Beier, S., Flade, I., Górska, A., El-Hadidi, M., Mitra, S., Ruscheweyh, H.J., Tappu, R. (2016). MEGAN Community Edition – Interactive exploration and analysis of large-scale microbiome sequencing data. *PLoS Computational Biology*, 12(6), e1004957.

iHMP Research Network Consortium, I.H. (2019). The integrative human microbiome project. *Nature*, 569, 641–648.

Imelfort, M., Parks, D., Woodcroft, B.J., Dennis, P., Hugenholtz, P., Tyson, G.W. (2014). GroopM: An automated tool for the recovery of population genomes from related metagenomes. *PeerJ*, 2, e603.

Kanehisa, M. (2004). The KEGG resource for deciphering the genome. *Nucleic Acids Research*, 32(90001), 277D–280.

Keegan, K.P., Glass, E.M., Meyer, F. (2016). MG-RAST, a metagenomics service for analysis of microbial community structure and function. *Microbial Environmental Genomics (MEG)*, 1399, 207–233.

Kim, D., Song, L., Breitwieser, F.P., Salzberg, S.L. (2016). Centrifuge: Rapid and sensitive classification of metagenomic sequences. *Genome Research*, 26(12), 1721–1729.

Kolmogorov, M., Rayko, M., Yuan, J., Polevikov, E., Pevzner, P. (2019). metaFlye: scalable long-read metagenome assembly using repeat graphs. bioRxiv p. 637637.

Kreimer, A., Doron-Faigenboim, A., Borenstein, E., Freilich, S. (2012). NetCmpt: A network-based tool for calculating the metabolic competition between bacterial species. *Bioinformatics*, 28(16), 2195–2197.

Laczny, C.C., Sternal, T., Plugaru, V., Gawron, P., Atashpendar, A., Margossian, H.H., Coronado, S., der Maaten, L.V., Vlassis, N., Wilmes, P. (2015). VizBin – An application for reference-independent visualization and human-augmented binning of metagenomic data. *Microbiome*, 3(1).

Langmead, B. and Salzberg, S.L. (2012). Fast gapped-read alignment with Bowtie 2. *Nature Methods*, 9(4), 357.

Legendre, P. and Cáceres, M.D. (2013). Beta diversity as the variance of community data: Dissimilarity coefficients and partitioning. *Ecology Letters*, 16(8), 951–963.

Leung, H.C., Yiu, S.-M., Parkinson, J., Chin, F.Y. (2013). IDBA-MT: De novo assembler for metatranscriptomic data generated from next-generation sequencing technology. *Journal of Computational Biology*, 20(7), 540–550.

Leung, H.C., Yiu, S.-M., Chin, F.Y. (2014). IDBA-MTP: A hybrid metatranscriptomic assembler based on protein information. *International Conference on Research in Computational Molecular Biology*, 160–172.

Levy, R., Carr, R., Kreimer, A., Freilich, S., Borenstein, E. (2015). NetCooperate: A network-based tool for inferring host-microbe and microbe-microbe cooperation. *BMC Bioinformatics*, 16(1).

Li, B. and Dewey, C.N. (2011). RSEM: Accurate transcript quantification from RNA-seq data with or without a reference genome. *BMC Bioinformatics*, 12(1), 323.

Li, D., Liu, C.M., Luo, R., Sadakane, K., Lam, T.W. (2015). MEGAHIT: An ultra-fast single-node solution for large and complex metagenomics assembly via succinct de Bruijn graph. *Bioinformatics*, 31(10), 1674–1676.

Liu, B. and Pop, M. (2010). Identifying differentially abundant metabolic pathways in metagenomic datasets. *Lecture Notes in Computer Science* (including subseries Lecture Notes in Artificial Intelligence and Lecture Notes in Bioinformatics), 6053 LNBI(Suppl. 2), 101–112.

Lloyd-Price, J., Mahurkar, A., Rahnavard, G., Crabtree, J., Orvis, J., Hall, A.B., Brady, A., Creasy, H.H., McCracken, C., Giglio, M.G., McDonald, D., Franzosa, E.A., Knight, R., White, O., Huttenhower, C. (2017). Strains, functions and dynamics in the expanded human microbiome project. *Nature*, 550(7674), 61.

Locey, K.J. and Lennon, J.T. (2016). Scaling laws predict global microbial diversity. *Proceedings of the National Academy of Sciences*, 113(21), 5970–5975.

Luo, C., Knight, R., Siljander, H., Knip, M., Xavier, R.J., Gevers, D. (2015). ConStrains identifies microbial strains in metagenomic datasets. *Nature Biotechnology*, 33(10), 1045–1052.

Maillet, N., Lemaitre, C., Chikhi, R., Lavenier, D., Peterlongo, P. (2012). Compareads: Comparing huge metagenomic experiments. *BMC Bioinformatics*, 13(Suppl. 19), S10.

Maillet, N., Collet, G., Vannier, T., Lavenier, D., Peterlongo, P. (2014). Commet: Comparing and combining multiple metagenomic datasets. *Proceedings – 2014 IEEE International Conference on Bioinformatics and Biomedicine, IEEE BIBM 2014*, IEEE, 94–98.

McDowall, J. and Hunter, S. (2011). InterPro protein classification. *Methods in Molecular Biology*, 694, 37–47.

Menzel, P., Ng, K.L., Krogh, A. (2016). Fast and sensitive taxonomic classification for metagenomics with Kaiju. *Nature Communications*, 7.

Mitchell, A.L., Almeida, A., Beracochea, M., Boland, M., Burgin, J., Cochrane, G., Crusoe, M.R., Kale, V., Potter, S.C., Richardson, L.J. (2019). MGnify: The microbiome analysis resource in 2020. *Nucleic Acids Research*, 48(D1), D570–D578.

Namiki, T., Hachiya, T., Tanaka, H., Sakakibara, Y. (2012). MetaVelvet: An extension of Velvet assembler to de novo metagenome assembly from short sequence reads. *Nucleic Acids Research*, 40(20), e155.

Nurk, S., Meleshko, D., Korobeynikov, A., Pevzner, P.A. (2017). metaSPAdes: A new versatile metagenomic assembler. *Genome Research*, 27(5), 824–834.

Ondov, B.D., Treangen, T.J., Melsted, P., Mallonee, A.B., Bergman, N.H., Koren, S., Phillippy, A.M. (2016). Mash: Fast genome and metagenome distance estimation using MinHash. *Genome Biology*, 17(1), 132.

Ounit, R., Wanamaker, S., Close, T.J., Lonardi, S. (2015). CLARK: Fast and accurate classification of metagenomic and genomic sequences using discriminative k-mers. *BMC Genomics*, 16(1), 236.

Pace, N.R., Stahl, D.A., Lane, D.J., Olsen, G.J. (1986). The analysis of natural microbial populations by ribosomal RNA sequences. In *Advances in Microbial Ecology*, Marshall, K.C. (ed.). Springer.

Parks, D.H., Imelfort, M., Skennerton, C.T., Hugenholtz, P., Tyson, G.W. (2015). CheckM: Assessing the quality of microbial genomes recovered from isolates, single cells, and metagenomes. *Genome Research*, 25(7), 1043–1055.

Paten, B., Novak, A.M., Eizenga, J.M., Garrison, E. (2017). Genome graphs and the evolution of genome inference. *Genome Research*, 27(5), 665–676.

Peng, Y., Leung, H.C.M., Yiu, S.M., Chin, F.Y.L. (2012). IDBA-UD: A de novo assembler for single-cell and metagenomic sequencing data with highly uneven depth. *Bioinformatics*, 28(11), 1420–1428.

Proctor, L. (2019). Priorities for the next 10 years of human microbiome research. *Nature*, 569(7758), 623–625.

Pruesse, E., Peplies, J., Glöckner, F.O. (2012). SINA: Accurate high-throughput multiple sequence alignment of ribosomal RNA genes. *Bioinformatics*, 28(14), 1823–1829.

Quast, C., Pruesse, E., Yilmaz, P., Gerken, J., Schweer, T., Yarza, P., Peplies, J., Glöckner, F.O. (2013). The SILVA ribosomal RNA gene database project: Improved data processing and web-based tools. *Nucleic Acids Research*, 41(D1), D590–D596.

Rappé, M.S. and Giovannoni, S.J. (2003). The uncultured microbial majority. *Annual Review of Microbiology*, 57(1), 369–394.

Rizk, G., Lavenier, D., Chikhi, R. (2013). DSK: k-mer counting with very low memory usage. *Bioinformatics*, 29(5), 652–653.

Roesch, L.F., Fulthorpe, R.R., Riva, A., Casella, G., Hadwin, A.K., Kent, A.D., Daroub, S.H., Camargo, F.A., Farmerie, W.G., Triplett, E.W. (2007). Pyrosequencing enumerates and contrasts soil microbial diversity. *ISME Journal*, 1(4), 283–290.

Sankar, S.A., Lagier, J.C., Pontarotti, P., Raoult, D., Fournier, P.E. (2015). The human gut microbiome, a taxonomic conundrum. *Systematic and Applied Microbiology*, 38(4), 276–286.

Schloss, P.D., Westcott, S.L., Ryabin, T., Hall, J.R., Hartmann, M., Hollister, E.B., Lesniewski, R.A., Oakley, B.B., Parks, D.H., Robinson, C.J., Sahl, J.W., Stres, B., Thallinger, G.G., Van Horn, D.J., Weber, C.F. (2009). Introducing mothur: Open-source, platform-independent, community-supported software for describing and comparing microbial communities. *Applied and Environmental Microbiology*, 75(23), 7537–7541.

Schouls, L.M., Schot, C.S., Jacobs, J.A. (2003). Horizontal transfer of segments of the 16S rRNA genes between species of the *Streptococcus anginosus* group. *Journal of Bacteriology*, 185(24), 7241–7246.

Sczyrba, A., Hofmann, P., Belmann, P., Koslicki, D., Janssen, S., Dröge, J., Gregor, I., Majda, S., Fiedler, J., Dahms, E., Bremges, A. (2017). Critical assessment of metagenome interpretation – A benchmark of metagenomics software. *Nature Methods*, 14(11), 1063–1071.

Sedlazeck, F.J., Lee, H., Darby, C.A., Schatz, M.C. (2018). Piercing the dark matter: Bioinformatics of long-range sequencing and mapping. *Nature Reviews Genetics*, 19(6), 329–346.

Segata, N. (2018). On the road to strain-resolved comparative metagenomics. *mSystems*, 3(2), e00190–17.

Seshadri, R., Kravitz, S.A., Smarr, L., Gilna, P., Frazier, M. (2007). Camera: A community resource for metagenomics. *PLoS Biology*, 5(3), e75.

Simpson, J.T., Wong, K., Jackman, S.D., Schein, J.E., Jones, S.J., Birol, I. (2009). ABySS: A parallel assembler for short read sequence data. *Genome Research*, 19(6), 1117–1123.

Sultan, M., Amstislavskiy, V., Risch, T., Schuette, M., Dökel, S., Ralser, M., Balzereit, D., Lehrach, H., Yaspo, M.-L. (2014). Influence of RNA extraction methods and library selection schemes on RNA-seq data. *BMC Genomics*, 15(1), 675.

Teeling, H., Meyerdierks, A., Bauer, M., Amann, R., Glöckner, F.O. (2004). Application of tetranucleotide frequencies for the assignment of genomic fragments. *Environmental Microbiology*, 6(9), 938–947.

Tiwari, R., Nain, L., Labrou, N.E., Shukla, P. (2018). Bioprospecting of functional cellulases from metagenome for second generation biofuel production: A review. *Critical Reviews in Microbiology*, 44(2), 244–257.

Truong, D.T., Franzosa, E.A., Tickle, T.L., Scholz, M., Weingart, G., Pasolli, E., Tett, A., Huttenhower, C., Segata, N. (2015). MetaPhlAn2 for enhanced metagenomic taxonomic profiling, *Nature Methods*, 12, 902–903.

Truong, D.T., Tett, A., Pasolli, E., Huttenhower, C., Segata, N. (2017). Microbial strain-level population structure & genetic diversity from metagenomes. *Genome Research*, 27(4), 626–638.

Turnbaugh, P.J., Ley, R.E., Hamady, M., Fraser-Liggett, C.M., Knight, R., Gordon, J.I. (2007). The human microbiome project. *Nature*, 449(7164), 804.

Ulyantsev, V.I., Kazakov, S.V., Dubinkina, V.B., Tyakht, A.V., Alexeev, D.G. (2016). Metafast: Fast reference-free graph-based comparison of shotgun metagenomic data. *Bioinformatics*, 32(18), 2760–2767.

Venter, J.C., Remington, K., Heidelberg, J.F., Halpern, A.L., Rusch, D., Eisen, J.A., Wu, D., Paulsen, I., Nelson, K.E. (2004). Environmental genome shotgun sequencing of the Sargasso Sea. *Science*, 304(5667), 66–74.

Vollmers, J., Wiegand, S., Kaster, A.-K. (2017). Comparing and evaluating metagenome assembly tools from a microbiologist's perspective-not only size matters! *PloS One*, 12(1), e0169662.

Wang, Z. and Wu, M. (2013). A phylum-level bacterial phylogenetic marker database. *Molecular Biology and Evolution*, 30(6), 1258–1262.

Welch, D.B. and Huse, S.M. (2011). Microbial diversity in the deep sea and the underexplored "rare biosphere". *Handbook of Molecular Microbial Ecology II: Metagenomics in Different Habitats*, 103(32), 243–252.

Wood, D.E. and Salzberg, S.L. (2014). Kraken: Ultrafast metagenomic sequence classification using exact alignments. *Genome Biology*, 15(3), R46.

Wu, Y.-W., Tang, Y.-H., Tringe, S.G., Simmons, B.A., Singer, S.W. (2014). MaxBin: An automated binning method to recover individual genomes from metagenomes using an expectation-maximization algorithm. *Microbiome*, 2(1), 26.

Xia, L.C., Cram, J.A., Chen, T., Fuhrman, J.A., Sun, F. (2011). Accurate genome relative abundance estimation based on shotgun metagenomic reads. *PloS One*, 6(12), e27992.

Ye, Y. and Tang, H. (2016). Utilizing de Bruijn graph of metagenome assembly for metatranscriptome analysis. *Bioinformatics*, 32(7), 1001–1008.

Zhu, W., Lomsadze, A., Borodovsky, M. (2010). Ab initio gene identification in metagenomic sequences. *Nucleic Acids Research*, 38(12).

6

RNA Folding

Yann PONTY[1] and Vladimir REINHARZ[2]

[1] *LIX UMR 7161, Polytechnic School, Polytechnic Institute of Paris, France*
[2] *Department of Computer Science, University of Quebec, Montreal, Canada*

6.1. Introduction

RNAs are molecules that are essential to any living organism. They are composed of nucleotides named Adenine, Cytosine, Guanine and Uracile, and usually represented as sequences over an $\{A, C, G, U\}$ alphabet. Such sequences differ slightly from DNA, itself encoded on an $\{A, C, G, T\}$ alphabet, since thymines are replaced by uracile upon transcription. Functional RNA molecules feature a wide variety of sizes, ranging from 25 nucleotides (nts) for the aptly named micro-RNAs, to dozens of thousands for viruses using RNA as its primary genomic material. For instance, HIV-1 encodes its function in a single-stranded RNA of approximately 9,500 nts, while the genome of SARS-CoV 2, responsible for the Covid-19 pandemic, consists of an RNA molecule of more than 30,000 nts.

This length variation reflects a wide functional diversity. Acting as mediators, messenger RNAs consist of slices of the genetic information contained in the DNA, and are used as a template for the synthesis of proteins. RNAs also play an integral part in the ribosome, a large multi-molecular

From Sequences to Graphs,
coordinated by Annie CHATEAU and Mikaël SALSON.
© ISTE Ltd 2022.

assembly which translates messenger RNAs into proteins. They also regulate gene expression at a quantitative level, for example, through the process of RNA interference, where small single-stranded RNAs bind to messenger RNAs, preventing the ribosome from binding to then, and thus inhibiting the synthesis of associated proteins.

Far from being exhaustive, this list of functions is also constantly growing, mirroring our ever-increasing discovery of novel RNAs. The RFAM database (Kalvari et al. 2017), which lists and organizes documented RNAs into functional families, has been experiencing a constant growth since its creation in 2002. As of 2022, RFAM lists more than 4,000 functional families, as shown in Figure 6.1.

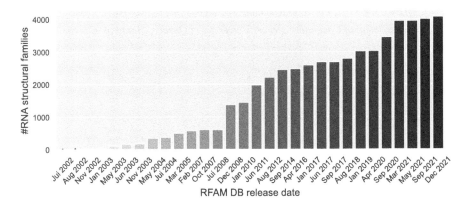

Figure 6.1. *Evolution of the number of functional RNA families, indexed in the RFAM database (Kalvari et al. 2017). The strong increase in the number of families in 2009 coincides with the democratization of the RNA-seq technology ENCODE (2007)*

6.1.1. *RNA folding*

Unlike DNA, RNA is synthesized as a single molecule and does not necessarily adopt a regular double-helix structure like DNA. On the contrary, RNA is initially *single-stranded* during its synthesis, and folds back on itself through a process that is subject to nanoscale fluctuations. It is stabilized in some of its conformations, or structures, by the formation of *base pairs*, connecting some of those nucleotides through hydrogen bonds.

Among non-coding RNAs, which act directly as RNAs and not through translation into proteins, a well-defined structure often constitutes an essential determinant of function. Consequently, across many functional families, the adoption of a precise structure is more conserved throughout evolution than a certain nucleotide sequence. Predicting the functional structure of an RNA therefore represents a necessary first step to understand its mode(s) of action, and to figure out its role within the broader context of biological systems.

6.1.1.1. *Paradigms for folding prediction*

From a perspective inspired by statistical physics, illustrated by Figure 6.2, RNA is initially transcribed in an essentially unstructured form (A). It then fluctuates in a stochastic manner, moving between its different states, also known as *structures* or *conformations*. The system eventually reaches *thermodynamic equilibrium*, where the probability of observing an RNA in a given conformation ceases to evolve with time.

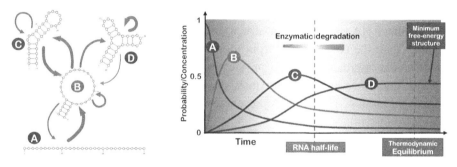

Figure 6.2. *Main paradigms for RNA folding prediction. The folding process can be abstracted as a continuous time Markov process (left), whose states (A–D) represent the main conformations adopted by a toy RNA. Left for sufficient time, the process converges to a thermodynamic equilibrium (right) where the probability of observing RNA in a given structure depends only on its free energy. The most probable structure is then the one with minimum free energy, but others may sometimes dominate the thermodynamic equilibrium. For a color version of this figure, see www.iste.co.uk/chateau/graphs.zip*

At the thermodynamic equilibrium, the set of structures possibly adopted by an RNA ω follows a *Boltzmann distribution*, such that a structure S is observed with probability

$$\mathbb{P}(S \mid \omega) = \frac{e^{-E(S)/RT}}{\mathcal{Z}}$$

where R is the Boltzmann constant, $E(S)$ is the *free energy* of S, T is the temperature, and $\mathcal{Z}$ is the *partition function*, a crucial quantity which can be seen here as a renormalization constant. This distribution maximizes the entropy given the average, measurable energy of the system.

This distribution motivates a focus, shared by many predictive approaches, on the *minimum free-energy (MFE) structure*. Indeed, the MFE probably possesses the highest probability in the Boltzmann distribution, and thus represents the most likely structure to be observed by its potential partners in the cellular environment.

However, although maximal among structures, the MFE probability may be very small in absolute terms and, in the absence of evolutionary pressure, is even assumed to decrease exponentially with the length of the RNA. Rather than focusing on a single poorly representative structure, some approaches will instead consider the expected properties of folding at *thermodynamic equilibrium*. For instance, in Figure 6.2, the outermost helix, involving both ends of the RNA, is present in structures B–D. It is therefore much more probable than the two apical hairpin loops, only found in the MFE structure D. Ensemble approaches, based on the explicit computation of the partition function and/or sampling techniques, make it possible to calculate these average properties, as well as representative structures (e.g. centroids of the dominant clusters).

More recent works focus on the *kinetics* of RNA, considering the properties of RNA folding before it reaches the thermodynamic equilibrium. Indeed, several phenomena (co-transcriptional folding (Lai et al. 2013), multi-stable RNAs (Findeiß et al. 2017)) exhibit a dependency on the initial distribution, refuting the hypothesis of convergence to an equilibrium. This out-of-equilibrium behavior can be explained by the limited life span of RNA, induced by an enzymatic degradation which prevents RNA from overcoming some *energy barriers* in time comparable to its *half-life*.

Finally, evolution can help predict the functional structure of RNA, by postulating the existence of selection pressure constraining the structure of *homologous RNAs* to adopt the same function. From a reverse point of view, a collection of homologous RNAs is likely to collectively adopt a common structure. This induces additional constraints, which supplement the energy model to inform the prediction of a shared structure.

6.1.2. *Secondary structure*

It is generally accepted that RNA adopts its functional structure through a folding process that is hierarchical in nature. RNA initially adopts a tree-like structure called the *secondary structure*, through a set of canonical pairings. In a second stage, RNA adopts a complex three-dimensional structure made possible by weaker stabilizing motifs.

Among these, we can find non-canonical bonds and complex topological patterns called *pseudoknots*, consisting of base pairs that are crossing when drawn in the upper half-plane. For this reason, structure prediction often starts with the critical guess of one (or more) candidate secondary structure(s). This initial prediction is then completed by additional crossing elements, and finally by the three-dimensional arrangement of these patterns.

Formally, a secondary structure is a set $S \subset [1, n]^2$ of base pairs $(i, j), 1 \leq i < j \leq n$, satisfying the following constraints:

1) Minimum distance θ: if $(i, j) \in S$, it then follows that $j - i > \theta$.

2) Monogamy: any position is involved in *at most* one pair of S.

3) Forbidden crossings: if $(i, j), (k, l) \in S$ such that $i < k$, it then follows that $i < k < l < j$ or $i < j < k < l$.

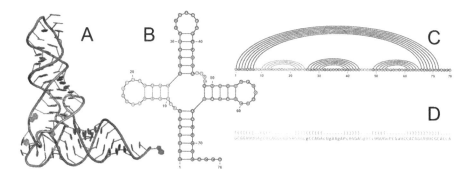

Figure 6.3. *Representation of the secondary structure associated with the 3D folding of a transfer RNA (PDB 1EHZ, chain A). For a color version of this figure, see www.iste.co.uk/chateau/graphs.zip*

Under the aforementioned restrictions, the secondary structure can be represented in several forms, as illustrated in Figure 6.3. From a 3D RNA structure in the Protein Data Bank (PDB (Berman et al. 2000) – A), a secondary structure can be extracted, for example, using the DSSR program (Lu et al. 2015). It can then be drawn without crossing as an outerplanar graph (B), or an arc-annotated sequence (C). Ultimately, a secondary structure can be represented very compactly using the *dot-bracket notation* (D), that is, a sequence $t \in \{(,), \bullet\}^*$ such that:

– there are as many opening and closing parentheses ($|t|_(= |t|_)$);

– for any prefix $t' \sqsubseteq t$, we have $|t'|_(\geq |t'|_)$.

In this setting, each opening parenthesis is unambiguously associated with a closing parenthesis, representing a base pair. The positions presenting a character $\bullet$ are then left free of interactions, or *unpaired*.

We finally describe the set of candidate structures, possibly adopted by an RNA sequence $\omega \in \{A, C, G, U\}^n$. A secondary structure S is *compatible* with ω if any base pair $(i, j) \in S$ is *canonical*, that is, either a *Watson–Crick* (G-C or A-U) or *Wobble* base pair. More formally:

$$(\omega_i, \omega_j) \in \{(G, C), (C, G), (A, U), (U, A), (G, U), (U, G)\} .$$

The set of structures compatible with the RNA ω is denoted by $\mathcal{S}_\omega$ (or simply $\mathcal{S}$ when clear from the context), and $\mathcal{S}_{i,j}$ represents the set of secondary structures that are compatible with the region $[i, j]$ of ω.

6.1.2.1. *Energy model and structure space decomposition*

RNA stability is physically determined by its free energy, expressed in kcal.mol^{-1}. The lower the free energy, the more stable an RNA structure is. The free energy of a structure depends largely on its base pairs, and their interaction in the form of patterns stabilizing the RNA structure.

In order to illustrate the different algorithmic approaches available for structure prediction, we will consider a *simple energy model*, defined additively over base pairs. More precisely, letting S be a secondary structure for a sequence ω, we have:

$$E(S) := \sum_{(i,j) \in S} E_{i,j}^\omega$$

where $E_{i,j}^\omega$ is the energy difference associated with the creation of the pair (i, j).

An energy of -1 can be associated with canonical base pairs (G-C, A-U and G-U), and energy of $+\infty$ can be associated with the invalid base pair. In other words, in this simple model, minimizing the free energy coincides with maximizing the number of canonical pairs. Alternatively, we may consider an energy model that fosters base pairs considered to be more stable (G-C $\to -3$, A-U $\to -2$), disadvantaging those that are more transient (G-U $\to -1$).

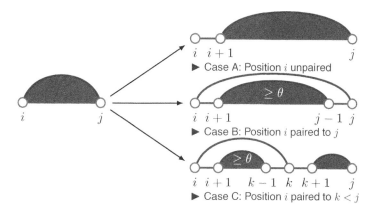

Figure 6.4. *Decomposition of the space of secondary structures, possibly adopted by an RNA on a region $[i, j]$, $1 \leq i < j \leq n$, given a minimal base pair distance of θ nucleotides*

As shown in Figure 6.4, it is possible to decompose the secondary structures of $\mathcal{S}_{i,j}$ compatible with a region $[i, j]$ of a RNA ω. For this purpose, we consider the status of nucleotide i in a structure formed over $[i, j]$:

Case A: Either i is unpaired and followed by a secondary structure formed independently over the region $[i + 1, j]$.

Case B: Or i is paired to a position j, $j - i > \theta$, and any secondary structure is formed over the region $[i + 1, j - 1]$.

Case C: Or i is paired to a position $k < j$, $k - i > \theta$, and two structures are then formed in regions $[i + 1, k - 1]$ and $[k + 1, j]$. These latter are independent, due to pseudoknots being forbidden.

It can be shown that this decomposition is *complete*, that is, any structure of $\mathcal{S}_{i,j}$ is generated/decomposed by one of the three cases above. Moreover, it is *unambiguous*, and any structure of $\mathcal{S}_{i,j}$ can be uniquely generated/decomposed through a recursive application of the three cases. Finally, it is *correct* for our simple energy model, as it explicitly scores base pairs, thus making it possible to capture our energy model.

6.2. Optimization for structure prediction

6.2.1. *Computing the minimum free-energy (MFE) structure*

The *minimum free-energy (MFE) structure* represents the most stable structure among all of the structures adopted by a sequence. It is also the most probable structure at the thermodynamic equilibrium and, as such, represents a reasonable candidate while searching for the functional conformation for a given RNA.

Nonetheless, to determine this structure, we must overcome a combinatorial explosion of the number of secondary structures, which is asymptotically equivalent to $\sim 1.8^n$ (Zuker and Sankoff 1984), on average, for an RNA sequence of length n. The computation of a minimum energy structure thus represents a potentially difficult, combinatorial optimization problem which can be defined as follows:

Problem 6.1. Free-energy minimization

Input: Sequence $\omega \in \{A, C, G, U\}^+$, $|\omega| = n$.
Output: Secondary structure $S^\star$ such that

$$E(S^\star) = \min_{S \in \mathcal{S}} E(S)$$

A dynamic programming scheme for this problem is based on the decomposition introduced in section 6.1.2.1. With this scheme, we are looking into the minimal energy $m_{i,j}$ accessible by folding the $[i, j]$ region within the input RNA. In any structure over $[i, j]$, and thus any minimum energy structure, only three options are possible for position i: either i is free, and the structure minimum energy is found by optimizing the energy over $[i+1, j]$; or i is paired to j, and an optimal folding forms over $[i + 1, j - 1]$; or position i is paired to some $k < j$, and two optimal and independent folds form over $[i + 1, k - 1]$ and $[k + 1, j]$.

It follows that, for a region $[i, j]$ such that $j - i > \theta$, the MFE $m_{i,j}$ over the region $[i, j]$ obeys:

$$m_{i,j} = \min \begin{cases} m_{i+1,j} & \blacktriangleright \text{CaseA:Pos.iisfree} \\ E_{i,j}^{\omega} + m_{i+1,j-1} & \blacktriangleright \text{CaseB:Pair(i,j)} \\ \min_{k=i+\theta+1}^{j-1} E_{i,k}^{\omega} + m_{i,k-1} + m_{k+1,j} & \blacktriangleright \text{CaseC:Pair(i,k),k>j} \end{cases}$$

[6.1]

When $j - i \leq \theta$, we get $m_{i,j} = 0$ because the region is then too small to contain a base pair.

We need to formulate an algorithm to efficiently compute this recurrence. Moreover, we also want to produce an MFE structure, and not just its energy, so we need to find an algorithm to reconstruct the chosen structure. Two algorithms are thus necessary, with quite similar structures:

– Algorithm 6.1 computes the minimum energy associated with each region $[i, j]$ in the sequence, as described in the system [6.1].

– Algorithm 6.2 backtracks, to reconstruct a minimum energy structure $S^{\star}$ for the sequence ω.

6.2.1.1. *Correctness of the algorithms*

PROPOSITION 6.1.– *Algorithm 6.1 returns a matrix* m *which contains at position* $m_{i,j}$ *the minimum energy of the subsequence* $\omega_{i,j}$.

PROOF.– We will directly show that, at each step of the computation, the value obtained for $m_{i,j}$ is correct. First, as mentioned in section 6.1.2, there can be no base pair over a region of length smaller than $\theta + 2$. We can therefore initialize $m_{i,j}$ with 0 for all regions $[i, j]$ such that $j - i + 1 < \theta + 2$, equivalent to $j - i \leq \theta$, which is achieved by the double loop starting at line 3.

Now, in the loop starting at line 6, we fill in the matrix m one cell at a time. We iterate over the regions $[i, j]$ in ascending order on i (and then on j). In this way, we can guarantee that, by the time we compute an accurate $[i, j]$, the values $m_{i',j'}$ such that $i' < i$ have already been computed.

We are then going to assume these values $m_{i',j'}$, $i < i'$ are correct, and show that this implies the correction of $m_{i,j}$. In order to obtain the value of $m_{i,j}$, there are only three possible cases to consider:

ALGORITHM 6.1. Filling the minimum energy matrix

Input   : ω – RNA of size n
Output : m – Matrix m, filled according to [6.1]

1 **Function** FillMatrix (ω):
2 $\quad$ $m \leftarrow$ EmptyMatrix $(n \times n)$
$\quad$ // Initialize with 0 all the values of the diagonal up to θ.
3 $\quad$ **for** $i \leftarrow 1$ **to** n **do**
4 $\quad\quad$ **for** $j \leftarrow i$ **to** $\min (i + \theta, n)$ **do**
5 $\quad\quad\quad$ $m_{i,j} \leftarrow 0$

6 $\quad$ **for** $i \leftarrow n$ **to** 1 **do**
7 $\quad\quad$ **for** $j \leftarrow i + \theta + 1$ **to** n **do**
$\quad\quad\quad$ ▶ Case A: position i left without partner $\quad\quad\quad\quad$;
8 $\quad\quad\quad$ $m_{i,j} \leftarrow m_{i+1,j}$;
$\quad\quad\quad$ ▶ Case B: positions i and j form a base pair $\quad\quad\quad$;
9 $\quad\quad\quad$ $m_{i,j} \leftarrow \min \left(m_{i,j}, m_{i+1,j-1} + E_{i,j}^{\omega} \right)$
$\quad\quad\quad$ ▶ Case C: position i paired to $k < j$ $\quad\quad\quad\quad\quad$;
10 $\quad\quad\quad$ **for** $k \leftarrow i + \theta + 1$ **to** $j - 1$ **do**
11 $\quad\quad\quad\quad$ $m_{i,j} \leftarrow \min \left(m_{i,j}, m_{i+1,k-1} + m_{k+1,j} + E_{i,k}^{\omega} \right)$

12 $\quad$ **return** m

Case A: An optimal structure leaves position i without a partner. The optimal structure is then composed of the base pairs of an independent folding on $[i + 1, j]$, whose energy can be found in $\omega_{i+1,j}$. Since $i + 1 > i$, this value was already computed and can be assumed to be correct.

Case B: An optimal structure pairs the positions i and j. In this case, the optimal structure is composed of a pair (i, j), of energy $E_{i,j}^{\omega}$, and an optimal folding over $[i + 1, j - 1]$, of energy found in $m_{i+1,j-1}$. It can be assumed that the latter is correctly computed because $i + 1 > i$.

Case C: An optimal structure pairs the positions i and $k < j$. The pair (i, k) thus delimits two regions $[i + 1, k - 1]$ and $[k + 1, j]$, where the RNA forms independent folds (pseudoknots not being allowed). These two regions start after i, and their minimum energies can thus be found in $m_{i+1,k-1}$ and $m_{k+1,j}$. The sum of these terms is therefore completed by the contribution $E_{i,k}^{\omega}$ of the pair to obtain the minimum energy.

Given that any structure falls into one of these categories, the value assigned to $m_{i,j}$ indeed represents the structure having minimum energy over $[i, j]$. The correction of $m_{i,j}$ can thus be inferred and, by induction, the correction of the computation over any region ensues. □

ALGORITHM 6.2. Backtracking for the minimum energy structure.

Input : $[i, j]$ – Region under consideration

m – Dyn. prog. matrix, previously computed according to equation [6.1]

ω – RNA of length n

Output : S^* – Structure minimizing free energy

1 **Function** Backtrack (i, j, m, ω):
2   **if** $j - i \leq \theta$ **then**
3   **return** $\overbrace{\bullet \ldots \bullet}^{j-i+1}$ // The empty structure has minimum energy
4   **else**
     ▶ Case A: position i left without partner   ;
5   **if** $m_{i,j} = m_{i+1,j}$ **then**   // Min. energy achieved by struct. where i is free
6        $S_i^* \leftarrow$ Backtrack $(i + 1, j, m, \omega)$
7   **return** $\bullet\, S_i^*$
     ▶ Case B: positions i and j form a base pair   ;
8   **if** $m_{i,j} = m_{i+1,j-1} + E_{i,j}^{\omega}$ **then** // Min. energy achieved by struct. pairing i and j
9        $S_{i,j}^* \leftarrow$ Backtrack $(i + 1, j - 1, m, \omega)$
10   **return** $(S_{i,j}^*)$
     ▶ Case C: position i paired to $k < j$;
11   **for** $k \leftarrow i + \theta + 1$ **to** $j - 1$ **do**
12   **if** $m_{i,j} = m_{i+1,k-1} + m_{k+1,j} + E_{i,k}^{\omega}$ **then** // Optimal struct. pairing i and k
13          $S_1^* \leftarrow$ Backtrack $(i + 1, k - 1, m, \omega)$
14          $S_2^* \leftarrow$ Backtrack $(k + 1, j, m, \omega)$
15   **return** $(S_1^*)\, S_2^*$

PROPOSITION 6.2.– *Let* m *be the matrix computed by Algorithm 6.1, the function* Backtrack(i, j, m, ω) *of Algorithm 6.2 returns a minimal energy structure over the region* $[i, j]$.

PROOF.– By Proposition 6.1, we know that $m_{i,j}$ contains the minimum energy for any region $[i, j]$. Then, there are four possible cases for the optimal structure:

Case 0: Sequence too short $i - j < \theta$. We know that if the regions contain less than $\theta + 2$ nucleotides, it cannot form a base pair. The structure without base pair, returned at line 2, is therefore the only compatible structure, and thus has minimal energy.

Case A: Position i left without a partner. In this case, we have $m_{i,j} = m_{i+1,j}$, and the optimal structure which starts with a free position, followed by an optimal structure over $[i+1, j]$. Such a structure has energy $m_{i+1,j}$, and is thus also of minimal energy for $[i, j]$.

Case B: Paired positions i and j. In this case, we have $m_{i,j} = m_{i+1,j-1} + E_{i,j}^{\omega}$, with the latter coinciding with the energy of the structure pairing i to j, and forming an optimal folding on $[i+1, j-1]$, which the algorithm returns.

Case C: Position i paired to $k < j$. In this final case, we have that $m_{i,j} = m_{i+1,k-1} + m_{k+1,j} + E_{i,k}^{\omega}$. This optimal energy is indeed that of the structure, returned by the algorithm, containing the pair (i, k), and two optimal folds on regions $[i+1, k-1]$ and $[k+1, j]$.

As the cases below cover all possible structures, we can conclude that the returned structure indeed has optimal energy over its region.   □

6.2.1.2. *Complexity analysis*

The overall complexity of the above algorithm for producing a minimum energy secondary structure is $\Theta(n^3)$ in time, and $\Theta(n^2)$ in memory.

For FillMatrix, after allocating space for the matrix m in $\Theta(n^2)$, which bounds the memory complexity, the initialization takes $\Theta(n)$ time, due to the iterations of the innermost loop being bounded by a constant θ. The main contribution to the complexity is due to the three nested **for** loops (line 6 and following). The first two loops enumerate all regions $[i, j]$ such that $j - i > \theta$, and the last one chooses $k \in [i + \theta + 1, j - 1]$. Each of these loops is executed at most n times, and the time complexity is $\mathcal{O}(n^3)$, that is, asymptotically bounded by $C\,n^3$ where C is a constant.

To prove the asymptotic equivalent, and thus the complexity in $\Theta(n^3)$, we may consider triplets (i, k, j) associated with the innermost loop executions (line 10). We note that such triplets correspond to choosing three distinct elements among $n - C'$, C' being a constant, and are therefore counted by:

$$\binom{n - C'}{3} = \frac{(n - C')(n - C' - 1)(n - C' - 2)}{3!} = \frac{n^3}{6} + \mathcal{O}(n^2) \in \Theta(n^3).$$

To determine the complexity of Backtrack, it is clear that, excluding the recursive calls, the number of operations performed by the algorithm is linear on the size of the region $[i, j]$. Moreover, the recursive calls involve subregions whose cumulative size is decreasing. It follows that, in the tree of recursive calls, the total number of iterations of the innermost loop, summed over all calls at depth p, remains bounded by n. Since the size of regions is strictly decreasing during successive recursive calls, the depth of the tree is bounded by n. The worst-case complexity is then $\Theta(n^2)$, and the complexity of Backtrack remains dominated by that of FillMatrix.

6.2.1.3. *Going further*

Despite its simplicity, this model already produces informative predictions, as can be seen in section 6.4.2. They can also be substantially improved by considering a more realistic energy model (see section 6.4.1). This requires a more complex algorithm, but very similar in principle to the one presented here.

Although the algorithm is commonly attributed to Nussinov et al. (1978), this seminal contribution was slightly different and, importantly, ambiguous: despite being correct for the minimization, it did not allow the computation of the partition function introduced in section 6.3.1. The version presented here is inspired by previous combinatorial works by Waterman (1978).

The algorithm can also be used to *predict the interaction of two RNAs*. Indeed, complexes can be predicted by running the algorithm on the concatenation of two RNAs, interspersed with θ anonymized nucleotides (N) to enable the full pairing of both RNAs. A minimum energy complex is then obtained, composed of both intramolecular base pairs (within a single RNA) and some intermolecular base pairs (involving both RNAs). However, since pseudoknots are forbidden, interactions remain limited to positions in the outer face of each of the two RNA (intramolecular) structures. More sophisticated dynamic programming schemes (Mückstein et al. 2006) have therefore been introduced to capture more realistic conformation spaces, allowing, for example, the interaction of loops.

The algorithm can also be used to *simplify* a pseudoknotted structure $S^{\sqcap}$, in order to recover a maximal non-crossing subset of base pairs. To this end, it is sufficient to adopt an energy model where $E_{i,j}^{\omega} := -1$ if $(i, j) \in S^{\sqcap}$, and $E_{i,j}^{\omega} := +\infty$ otherwise. Minimizing the energy is then equivalent to maximizing the number of pairs retained from $S^{\sqcap}$ such that pseudoknots are removed while arguably maximizing the residual structural information.

6.2.2. *Listing (sub)optimal structures*

Although fruitful, the energy minimization paradigm remains highly sensitive to the intrinsically imperfect inaccuracy of energy models. It is potentially impacted by measurement errors involved in the energy parameters, including the individual contributions of base pairs and, more generally, structural motifs.

Consequently, a structure S may be marginally more stable than an alternative structure S', and still returned by an energy minimization algorithm. This may occur despite the energy distance $|E(S') - E(S)|$ being arbitrarily small, much smaller than the experimental imprecision of the protocols used to calibrate the energy model. In such a case, it seems arbitrary to produce a structure S as representative of the folding process, especially when slightly suboptimal structures significantly differ.

This motivates the consideration of Δ-*admissible suboptimal structures*, that is, structures compatible with the input RNA that are located within at most Δ kcal.mol^{-1} of the MFE structure. This problem was initially considered by Zuker (1989), in a version restricted to sets of structures having no pairwise base pairs in common. Nevertheless, due to its greedy nature, this strategy turned out to be highly dependent on the order of produced structures, and was found to overlook important stable structures.

A more satisfactory, exhaustive version of the problem was subsequently considered by Wuchty et al. (1999).

Problem 6.2. Δ-suboptimal structures

Input: Sequence $\omega \in \{A, C, G, U\}^+$; Tolerance $\Delta \in \mathbb{R}^+$.
Output: Set $\mathcal{S}_\Delta$ of secondary Δ-admissible structures, having energy within Δ of minimum energy:

$$\mathcal{S}_\Delta = \{S \text{ such that } E(S) - \text{MFE}(\omega) \leq \Delta\}$$

A first idea, natural in the context of dynamic programming, consists of computing the exhaustive list of the Δ-suboptimal structures realizable over each region $[i, j]$. The lists associated with the different regions should then be stored in the cells of a specific matrix, and can be computed recursively. However, such a strategy would result in a memory complexity in $\Theta(n^3 \times$

M), where M is the number of Δ-suboptimal structures, and would quickly become prohibitive even for small RNAs.

Wuchty et al. (1999)'s algorithm modifies the backtrack phase to generate all suboptimal structures, while guaranteeing that each recursive call generates at least one admissible suboptimal structure. To this purpose, a parameter Δ, representing a *residual tolerance*, is introduced in the backtrack function. While inspecting cases in the dynamic programming, this parameter is used to decide whether or not a given case may contribute an admissible suboptimal. It is updated in the recursive calls to reflect the fact that choosing a given DP case may already *consume* some tolerance. The modified backtrack is summarized in Algorithm 6.3, and must be preceded by the DP computation of the MFE matrix (Algorithm 6.1) to obtain all the Δ suboptimal structures.

6.2.2.1. *Correctness of the algorithm*

PROPOSITION 6.3.– *For any tolerance $\Delta \geq 0$, and any region $\sigma := \{[1, n]\}$, Algorithm 6.3 returns the set of Δ-suboptimal structures such that $E(S) \leq m_{1,n} + \Delta$.*

PROOF.– Let us begin by noticing that, whenever invoked with $\Delta \geq 0$, Subopts will only pass positive values to Δ upon its subsequent recursive calls, as can be verified in lines 11, 14 and 18. We thus assume without loss of generality that $\Delta \geq 0$, and consider the following generalization of Proposition 6.3.

LEMMA 6.1.– *Consider an RNA ω of length n, and opt for the matrix of the minimal energies associated with regions. Then, for any list σ, any structure S_p and any residual tolerance $\Delta \geq 0$, the call to Subopts $(\sigma, S_p, \Delta, m, \omega)$ returns the set of every structure S compatible with ω and extending S_p with structures for every region of σ, such that*

$$E(S) \leq \Delta + \sum_{[i,j] \in \sigma} m_{i,j} + \sum_{(a,b) \in S_p} E_{a,b}^{\omega}. \qquad [6.2]$$

To prove Lemma 6.1, let us consider the *cumulative length $l(\sigma) :=$* $\sum_{[i,j] \in \delta} j - i + 1$ of the regions in σ. First of all, it can be seen that when $l(\sigma) = 0$ ($\sigma = \varnothing$), the structure S_p returned by the algorithm is such that

$$E(S_p) = \sum_{(a,b) \in S_p} E_{a,b}^{\omega} \leq \sum_{(a,b) \in S_p} E_{a,b}^{\omega} + \Delta$$

and thus satisfies the conditions of equation [6.2]. Moreover, it is the only possible extension of the input structure. This allows us to conclude with the validity of Lemma 6.1 when $l = 0$, thus providing the base case of an inductive proof.

ALGORITHM 6.3. Backtracking for Δ-suboptimal structures.

Input	$: \sigma$ – Set of regions being considered (initially $\sigma = \{[1, n]\}$)
	S_p – Partial secondary structure (initially $S_p = \varnothing$)
	Δ – Residual tolerance $\Delta \geq 0$
	m – Dyn. prog. matrix, previously computed according to equation [6.1]
	ω – RNA of size n
Output	$: S_\Delta$ – Δ-suboptimal structures over the region $[i, j]$

1 **Function** Subopts $(\sigma, S_p, \Delta, m, \omega)$:
2   **if** $\sigma = \varnothing$ **then**
3 | **return** $\{S_p\}$ // The partial structure S_p is Δ suboptimal
4   **else**
5       $[i, j] \leftarrow \text{pop}(\sigma)$ // Removes the first region of the stack σ
6   **if** $j - i \leq \theta$ **then**
7 | **return** Subopts $(\sigma, S_p, \Delta, m, \omega)$ // Processing other regions in σ
8   **else**
9         $\mathcal{A} \leftarrow \varnothing; \mathcal{B} \leftarrow \varnothing; \mathcal{C} \leftarrow \{\varnothing\}_{k=i}^{j}$
          ► Case A: position i left without partner   ;
10        $\delta_i \leftarrow m_{i+1,j} - m_{i,j}$ // Minimum distance to optimal if i free
11   **if** $\Delta - \delta_i \geq 0$ **then**   // $\exists$ struct. Δ-suboptimal where i is free
12 | $\mathcal{A} \leftarrow$ Subopts $([i + 1, j] \circ \sigma, S_p, \Delta - \delta_i, m, \omega)$
          ► Case B: positions i and j form a base pair   ;
13        $\delta_{i,j} \leftarrow (m_{i+1,j-1} + E_{i,j}^\omega) - m_{i,j}$ // Min. distance to opt. if (i, j) paired
14   **if** $\Delta - \delta_{i,j} \geq 0$ **then**   // $\exists$ struct. Δ-suboptimal pairing i and j
15 | $\mathcal{B} \leftarrow$ Subopts $([i + 1, j - 1] \circ \sigma, \{(i,j)\} \cup S_p, \Delta - \delta_{i,j}, m, \omega)$
          ► Case C: position i paired to $k < j$;
16   **for** $k \leftarrow i + \theta + 1$ **to** $j - 1$ **do**
17          $\delta_{i,k} \leftarrow (m_{i+1,k-1} + m_{k+1,j} + E_{i,k}^\omega) - m_{i,j}$ // Min. dist. if (i, k)
            paired
18   **if** $\Delta - \delta_{i,k} \geq 0$ **then**   // $\exists$ struct. Δ-suboptimal pairing i and k
19 | $\sigma_k \leftarrow [i + 1, k - 1] \circ [k + 1, j] \circ \sigma$
20 | $\mathcal{C}_k \leftarrow$ Subopts $(\sigma_k, \{(i,k)\} \cup S_p, \Delta - \delta_{i,k}, m, \omega)$
21   **return** $\mathcal{A} \cup \mathcal{B} \cup \bigcup_{k=i}^{j} \mathcal{C}_k$

Next, we assume the correction of Lemma 6.1 for any list of regions σ having cumulative length $l < l^\star$, for any value $\Delta \geq 0$ and any structure S_p.

Consider a list of regions $\sigma := [i, j] \circ \sigma'$ of cumulative length $l^\star$. The minimal energy accessible from a pair (σ, S_p) is

$$m(\sigma, S_p) := \sum_{[i,j] \in \sigma} m_{i,j} + \sum_{(a,b) \in S_p} E^\omega_{a,b}.$$

The choice of a decomposition case over $[i, j]$ can be seen as committing to a subset of structures, which may or may not include the local MFE, so the minimum accessible energy is $m' \geq m(\sigma, S_p)$. In other words, an *optimality loss*

$$\delta := m' - m(\sigma, S_p) \geq 0$$

results from the choice of a decomposition case.

If $\delta > \Delta$, then, in any structure S resulting from successive recursive calls, we have $E(S) \geq m' = m(\sigma, S_p) + \delta > m(\sigma, S_p) + \Delta$, so S should not be returned by the algorithm. It follows that $\mathcal{A}$ (respectively, $\mathcal{B}$ and $\mathcal{C}_k$) is empty when $\delta > \Delta$ (lines 11, 14 and 18).

When $\delta \leq \Delta$, the produced subset depends on the decomposition case:

Case A (i free): The minimal energy of a structure leaving i unpaired is given by

$$m([i + 1, j] \circ \sigma', S_p) = \sum_{[x,y] \in \sigma'} m_{x,y}$$
$$+ \sum_{(a,b) \in S_p} E^\omega_{a,b} = m(\sigma, S_p) + m_{i+1,j} - m_{i,j}.$$

It thus follows that $\delta = m([i+1, j] \circ \sigma', S_p) - m(\sigma, S_p) = m_{i+1,j} - m_{i,j} \geq 0$. Since $l([i+1, j] \circ \sigma') = l(\sigma) - 1 < l^\star$, the induction hypothesis applies to the recursive call on σ' and S_p. This thus produces all the structures S extending S_p on $[i + 1, j] \circ \sigma'$, such that

$$E(S) \leq m([i + 1, j] \circ \sigma', S_p) + \Delta - \delta = m(\sigma, S_p) + \Delta.$$

The set $\mathcal{A}$ thus coincides with the restriction of the extensions of S_p over σ, where i is left unpaired.

Case B (i **paired to** j): The case where i is paired to j is similar, but induces a loss of optimality $\delta = E_{i,j}^\omega + m_{i+1,j-1} - m_{i,j}$. We still have $l([i + 1, j - 1] \circ \sigma') = l(\sigma) - 2 < l^\star$ and the induction hypothesis implies correcting the recursive call, which thus produces all the S structures, as extensions of $S_p \cup \{(i,j)\}$ on $[i + 1, j - 1] \circ \sigma'$ such that

$$E(S) \leq m([i + 1, j - 1] \circ \sigma', \{(i,j)\} \cup S_p) + \Delta - \delta = m(\sigma, S_p) + \Delta.$$

The structures in $\mathcal{B}$ thus extend S_p on σ and satisfy [6.2] while pairing i with j.

Case C (i **paired to** $k < j$): When i is paired to $k < j$, we have $\delta = E_{i,k}^\omega + m_{i+1,k-1} + m_{k+1,j} - m_{i,j}$. For any k, the recursive call is made on $\sigma_k := [i + 1, k - 1] \circ [k + 1, j] \circ \sigma$, such that $l(\sigma_k) = l(\sigma) - 2$. The induction hypothesis thus applies, and the set of all structures extending $S_p \cup \{(i,k)\}$ over σ_k is obtained such that

$$E(S) \leq m(\sigma_k, \{(i,k)\} \cup S_p) + \Delta - \delta = m(\sigma, S_p) + \Delta.$$

The set $\mathcal{C}_k$ thus indeed represents the extensions of S_p on σ, verifying [6.2], and pairing i and k.

Remember that any structure over $[i, j]$ is generated by one of the three cases above. The assumed correctness of the algorithm, for any σ such that $l(\sigma) < l^\star$, thus extends to σ such that $l(\sigma) = l^\star$. In conjunction with the proven correctness when $l(\sigma) = 0$, this concludes the induction, and shows the validity of Lemma 6.1.

Finally, notice that for $\sigma = \{[1, n]\}$ and $S_p = \varnothing$, we obtain all structures such as

$$E(S) \leq \Delta + \sum_{[i,j] \in \sigma} m_{i,j} + \sum_{(a,b) \in S_p} E_{a,b}^\omega = m_{1,n} + \Delta$$

so the correction of Lemma 6.1 implies Property 6.3.   □

6.2.2.2. *Complexity analysis*

The combinatorial explosion of the Δ-optimal structures produced by the algorithm, in exponential number on Δ and n, does not allow for a fine complexity analysis according to the input parameters only. The complexity is therefore considered as a function of the number M of returned structures, and we show that Subopts can be executed in time $\mathcal{O}(M \times n^2)$.

We first focus on the structure of the tree T of recursive calls. Initially called with $\Delta \geq 0$, Subopts only makes recursive calls where $\Delta \geq 0$, as seen in lines 11, 14 and 18 of the pseudocode. Moreover, when $\sigma \neq \varnothing$ and $\Delta \geq 0$, at least one of the tests contributes a structure, so the leaves of T correspond to the case $\sigma = \varnothing$, producing a single structure $\{S_p\}$ (line 3). These structures are pairwise distinct (unambiguous decomposition), and thus in number M since any structure produced is propagated and backtracks to the root of T, where it is returned. Moreover, the height of T is at most n, since the cumulative size of the regions involved in σ is strictly decreasing during the successive recursive calls. The number of internal (non-root) nodes is therefore at most M because, at any depth $p \leq n$, the number of nodes at depth p is bounded by M (otherwise there would exist more than M leaves in T).

We obtain the predicted complexity of $\mathcal{O}(M \times n^2)$, noting that, excluding recursive calls, each run of Subopts requires, at worst, a linear number of elementary operations. For this purpose, suitable data structures will, however, have to be chosen, allowing addition to lists/stacks, and the set disjoint union in $\mathcal{O}(1)$ time. In practice, basic lists represent reasonable candidates, resulting in a relatively easy implementation.

6.2.2.3. *Going further*

The fundamental principle of the algorithm, which consists of updating a tolerance Δ according to the choices made during the backtrack, generalizes previous works by Waterman and Byers (1985), and can be slightly improved using techniques derived from natural language processing (Huang and Chiang 2005).

The suboptimal backtrack can be adapted to any algorithm based on an unambiguous dynamic programming scheme. It remains valid for an ambiguous decomposition, albeit generating some structures redundantly. However, this multiplicity typically introduces an exponential overhead in n, thus restricting its practical use and motivating the search for alternative unambiguous DP schemes.

6.2.3. *Comparative prediction: simultaneous alignment/folding of RNAs*

Comparative folding represents a final category of methods for structure prediction. It takes advantage of an evolutionary pressure towards structure conservation, observed within many functional families of non-coding RNAs. When a multiple sequence alignment is available for homologous RNAs, then a fruitful approach consists of folding the alignment, thereby simultaneously predicting a structure for all of its RNAs. This approach, which can be tackled using a variant of the Nussinov algorithm, optimizes the cumulative free energy while including substantial bonuses to reward *compensatory mutations*, that is, pairs of positions in the alignment that mutate, yet preserve the possibility to form base pairs.

Unfortunately, while the consideration of a structural alignment structure greatly improves the quality of predictions, such an alignment may be difficult to build in the absence of a joint structure. This induces a circular dependence since the alignment depends on the structure, and vice versa, so it is unclear where to start (chicken and egg paradox). The pioneering work of Sankoff (1985), at the origin of multiple algorithms and dozens of methods and software, works around the issue by solving the folding and alignment problems simultaneously. More precisely, it introduces the problem of determining the alignment/structure pair that optimizes a combination of free energy, conservation and compensatory mutations.

Similarly to multiple sequence alignment, the simultaneous alignment/folding problem is generally NP-hard (Wang and Jiang 1994) for an arbitrary number of sequences, so a polynomial-time algorithm seems highly unlikely. Yet, the restriction of the problem to a pair of homologous RNAs is already relevant and informative. Indeed, an algorithm for the pairwise alignment can be leveraged in a popular heuristics for the multiple RNA alignment problem, which progressively incorporates sequences into a partial multiple sequence alignment. Interestingly, the alignment/folding of an RNA pair admits an exact solution in $\Theta(n^6)$, based on a product of two dynamic programming schemes, visually described in Figure 6.5.

6.2.4. *Joint alignment/folding model*

Let us now describe more precisely the notion of *joint alignment/folding* of a pair (u, v) of RNAs. Let us recall that an *alignment* of two RNA sequences can be defined as a pair of character strings $A = (u', v')$ from an extended alphabet $\{A, C, G, U, -\}$, where the character $-$ represents an insertion/deletion (indel) such that:

– the two sequences (u', v') have equal length $|u'| = |v'| \geq \max(|u|, |v|)$;

– u (respectively v) is obtained from u' (respectively v') by removing the indels (–).

For instance, the RNA sequences $u :=$ ACGU and $v :=$ AGAU admit (among others) the following alignments:

$$A_1 := \begin{array}{c} \quad\; 1\; 2\; 3 \quad 4 \\ \hline u' \to \text{A C G - U} \\ v' \to \text{A - G A U} \\ \hline \quad\; 1 \quad 2\; 3\; 4 \end{array} \qquad A_2 := \begin{array}{c} 1\; 2\; 3\; 4 \\ \hline \text{A C G U} \\ \text{A G A U} \\ \hline 1\; 2\; 3\; 4 \end{array} \qquad A_3 :=$$

$$\begin{array}{c} 1\; 2\; 3\; 4 \\ \hline \text{A C G U - - - -} \\ \text{- - - - A G A U} \\ \hline \quad\quad\quad\; 1\; 2\; 3\; 4 \end{array}$$

Each of the alignments induces a set of *correspondences*, called *(mis)matches*, each involving a position in the two RNAs. For example, alignment A_1 above induces the set of matches $\{(1,1),(3,2),(4,4)\}$, alignment A_2 induces the matches $\{(1,1),(2,2),(3,3),(4,4)\}$ and A_3 has no matches ($\varnothing$).

Not all alignments are equally realistic, and evolutionary models can be inferred associate a probability with any alignment. Within the *maximal parsimony paradigm*, such probabilities are generally defined as the product of independent probabilities, associated with evolutionary events suggested by the alignment.

For instance, the match $(1,1)$ in A_1 suggests the presence of A in the (common) ancestral sequence, while the C in the second column could have been recently acquired by u (or lost by v). Finally, the matching of two distinct nucleotides, for example, in the second column of A_2, suggests a mutation following the speciation/duplication of the RNA being considered.

The probabilities of these events can be estimated, and the probability of an alignment is obtained by multiplying the probabilities of the events implied by the columns of the alignment:

$$\mathbb{P}(A \mid u, v) = \prod_{\substack{\left[\begin{smallmatrix} x \\ y \end{smallmatrix}\right] \in A}} \mathbf{P}\mu_{x,y} \prod_{\substack{\left[\begin{smallmatrix} x \\ - \end{smallmatrix}\right] \in A}} \mathbf{P}\iota_x \prod_{\substack{\left[\begin{smallmatrix} - \\ y \end{smallmatrix}\right] \in A}} \mathbf{P}\delta_y$$

where $\mathbf{P}\mu_{x,y}$ represents the probability of a conservation/match $(x = y)$ or substitution/mismatch $(x \neq y)$. Meanwhile, $\mathbf{P}\iota_x$ (respectively $\mathbf{P}\delta_y$) represents the probability of an insertion into u (respectively v).

A joint alignment/folding (A, S) then simply adds a secondary structure S on top of an alignment $A = (u', v')$, with each base pair implicitly pairing nucleotides in the alignment columns. For any pair of bases (i, j) in S, at either (u'_i, u'_j) or (v'_i, v'_j) (or both) may form a base pair. In the case where both sequences can form the base pair, it is possible to reward or penalize an apparent co-evolution of the two positions. On the contrary, if only one of the sequences allows pairing, then its presence in a shared structure becomes less likely.

To capture this aspect, we note $S \rightsquigarrow (U, V)$, where U and V are the restrictions of S_A, induced by u and v, respectively, obtained by removing the indels ($-$) and the base pairs involving at least one indel. The probability for an alignment A, in conjunction with a common structure S for its two sequences, can then be (somewhat arbitrarily) defined as

$$\mathbb{P}(A, S \mid u, v) \propto \mathbb{P}(A \mid u, v)\,\mathbb{P}(U \mid u)\,\mathbb{P}(V \mid v) \prod_{(a,b) \in S} \mathbf{P}\pi^{u'_a, u'_b}_{v'_a, v'_b} \quad [6.3]$$

where $\mathbb{P}(S^\star \mid \omega)$ is the Boltzmann probability of $S^\star$ for a sequence ω, and $\mathbf{P}\pi^{x_1, y_1}_{x_2, y_2}$ is the probability of a *substitution of base pairs*, involving nucleotides (x_1, y_1) in u and (x_2, y_2) in v. This allows us to reward *compensatory mutations*, defined here as:

Columns $\begin{bmatrix} x \\ y \end{bmatrix}$ and $\begin{bmatrix} a \\ b \end{bmatrix}$, $x \neq y, a \neq b$ such that (x, a) and (y, b) can be paired.

Such mutations are often interpreted as indicating a positive selection pressure towards the formation of base pairs, and have been used in comparative RNA modeling since the early days of RNA research (Michel and Westhof 1990).

This probability $\mathbb{P}(A, S \mid u, v)$ should be maximized, which is equivalent to maximizing the right-hand side of equation [6.3]. In practice, to avoid issues related to numerical precision, a logarithmic version of the objective function is considered. Since the logarithm is a monotonously increasing function, optimizing the logarithm of the objective function is equivalent to optimizing the objective function. Moreover, partition function-induced terms contribute a constant factor that is independent of the structure or alignment. They can therefore be ignored for optimization purposes. The objective function then becomes

$$F(A, S) = \sum_{\substack{\boxed{\begin{array}{c} x \\ y \end{array}} \in A}} \mu_{x,y} + \sum_{\substack{\boxed{\begin{array}{c} x \\ - \end{array}} \in A}} \iota_x + \sum_{\substack{\boxed{\begin{array}{c} - \\ y \end{array}} \in A}} \delta_y$$

$$- (E(U, u) + E(V, v)) + \sum_{(a,b) \in S} \pi_{v'_a, v'_b}^{u'_a, u'_b} \qquad [6.4]$$

where μ, ι, δ and π represent the respective natural logarithms, multiplied by RT, respectively, from $\mathbf{P}\mu$, $\mathbf{P}\iota$, $\mathbf{P}\delta$ and $\mathbf{P}\pi$.

Problem 6.3. Combined alignment/folding

Input: $u, v \in \{A, C, G, U\}^\star$; matrices ι, δ, μ and π.
Output: Alignment/structure pair $(A^\star, S^\star)$ having max probability with respect to [6.4]:

$$F(A^\star, S^\star) = \max_{A,S} F(A, S)$$

6.2.4.1. *Algorithm and complexity*

The above problem can also be solved using a polynomial dynamic programming algorithm. It relies on simulating all possible alignments during folding, as illustrated in Figure 6.5. A dynamic programming equation can be immediately derived to compute the maximal *logarithmic score* $f_{k,l}^{i,j}$ achievable on the region $[i, j]$ of u, and region $[k, l]$ of v.

Namely, for empty regions on u and/or v, we have:

$$f_{k,l<l}^{i,j<i} := 0 \qquad \text{// Regions of } u \text{ and } v \text{ both empty}$$

$$f_{k,l\geq k}^{i,j<i} := -m_{k,l}^v + \sum_{c \in v_{k,l}} \delta_c$$

// Empty region of $v \rightarrow$ The region of u is folded and inserted

$$f_{k,l<k}^{i,j\geq i} := -m_{i,j}^u + \sum_{c \in u_{i,j}} \iota_c$$

// Empty region of $u \rightarrow$ The region of v is folded and deleted where $m^{\omega}_{i,j}$ represents the minimum energy of a folding of ω over the $[i,j]$ region, computed as seen in section 6.2.1. In addition to the energies induced by the independent foldings, the optimal scores must take into account the full insertion/deletion of the non-empty region, hence the above sums.

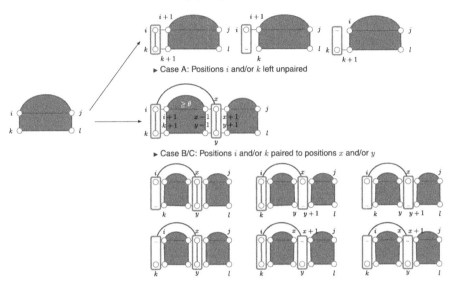

▶ Case A: Positions i and/or k left unpaired

▶ Case B/C: Positions i and/or k paired to positions x and/or y

Figure 6.5. *Decomposition of the combined alignment/folding space based on the Sankoff algorithm. For two RNA sequences restricted to regions $[i,j]$ and $[k,l]$, the decomposition distinguishes between leaving the first position unpaired, or pairing it to some other column*

In the general case, non-empty regions are considered in both u and v, and we have

$$
f^{i,j \geq i}_{k,l \geq k} := \max \begin{cases} \blacktriangleright \text{ Case A: Unpaired positions i and/or k} \\ \displaystyle\max_{b_i,b_k \in \{0,1\}^2} b_i\,\overline{b_k}\,\iota_{u_i} + \overline{b_i}\,b_k\,\delta_{v_k} + b_i\,b_k\,\mu_{u_i,v_k} + f^{i+b_i,j}_{k+b_k,l} \\ \blacktriangleright \text{ Case B/C: Pairings (i,x) and/or (k,y)} \\ \displaystyle\max_{\substack{\binom{x}{y}=\binom{i+\theta+1}{k+\theta+1}; \\ \binom{b_i,b_x}{b_k,b_y} \in [0,1]^4 \\ b_i b_x + b_k b_y \geq 1}}^{\binom{j}{l}} \begin{vmatrix} b_i\,\overline{b_k}\,\iota_{u_i} + \overline{b_i}\,b_k\,\delta_{v_k} + b_x\,\overline{b_y}\,\iota_{u_x} + \overline{b_x}\,b_y\,\delta_{v_y} \\ + b_i\,b_k\,\mu_{u_i,v_k} + b_x\,b_y\,\mu_{u_x,v_y} \\ + b_i\,b_x\,b_k\,b_y\,\pi^{u_i,u_x}_{v_k,v_y} \\ + b_i\,b_x\,E^u_{i,x} + b_k\,b_y\,E^v_{k,y} \\ + f^{i+b_i,x-b_x}_{k+b_k,y-b_y} + f^{x+1,j}_{y+1,l} \end{vmatrix} \end{cases}
$$

$$[6.5]$$

where $\overline{b_p} := (1 - b_p)$ for any position p.

Each of the b_p reflects the implication ($b_p = 1$) or not ($b_p = 0$) of a position p in a column of the generated alignment. Such Boolean variables are used to factor the (otherwise numerous) cases in the decomposition, inferred by the enumeration of the alignments, only incorporating relevant terms in each case.

For example, consider the term $b_i\, b_k\, \mu_{u_i,v_k}$. If the positions i and k are both aligned ($b_i = b_k = 1$), we then have $b_i\, b_k\, \mu_{u_i,v_k} = \mu_{u_i,v_k}$, corresponding to the conservation/substitution term expected for a match of i and k. On the other hand, if one of the two positions remains unaligned ($b_i = 0$ or $b_k = 0$), then we have $b_i\, b_k\, \mu_{u_i,v_k} = 0$, and the score does not include any contribution from the match.

Similarly, we have:

$b_p\, \overline{b_q}\, \iota_{u_p} \rightarrow$ Insertion score only if p without partner ($\overline{q}$);

$\overline{b_p}\, b_q\, \delta_{u_q} \rightarrow$ Deletion score only if q without partner ($\overline{p}$);

$b_p\, b_q\, b_r\, b_s\, \pi_{v_r,v_s}^{u_p,u_q} \rightarrow$ Base pair substitution score only if the four positions involved are pairwise aligned;

$b_p\, b_q\, E_{p,q}^{\omega} \rightarrow$ Energy of the base pair only if the pair is populated.

A variant of the Sankoff algorithm then computes the terms of this recurrence using dynamic programming. In its outermost loop, it processes (pairs of) regions by the increasing order of their *cumulative size* $N(i,j,k,l)$, defined such that:

$$N(i,j,k,l) = |[i,j]| + |[k,l]| = j - i + k - l + 2$$

and in any order for the other indices/loops. A backtracking then completes the algorithm, and reconstructs the optimal folding/alignment.

Each run of this algorithm requires a $\Theta(n^6)$ time for two sequences u and v of equal length n, and $\Theta(n^4)$ in memory. More precisely, the time complexity of this algorithm is $\Theta(|u|^3 \cdot |v|^3)$, and its memory complexity is $\Theta(|u|^2 \cdot |v|^2)$. The decomposition underlying the Sankoff algorithm can also be generalized to M sequences, but the time complexity then increases to $\Theta(n^{3M})$, while the memory requirement scales to $\Theta(n^{2M})$.

6.2.4.2. *Going further*

The principle behind the Sankoff algorithm is at the core of virtually every approach for comparative prediction. The quality of its predictions is far superior to those obtained using energy minimization and (as of 2022) machine learning. However, its high complexity, especially in terms of memory, prevents its direct use for RNAs longer than ~ 100 nucleotides. Consequently, various computational tricks and heuristics can be found in modern implementations to support multiple (long) sequences without substantially sacrificing the predictive capability (see SPARSE (Will et al. 2015), currently at the state of the art despite its modest $\Theta(n^2)$ complexity).

The alignment model can be extended in a number of directions:

– First of all, the Sankoff algorithm can be extended to the full nearest-neighbor energy model introduced by Turner and Mathews (2010). It can also support more complex evolutionary models, for example, taking a phylogenetic tree as input, in order to consider evolutionary distances and speciation events while interpreting a compensatory mutation.

– The cost associated with a sequence of g consecutive indels can be defined as an affine function $\alpha \times g + \beta$, instead of an implicit $\alpha' \times g$ in our model. The new objective function can be optimized using a variant of the Sankoff algorithm having the same complexity (up to constants) owing to a generic technique devised by Gotoh (1982). A similar trick can be used to remove the ambiguity induced by the alignment (essentially due to the commutativity of the indels), unlocking the door to alignment under the assumption of preservation of the Boltzmann ensemble (Will et al. 2012).

6.3. Analyzing the Boltzmann ensemble

6.3.1. *Computing the partition function*

As seen in section 6.2.2, suboptimal structures can be produced, and provide a sense of the diversity of almost-optimal structures. However, while they may be useful in modeling to suggest alternative structures, it is impossible to judge whether or not suboptimals accurately reflect the full diversity explored by the folding process. Indeed, at the thermodynamic equilibrium, the MFE structure is typically associated with a probability which, despite being maximal by definition, remains abysmally small. Moreover, suboptimal structures produced by the algorithm for a given tolerance Δ may be extremely similar without being fully representative of the Boltzmann ensemble. It follows that, for a given tolerance, the list of suboptimals is typically biased towards the MFE and its trivial variations. It may overlook the existence of alternative conformations, represented by a large number of similar structures whose accumulated probability may exceed the MFE (+ variations) probability.

Let us formalize the notion of being representative of the folding space, also called the *Boltzmann ensemble*, using concepts from statistical mechanics. To this end, remember that at the thermodynamic equilibrium, the set of all possible structures $S \in \mathcal{S}_\omega$ for an RNA ω is expected to follow a *Boltzmann distribution*:

$$\mathbb{P}(S \mid \omega) = \frac{e^{-\frac{E(S)}{RT}}}{\mathcal{Z}} \tag{6.6}$$

where T is the temperature (K), R is the Boltzmann constant (1.987×10^{-3} kcal.mol^{-1}.K^{-1}) and $\mathcal{Z}$ is the *partition function*, defined as

$$\mathcal{Z} = \sum_{S \in \mathcal{S}} e^{-E(S)/RT}. \tag{6.7}$$

The partition function is essential to adopt a statistical perspective over the Boltzmann ensemble. For example, the probability of the MFE structure, giving us an idea of its prevalence, is given by $e^{-m_{1,n}/RT}/\mathcal{Z}$. More generally, computing the partition function is an essential prerequisite to sample the ensemble, as shown in section 6.3.2, or to accurately compute average ensemble properties, as described in section 6.3.3.

In practice, we must not only compute $\mathcal{Z}$, but also $\mathcal{Z}_{i,j}$, the partition function restricted to the set $\mathcal{S}_{i,j}$ of structures adopted on a region $[i,j]$. Note that $\mathcal{Z} := \mathcal{Z}_{1,n}$, so these (partial) partition functions can be used to find the global partition function of the system. Computation for all regions $[i,j]$ therefore represents a potentially complex, weighted counting problem defined as follows.

Problem 6.4. Computation of the partition function $\mathcal{Z}$

Input: Sequence $\omega \in \{A, C, G, U\}^+$, $|\omega| = n$.
Output: Partition function $\mathcal{Z}_{i,j}$ for any region $[i,j]$, defined as

$$\mathcal{Z}_{i,j} = \sum_{S \in \mathcal{S}_{i,j}} e^{-E(S)/RT}$$

While the number of terms in the sum grows exponentially with the sequence length n, it is in fact possible to compute $\mathcal{Z}$ very efficiently, in time only polynomial in n, as done by Algorithm 6.4.

ALGORITHM 6.4. Computation of the partition function $\mathcal{Z}$

Input : ω	– RNA of size n
Output : $\mathcal{Z}$	– Partition function Z

1 **Function** `PartitionFunction`(ω):
2      $\mathcal{Z} \leftarrow$ `EmptyMatrix`($n \times n$)
       // Initialize to 1 all the values of the diagonal up to θ
3   **for** $i \leftarrow 1$ **to** n **do**
4   **for** $j \leftarrow i$ **to** $\min(i + \theta, n)$ **do**
5              $\mathcal{Z}_{i,j} \leftarrow 1$
6   **for** $i \leftarrow n$ **to** 1 **do**
7   **for** $j \leftarrow i + \theta + 1$ **to** n **do**
             ▶ Case A: position i left without partner
8              $\mathcal{Z}_{i,j} \leftarrow \mathcal{Z}_{i+1,j}$
             ▶ Case B: positions i and j form a base pair
9              $\mathcal{Z}_{i,j} \leftarrow \mathcal{Z}_{i,j} + \mathcal{Z}_{i+1,j-1} \times e^{-E_{i,j}^{\omega}/RT}$
             ▶ Case C: position i paired to $k < j$
10   **for** $k \leftarrow i + \theta + 1$ **to** $j - 1$ **do**
11                  $\mathcal{Z}_{i,j} \leftarrow \mathcal{Z}_{i,j} + \mathcal{Z}_{i+1,k-1} \times \mathcal{Z}_{k+1,j} \times e^{-E_{i,k}^{\omega}/RT}$
12   **return** $\mathcal{Z}$

In fact, we already introduced a correct polynomial algorithm for the problem in section 6.2.1, up to a simple change of algebra! Indeed, our implementation of `FillMatrix` in Algorithm 6.1 can be slightly modified to calculate $\mathcal{Z}_{i,j}$ instead of $m_{i,j}$. Towards that, we simply have to replace sums by products, minimizations by sums and transform constant energy terms into their Boltzmann factor:

$$\min \rightarrow + \qquad\qquad + \rightarrow \times \qquad\qquad E \rightarrow e^{-E/RT}$$

We finally obtain Algorithm 6.4, which computes the partition functions $\mathcal{Z}_{i,j}$.

6.3.1.1. *Correctness of the algorithms*

Let us start with a purely technical observation, which will represent the basis of our proof by induction. Precisely, let $E(S) = E_1 + \cdots + E_l$ be the energy of a structure S, which can be decomposed into l terms; we then have

$$\prod_{i=1}^{l} e^{-E_i/RT} = e^{-\sum_{i=1}^{l} E_i/RT} = e^{-E(S)/RT} \qquad [6.8]$$

Equipped with this property, we can now establish the correction of the matrix filling procedure.

PROPOSITION 6.4.– *Algorithm 6.4 correctly computes the partition function of ω for each region.*

PROOF.– We proceed by *induction on the length of the region* $[i, j]$, and prove that the value computed in $Z_{i,j}$ coincides with the partition function restricted to the subsequence $\omega_{i,j}$. In the *base case*, when $i - j \leq \theta$, there is only one possible structure, with no base pair and therefore zero energy, whose Boltzmann factor is $e^{-0/RT} = 1$. Now, the initialization assigns the value 1 to $Z_{i,j}$ for any region of length at most $\theta + 1$, and we thus get the expected result.

We now assume the validity of the proposition for any region $[i', j']$ of length $j' - i' + 1 < n^\star$, meaning that the value $Z_{i',j'}$ coincides well with the partition function restricted to $\omega_{i',j'}$. Now, if we consider a region $[i, j]$ of length $n^\star$, while computing $Z_{i,j}$, we have three possible cases:

Case A: Position i left without a partner. Since $j - i + 1 < n^\star$, the induction assumption applies and, in conjunction with the lack of energy contribution from the unmatched positions, implies that:

$$Z_{i+1,j} = \sum_{S' \in \mathcal{S}_{i+1,j}} e^{\frac{-E(S')}{RT}} = \sum_{S' \in \mathcal{S}_{i+1,j}} e^{\frac{-E(\bullet S')}{RT}} = \sum_{S \in \bullet \mathcal{S}_{i+1,j}} e^{\frac{-E(S)}{RT}}.$$

In other words, $Z_{i+1,j}$ coincides with the partition function on $[i, j]$, restricted to structures letting i free. We will denote this restriction by $Z_{\bullet S}$ in the following.

Case B: Positions i paired with j. The induction hypothesis applies to $[i + 1, j - 1]$. Noting that the pair (i, j) provides an energy $E_{i,j}^\omega$, we get:

$$e^{\frac{-E_{i,j}^\omega}{RT}} \times Z_{i+1,j-1} = e^{\frac{-E_{i,j}^\omega}{RT}} \sum_{S' \in \mathcal{S}_{i+1,j-1}} e^{\frac{-E(S')}{RT}} = \sum_{S' \in \mathcal{S}_{i+1,j-1}} e^{\frac{-(E_{i,j}^\omega + E(S'))}{RT}}$$

$$= \sum_{S' \in \mathcal{S}_{i+1,j-1}} e^{\frac{-E((S'))}{RT}} = \sum_{S \in (S_{i+1,j-1})} e^{\frac{-E(S)}{RT}} \qquad [6.9]$$

The computation proposed in the algorithm thus captures all the structures pairing i to j, whose partition function is denoted by $\mathcal{Z}_{(S)}$.

Case C: Position i paired to $k < j$. In this case, the algorithm adds to the partition function a quantity $\sum_{i+\theta+1}^{j-1} e^{-E_{i,j}^\omega/RT} \mathcal{Z}_{i+1,k-1} \mathcal{Z}_{k+1,j}$ with correct contributions as follows from the induction hypothesis. We thus obtain:

$$e^{-\frac{E_{i,k}^\omega}{RT}} \mathcal{Z}_{i+1,k-1} \mathcal{Z}_{k+1,j} = e^{-\frac{E_{i,k}^\omega}{RT}} \sum_{S_1 \in \mathcal{S}_{i+1,k-1}} e^{-\frac{E(S_1)}{RT}} \sum_{S_2 \in \mathcal{S}_{k+1,j}} e^{-\frac{E(S_2)}{RT}}$$

$$= \sum_{S_1 \in \mathcal{S}_{i+1,k-1}} \sum_{S_2 \in \mathcal{S}_{k+1,j}} e^{-\frac{E_{i,k}^\omega + E(S_1) + E(S_2)}{RT}} = \sum_{S \in (\mathcal{S}_{i+1,k-1})\mathcal{S}_{k+1,j}} e^{-\frac{E(S)}{RT}}.$$

The term of the sum coincides with the definition of the partition function restricted to the structures pairing i to k, for a given value of k. By summing over all the values of k on $[i + \theta + 1, j - 1]$, we obtain the partition function $\mathcal{Z}_{(S_1)S_2}$ of all the structures pairing i to any position other than j.

It is easy to see that the decomposition is unambiguous, that is, the various cases cover pairwise disjoint sets of structures. Moreover, any structure over a region $[i, j]$ falls into one of these three categories. We conclude that:

$$\mathcal{Z}_{\bullet S} + \mathcal{Z}_{(S)} + \mathcal{Z}_{(S_1)S_2} = \sum_{\substack{S \in \bullet \mathcal{S}_{i+1,j} \cup (\mathcal{S}_{i+1,j-1}) \\ \cup (\mathcal{S}_{i+1,k-1})\mathcal{S}_{k+1,j}}} e^{-\frac{E(S)}{RT}} = \sum_{S \in \mathcal{S}_{i,j}} e^{-\frac{E(S)}{RT}}.$$

$$[6.10]$$

The validity of the computed partition function on any region of length $n < n^\star$ implies the correctness on regions of size $n^\star$, allowing us to conclude the induction.   □

The differences between Algorithms 6.1 and 6.4 lead to constant time/memory overheads: elementary energy terms are $e^{-E/RT}$ instead of E, while sums and products replace the minima and sums, all computable in constant time. We thus obtain an algorithm running in overall $\Theta(n^3)$ time and $\Theta(n^2)$ space complexity.

6.3.1.2. *Going further*

The change of algebra $(\min, +, E) \rightarrow (+, \times, e^{-E/RT})$ can, in principle, be adapted to any combinatorial problem solvable using dynamic programming.

However, in order for the modified algorithm to compute the true partition function, we must ensure that the underlying decomposition is complete – that it captures all the elements of the search space – and unambiguous – that it produces each element in a single way.

The number of secondary structures compatible with an RNA ω can also be easily obtained through a computation of a partition function. Indeed, assigning a very large value to the temperature T, we obtain

$$\mathcal{Z} := \mathcal{Z}_{1,n} = \sum_{s \in \mathcal{S}} e^{-E(S)/RT} \xrightarrow[T \to +\infty]{} \sum_{s \in \mathcal{S}} e^0 = \sum_{s \in \mathcal{S}} 1 = |\mathcal{S}|.$$

6.3.2. *Statistical sampling*

The partition function is an essential quantity to derive the statistical properties of the folding space. However, it essentially only gives access to the individual probabilities of the structures. Meanwhile, there is a large number of structures, growing exponentially with the sequence size n, all associated with probabilities that are exponentially small. Computing the statistical properties in a deterministic fashion, by going through the list of all structures while accounting for their individual probabilities, would then require exponential time.

To overcome this issue, while still granting access to statistics of the Boltzmann ensemble for a specific RNA, Ding and Lawrence (2003) introduce a *random generation algorithm*, also called *stochastic sampling*. The idea is to modify the backtracking step in order to produce a random structure, generated according to the *Boltzmann distribution*

$$\mathbb{P}(S \mid \omega) = \frac{e^{-E(S)/RT}}{\mathcal{Z}}$$

where $\mathcal{Z} = e^{-E(S)/RT}$ is the partition function, calculated as shown in section 6.3.1.

Problem 6.5. Sampling structures

Input: Sequence $\omega \in \{A, C, G, U\}^+$, $|\omega| = n$.
Output: Structure S with probability

$$\mathbb{P}(S) = \frac{p_S}{\mathcal{Z}} = \frac{e^{-E(S)/RT}}{\mathcal{Z}}$$

The *stochastic backtracking*, implemented as Algorithm 6.2, can be used to solve the problem in a simple energy model.

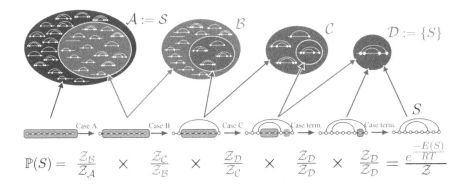

$$\mathbb{P}(S) = \frac{\mathcal{Z}_{\mathcal{B}}}{\mathcal{Z}_{\mathcal{A}}} \times \frac{\mathcal{Z}_{\mathcal{C}}}{\mathcal{Z}_{\mathcal{B}}} \times \frac{\mathcal{Z}_{\mathcal{D}}}{\mathcal{Z}_{\mathcal{C}}} \times \frac{\mathcal{Z}_{\mathcal{D}}}{\mathcal{Z}_{\mathcal{D}}} \times \frac{\mathcal{Z}_{\mathcal{D}}}{\mathcal{Z}_{\mathcal{D}}} = \frac{e^{\frac{-E(S)}{RT}}}{\mathcal{Z}}$$

Figure 6.6. *Principle of random generation using the recursive method. At each step, a decomposition case is chosen with probability proportional to its contribution in the partition function. The probability of generating a given structure S then equals the probability product over the chosen cases, and the consecutive numerators/denominators cancel out, leading S to be generated with Boltzmann probability. For a color version of this figure, see www.iste.co.uk/chateau/graphs.zip*

Its principle, illustrated by Figure 6.6, relies on a random choice, at each step of the generation, of a decomposition case with probability proportional to its contribution to the partition function. Namely, let us consider a region $[i, j]$ giving access to a set $\mathcal{S}_{i,j}$ of structures, and assume that each decomposition case gives access to a subset $\mathcal{S}' \subseteq \mathcal{S}_{i,j}$, associated with a partition function $\mathcal{Z}_{\mathcal{S}'} := \sum_{S \in \mathcal{S}'} e^{-E(S)/RT}$. Such a case will be chosen, a backtracked upon, with probability:

$$p_{\mathcal{S}'} = \frac{\mathcal{Z}_{\mathcal{S}'}}{\mathcal{Z}_{i,j}}$$

If a valid Boltzmann generator for $\mathcal{S}'$ is available and called, the probability of emitting a given structure $S' \in \mathcal{S}'$ for $[i, j]$ then becomes

$$\mathbb{P}(S' \mid [i, j]) = p_{\mathcal{S}'} \times \mathbb{P}(S' \mid \mathcal{S}') = \frac{\mathcal{Z}_{\mathcal{S}'}}{\mathcal{Z}_{i,j}} \times \frac{e^{-E(S')/RT}}{\mathcal{Z}_{\mathcal{S}'}} = \frac{e^{-E(S')/RT}}{\mathcal{Z}_{i,j}}$$

where we recognize the targeted probability when called for the full sequence ω with $[i, j] = [1, n]$.

6.3.2.1. *Correctness of the algorithm*

PROPOSITION 6.5.– *Let $\mathcal{Z}_{i,j}$ be the partition function of an RNA ω restricted to $[i,j]$. Then, a call to* RandomStruct$(i,j,\omega,\mathcal{Z})$ *returns some $S^\star \in \mathcal{S}_{i,j}$ with probability:*

$$\mathbb{P}(S^\star) = \frac{e^{-E(S^\star)/RT}}{\mathcal{Z}_{i,j}}$$

PROOF.– We proceed by *induction on the length of the regions* $[i,j]$. In the *base case*, when $i - j \le \theta$, there is only one possible structure $S^\star$, the empty structure. It is returned with probability 1 as described at line 2.

Let us now assume that the property holds for any region $[i,j]$ such that $j - i + 1 \le n - 1$. As we have seen for the computation of the partition function, we have:

$$\overbrace{\mathcal{Z}_{i,j}}^{S} = \overbrace{\mathcal{Z}_{i+1,j}}^{\bullet S_{i+1,j}} + \overbrace{E^{\omega}_{i,j} \times \mathcal{Z}_{i+1,j-1}}^{(S_{i+1,j-1})} + \sum_{k=i+\theta+1}^{j-1} \overbrace{E^{\omega}_{i,k} \times \mathcal{Z}_{i+1,k-1} \times \mathcal{Z}_{k+1,j}}^{(S_{i+1,k-1})S_{k+1,j}}.$$

$$[6.11]$$

Each term of the sum represents the contribution of a subset of possible structures for $S^\star$, associated with one of the decomposition cases. The random number a generated by Algorithm 6.5 is used to identify the decomposition case, so that each ends up being chosen with a probability proportional to its contribution.

Consider a structure $S^\star$ generated by the algorithm over a region $j-i+1 \le n$. There are three possible cases:

Case A: Position i without partner in $S^\star$. We have $S^\star = \bullet S'$, where S' is generated over $[i+1,j]$ with Boltzmann probability as per the induction hypothesis, and such that $E(S^\star) = E(S')$. Moreover, the probability of choosing this case is $\mathbb{P}(a \le \mathcal{Z}_{i+1,j}) = \mathcal{Z}_{i+1,j}/\mathcal{Z}_{i,j}$. The emission probability of generating $S^\star$ is therefore:

$$\mathbb{P}(S^\star) = \frac{\mathcal{Z}_{i+1,j}}{\mathcal{Z}_{i,j}} \cdot \mathbb{P}(S') = \frac{\mathcal{Z}_{i+1,j}}{\mathcal{Z}_{i,j}} \cdot \frac{e^{\frac{-E(S')}{RT}}}{\mathcal{Z}_{i+1,j}} = \frac{e^{\frac{-E(S')}{RT}}}{\mathcal{Z}_{i,j}} = \frac{e^{\frac{-E(S^\star)}{RT}}}{\mathcal{Z}_{i,j}}.$$

ALGORITHM 6.5. Generates a structure S with probability $e^{-E(S)/RT}/\mathcal{Z}$

Input	: $[i, j]$ – Region being considered
	$\mathcal{Z}$ – Partition function for each region, computed by Algorithm 6.4
	ω – RNA of size n
Output	: S – Random Boltzmann-distributed structure compatible with ω over $[i, j]$

1 **Function** RandomStruct$(i, j, \mathcal{Z}, \omega)$:

2   **if** $j - i \leq \theta$ **then return** $\overbrace{\bullet \ldots \bullet}^{j-i+1}$ // Empty structure is unique $\rightarrow$ Probability 1

3   **else**

4          $a \leftarrow$ random$(0, \mathcal{Z}_{i,j})$ // Random number, uniform drawn in $[0, \mathcal{Z}_{i,j}[$

         ▶ Case A: position i left without partner

5          $a \leftarrow a - \mathcal{Z}_{i+1,j}$ // Subtracting part. func. of all structures leaving i unpaired

6   **if** $a < 0$ **then**   // True when $a \in [0, \mathcal{Z}_{i+1,j}[\rightarrow$ Probability $\mathcal{Z}_{i+1,j}/\mathcal{Z}_{i,j}$

7             $S_i^\star \leftarrow$ RandomStruct $(i+1, j, \mathcal{Z}, \omega)$

8   **return** $\bullet\, S_i^\star$

         ▶ Case B: positions i and j form a base pair

9          $a \leftarrow a - \mathcal{Z}_{i+1,j-1} \times e^{-E_{i,j}^\omega/RT}$ // Subtracting part. func. of all structures pairing i to j

10   **if** $a < 0$ **then**   // True with prob. $\mathcal{Z}_{i+1,j} \times e^{-E_{i,j}^\omega/RT}/\mathcal{Z}_{i,j}$

11             $S_{i,j}^\star \leftarrow$ RandomStruct $(i+1, j-1, \mathcal{Z}, \omega)$

12   **return** $(\, S_{i,j}^\star)$

         ▶ Case C: position i paired to $k < j$

13   **for** $k \leftarrow i + \theta + 1$ **to** $j - 1$ **do**

14             $a \leftarrow a - \mathcal{Z}_{i+1,k-1} \times \mathcal{Z}_{k+1,j} \times e^{-E_{i,k}^\omega/RT}$ // Sub. part. fun. pairing i to $k < j$

15   **if** $a < 0$ **then**   // True with prob. $(\mathcal{Z}_{i+1,k-1} \times \mathcal{Z}_{k+1,j} \times e^{-E_{i,k}^\omega/RT})/\mathcal{Z}_{i,j}$

16                $S_1^\star \leftarrow$ RandomStruct $(i+1, k-1, \mathcal{Z}, \omega)$

17                $S_2^\star \leftarrow$ RandomStruct $(k+1, j, \mathcal{Z}, \omega)$

18   **return** $(\, S_1^\star)\, S_2^\star$

Case B: Positions i and j paired in $S^\star$. We have $S^\star = (S')$, where S' is generated over $[i+1, j-1]$ such that $E(S^\star) = E(S') + E_{i,k}^\omega$. The probability of choosing a such that it identifies this case is $\mathcal{Z}_{i+1,j-1} \times e^{-E_{i,j}^\omega/RT}/\mathcal{Z}_{i,j}$. The likelihood of generating $S^\star$ is therefore:

$$\mathbb{P}(S^\star) = \frac{\mathcal{Z}_{i+1,j-1} \times e^{\frac{-E_{i,j}^\omega}{RT}}}{\mathcal{Z}_{i,j}} \times \frac{e^{\frac{-E(S')}{RT}}}{\mathcal{Z}_{i+1,j-1}} = \frac{e^{\frac{E(S') + E_{i,j}^\omega}{RT}}}{\mathcal{Z}_{i,j}} = \frac{e^{\frac{-E(S^\star)}{RT}}}{\mathcal{Z}_{i,j}}.$$

Case C: Position i paired to $k < j$ in $S^\star$. In the last case, we have $S^\star = (S_1)S_2$, where S_1 and S_2 are generated over regions $[i+1, k-1]$ and

$[k+1, j]$, respectively, and $E(S^\star) = E^\omega_{i,k} + E(S_1) + E(S_2)$. The probability of choosing this case is then

$$\frac{\mathcal{Z}_{i+1,k-1} \times \mathcal{Z}_{k+1,j} \times e^{-E^\omega_{i,k}/RT}}{\mathcal{Z}_{i,j}}$$

and it follows that the probability of generating $S^\star$ is

$$\mathbb{P}(S^\star) = \frac{\mathcal{Z}_{i+1,k-1} \mathcal{Z}_{k+1,j} e^{\frac{-E^\omega_{i,k}}{RT}}}{\mathcal{Z}_{i,j}} \frac{e^{\frac{-E(S_1)}{RT}} e^{\frac{-E(S_2)}{RT}}}{\mathcal{Z}_{i+1,k-1} \mathcal{Z}_{k+1,j}}$$

$$= \frac{e^{-\frac{E^\omega_{i,k}+E(S_1)+E(S_2)}{RT}}}{\mathcal{Z}_{i,j}} = \frac{e^{-E(S^\star)/RT}}{\mathcal{Z}_{i,j}}.$$

As these three cases cover exhaustively and uniquely all the structures, the function `RandomStruct`$(i, j, \mathcal{Z}, \omega,)$ thus returns $S^\star \in \mathcal{S}_{i,j}$ with the expected probability. □

6.3.2.2. *Complexity*

Assuming that a random uniform number can be generated in constant time, the complexity of the `RandomStruct` algorithm is $\Theta(n^2)$, with a worst case similar to the one analyzed in section 6.2.1. It is thus possible to generate a sample of M structures in $\Theta(M.n^2)$ time after a preprocessing in $\Theta(n^3)$ time and $\Theta(n^2)$ space.

6.3.2.3. *Going further*

From a representative sample of structures, it is possible to estimate the statistical properties of a folding. For instance, to study how structured an RNA is, we can use the expected number of base pairs as a proxy, estimated from a random sample of structures $S_1, S_2, ..., S_M$ through a basic estimator:

$$\mathbb{E}(\#\mathrm{Pairs}(S)) = \frac{\sum_{i=1}^{M} \#\mathrm{Pairs}(S_i)}{M}$$

Sampling can also be combined with unsupervised machine learning (*clustering* algorithm), based on a notion of base pair distance, to identify dominant conformation(s) within the Boltzmann ensemble (Ding et al. 2005).

The average complexity of the algorithm is $\Theta(n\sqrt{n})$ (Ponty 2008). It can be significantly improved by simply changing the examination order of the k values in case C. For this, the original loop order

$$k := i + \theta + 1 \rightarrow i + \theta + 2 \rightsquigarrow \ldots \rightarrow j - 2 \rightarrow j - 1$$

can simply be replaced by a Boustrophedon order, converging from the extremities of the interval towards its center

$$k := i + \theta + 1 \rightarrow j - 1 \rightarrow i + \theta + 2 \rightarrow j - 2 \rightarrow \ldots$$

A highly technical analysis of the worst-case complexity allows us to conclude that the worst-case execution time then becomes $\mathcal{O}(n \log n)$ (Ponty 2008).

6.3.3. *Boltzmann probability of structural patterns*

Statistical sampling enables the estimation of statistical properties at thermodynamic equilibrium, while offering (probabilistic) guarantees regarding their accuracy, for instance, in the form of confidence intervals. It thus makes it possible, by generating enough structures, to satisfactorily address this question: *What is the average energy of a folding at thermodynamic equilibrium?*

However, confidence intervals, based on the law of large numbers, only allow us to control the absolute error. Sampling encounters issues, or becomes very costly when the objective is to estimate quantities having smaller or very diverse values. In particular, it does not provide a very satisfactory solution to this question: *What are the Boltzmann probabilities of all base pairs (i, j)?* More generally, it provides only, possibly noisy, probabilistic estimates for computing the probability of complex structural patterns at the thermodynamic equilibrium.

A major contribution of the seminal paper by McCaskill (1990) resides in an efficient computation of the *exact Boltzmann probability of a structural pattern* m:

$$\mathbb{P}(m \in S) := \sum_{\substack{S \in \mathcal{S} \\ \text{such that } m \in S}} \mathbb{P}(S \mid w) = \sum_{\substack{S \in \mathcal{S} \\ \text{such that } m \in S}} \frac{e^{-E(S)/RT}}{\mathcal{Z}} = \frac{\mathcal{Z}_m}{\mathcal{Z}}$$

where $\mathcal{Z}$ is the partition function and $\mathcal{Z}_m := \sum_{S \in \mathcal{S};m \in S} e^{-E(S)/RT}$ is the partition function restricted to structures featuring the motif m. Since $\mathcal{Z}$ is computable in $\Theta(n^3)$ time, as seen in section 6.3.1, the main remaining difficulty resides in computing $\mathcal{Z}_m$.

The algorithm proposed by McCaskill adapts the approach of the *Inside–Outside* algorithm (Lari and Young 1990), initially proposed in the context of automatic language processing. It is based on a non-ambiguous decomposition, illustrated in Figure 6.7, of all S structures containing $m \in S$ into:

– a decomposition-induced *production* P, applicable to a region $[i, j]$, creating an instance of the pattern m, and followed by one or more substructure(s) over region(s) $[i_1, j_1], [i_2, j_2] \ldots$;

– an *(inside) structure* S_r for each region $[i_r, j_r]$ produced by P;

– an *outside structure* S_E, defined over $[1, n]$ while leaving a *hole* in $[i, j]$.

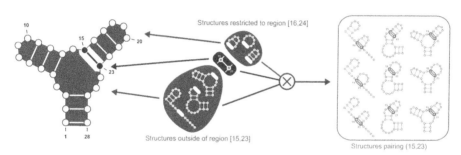

Figure 6.7. *Decomposition of structures featuring a structural pattern, here the base pair $(15, 23)$. Any structure featuring $(15, 23)$ contains an outside part (red) and an inside part (blue), both of which independently contribute to the stability. The set of structures containing the pair can be obtained as a Cartesian product of both, considering all combinations of inner and outer structures. For a color version of this figure, see www.iste.co.uk/chateau/graphs.zip*

PROPOSITION 6.6.– *Let $E(P)$ be the proper contribution of a production P to the free energy, and $\mathcal{Y}_{i,j}$ be the* outside partition function *with respect to the region $[i, j]$, such that*

$$\mathcal{Y}_{i,j} := \sum_{S_E \ external \ to \ [i,j]} e^{\frac{-E(S_E)}{RT}} \tag{6.12}$$

We then have

$$\mathcal{Z}_m = \sum_{\substack{P=([i,j]\rightarrow[i_1,j_1],\dots,[i_r,j_r]) \\ \text{such that } m \in P}} e^{\frac{-E(P)}{RT}} \mathcal{Y}_{i,j} \prod_r \mathcal{Z}_{i_r,j_r}. \tag{6.13}$$

PROOF.– Let us first note that, for any structure S featuring m, we have $E(S) = E(P) + E(S_E) + \sum_r E(S_r)$. Consider then the quantity

$$\Phi := \sum_{\substack{P=[i,j]\rightarrow[i_1,j_1],[i_2,j_2]\dots \\ \text{such that } m \in P}} e^{\frac{-E(P)}{RT}} \mathcal{Y}_{i,j} \prod_r \mathcal{Z}_{i_r,j_r}.$$

By replacing the partition functions by their respective definitions, we obtain

$$\Phi = \sum_{P;m\in P} e^{\frac{-E(P)}{RT}} \left(\sum_{\substack{S_E \text{ ext.} \\ \text{to } [i,j]}} e^{\frac{-E(S_E)}{RT}} \right) \prod_r \left(\sum_{\substack{S_r \\ \text{over } [i_r,j_r]}} e^{\frac{-E(S_r)}{RT}} \right)$$

$$= \sum_{P;m\in P} \sum_{S_E,S_1,S_2,\dots} e^{-\frac{E(P)+E(S_E)+\sum_r E(S_r)}{RT}} = \sum_{\substack{S\in\mathcal{S} \\ \text{such that } m\in S}} e^{-E(S)/RT} \equiv \mathcal{Z}_m.$$

$\square$

Remember that the (inside) partition functions $\mathcal{Z}_{i,j}$ can be computed in time $\Theta(n^3)$ (see section 6.3.1) simultaneously for all regions $[i,j]$. The only missing ingredient to compute $\mathcal{Z}_m$, and thus p_m, is the outside partition function $\mathcal{Y}$.

Problem 6.6. Outside partition function

Input: Sequence $\omega \in \{\text{A}, \text{C}, \text{G}, \text{U}\}^+$
Output: The *outside partition function* $\mathcal{Y}$ associated with each region $[i,j]$, defined as

$$\mathcal{Y}_{i,j} = \sum_{S_E \text{ outside } [i,j]} e^{-E(S_E)/RT}$$

Fortunately, $\mathcal{Y}$ follows a relatively simple formula, based on the decomposition described in Figure 6.8, which we establish by *inverting the rules* of the dynamic programming scheme. We then obtain, for $i > 1$:

$$
\mathcal{Y}_{i,j} = \sum
\begin{cases}
\mathcal{Y}_{i-1,j} & \blacktriangleright \text{Case } \overline{\text{A}}: \text{Pos. } i-1 \text{ is free} \\[2ex]
\text{// If } j < n \text{ and } j - i > \theta : & \blacktriangleright \text{Case } \overline{\text{B}}: \text{Pair } (i-1,j+1) \\
e^{\frac{-E^{\omega}_{i-1,j+1}}{RT}} \, \mathcal{Y}_{i-1,j-1} & \\[2ex]
\text{// If } j - i > \theta: & \blacktriangleright \text{Case } \overline{\text{C}}_{\text{G}}: \text{Pair } (i-1,j+1) \\
\displaystyle\sum_{k=j+2}^{n} e^{\frac{-E^{\omega}_{i-1,j+1}}{RT}} \, \mathcal{Y}_{i-1,k} \, \mathcal{Z}_{k+1,j} & \qquad\quad \text{in } [i-1, k > j] \\[2ex]
\displaystyle\sum_{h=1}^{i-\theta-2} e^{\frac{-E^{\omega}_{h,i-1}}{RT}} \, \mathcal{Y}_{h,j} \, \mathcal{Z}_{h+1,i-2} & \blacktriangleright \text{Case } \overline{\text{C}}_{\text{D}}: \text{Pair } (h,i-1) \\
& \qquad\quad \text{in } [h < i, j]
\end{cases}
$$

[6.14]

with $\mathcal{Y}_{1,n} := 1$ and $\mathcal{Y}_{1,j<n} := 0$. This equation can be computed for any interval using dynamic programming as described in Algorithm 6.6. The resulting algorithm has a time complexity in $\Theta(n^3)$ and a memory complexity in $\Theta(n^2)$.

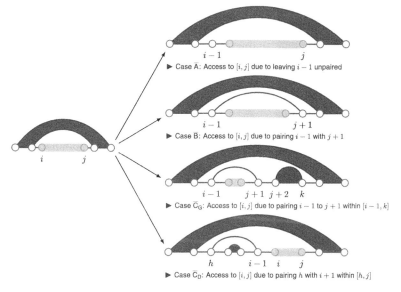

Figure 6.8. *Decomposition of structures outside a region $[i, j]$*

ALGORITHM 6.6. Outside partition function

Input : ω – RNA of size n
Output : $\mathcal{Z}$ – Matrix $\mathcal{Y}$, filled according to equation [6.14]

1 $\mathcal{Y} \leftarrow \texttt{EmptyMatrix}(n \times n)$
   // Initialize to 0 all the values of the diagonal up to θ
2 **for** $j \leftarrow 1$ **to** $n - 1$ **do** $\mathcal{Y}_{1,j} \leftarrow 0$
3 $\mathcal{Y}_{1,n} \leftarrow 1$
4 **for** $i \leftarrow 2$ **to** n **do**
5   **for** $j \leftarrow i$ **to** n **do**
         ▶ Case $\overline{\text{A}}$: position i left without partner
6        $\mathcal{Y}_{i,j} \leftarrow \mathcal{Y}_{i-1,j}$
         ▶ Case $\overline{\text{B}}$: positions i and j form a base pair
7   **if** $j < n$ **and** $j - i > \theta + 2$ **then**
8          $\mathcal{Y}_{i,j} \leftarrow \mathcal{Y}_{i,j} + e^{-E^{\omega}_{i-1,j+1}/RT} \times \mathcal{Y}_{i-1,j-1}$
         ▶ Case $\overline{\text{C}_{\text{G}}}$: position i paired to $k < j$
9   **if** $j < n$ **and** $j - i > \theta + 2$ **then**
10   **for** $k \leftarrow j + 2$ **to** n **do**
11           $\mathcal{Y}_{i,j} \leftarrow \mathcal{Y}_{i,j} + \mathcal{Y}_{i-1,k} \times e^{-E^{\omega}_{i-1,j+1}/RT} \times \mathcal{Z}_{k+1,j}$
         ▶ Case $\overline{\text{C}_{\text{D}}}$: position i paired to $k < j$
12   **for** $h \leftarrow 1$ **to** $i - \theta - 2$ **do**
13         $\mathcal{Y}_{i,j} \leftarrow \mathcal{Y}_{i,j} + \mathcal{Y}_{h,j} \times e^{-E^{\omega}_{h,i-1}/RT} \times \mathcal{Z}_{h+1,i-2}$

14 **return** $\mathcal{Y}$

To calculate the Boltzmann probability of a pattern, the transitions producing a particular pattern thus remain to be enumerated. In practical terms, the probability of leaving a position i free is given by

$$\mathbb{P}(i \text{ free}) = \frac{\mathcal{Y}_{i,i} + \sum_{j=i+1}^{n} \mathcal{Y}_{i,j} \mathcal{Z}_{i+1,j}}{\mathcal{Z}_{1,n}}.$$

Similarly, the probability of forming a base pair (i, j) is obtained by

$$\mathbb{P}(\text{pair }(i,j)) = \frac{e^{\frac{-E^{\omega}_{i,j}}{RT}} \mathcal{Y}_{i,j} \mathcal{Z}_{i+1,j-1} + \sum_{k=j+1}^{n} e^{\frac{-E^{\omega}_{i,j}}{RT}} \mathcal{Y}_{i,k} \mathcal{Z}_{i+1,j-1} \mathcal{Z}_{j+1,k}}{\mathcal{Z}_{1,n}}.$$

Here, these probabilities can typically be computed simultaneously for all the possible positions of the pattern in $\mathcal{O}(n^3)$ time.

6.3.3.1. *Going further*

In order to take advantage of an efficient algorithm, here in $\mathcal{O}(n^3)$ time, the pattern must be identifiable in the dynamic programming scheme. In the Nussinov decomposition, this constraint limits the list of eligible patterns to base pairs and unpaired positions. However, different types of loops can also be considered by more complex decompositions, for instance, those capturing the Turner energy model as seen in section 6.4.1.

The framework described above considers patterns (base pairs, unpaired positions) that appear at most once in each structure. However, the same calculation can be exactly used for a pattern m' that possibly occurs several times in a given structure. The value returned by the algorithm then simply becomes the *expectation of the number of occurrences of m'* in the Boltzmann distribution.

6.4. Studying RNA structure in practice

6.4.1. *The Turner model*

The base-pair-based free-energy model used throughout this chapter may appear oversimplistic and indeed is! Base pairs are actually not the main determinants of free energy, but the latter is thought to be dominated by the contributions of structural "blocks" (Xia et al. 1998) called *loops*, namely the closed regions appearing in the graph drawing of the secondary structure (see Figure 6.9). In particular, the *stackings* of two directly nested base pairs $(i, j) \rightarrow (i + 1, j - 1)$ often represent the main contributors to the free energy. Energies associated with the different types and contents of the loops have been precisely calculated and extrapolated from the results of optical melting curve experiments (Turner and Mathews 2010).

Although more complex, this energy model preserves a notion of *independence* of local patterns in the structure. For this reason, it can be captured by a decomposition, illustrated in Figure 6.9, which retains the same properties (completeness, unambiguity, correctness) as the simple base-pair-based decompositions presented in this chapter. All the methods and algorithmic approaches presented in this chapter can thus be adapted, with essentially the same complexity, to this more realistic model.

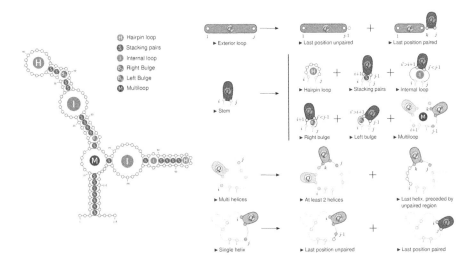

Figure 6.9. *Loops of the Turner energy model, illustrated using the structure of a 5s ribosomal RNA (left) and decomposition (right) of all secondary structures allowing for the expression of the loop-based energy model. For a color version of this figure, see www.iste.co.uk/chateau/graphs.zip*

The resulting gain in predictive accuracy is significant, as illustrated in Figure 6.10. We considered a structure/sequence database proposed by Mathews (2004), comprising RNAs having known structure. For each sequence, we used Algorithm 6.2 to produce a minimum energy structure, based on contributions G-C → -3, A-U → -2, and G-U → -1 (kcal.mol^{-1}). We also run a recent version of the RNAfold software (Lorenz et al. 2011), implementing energy minimization in the Turner model, to produce an alternative, hopefully more accurate, structure.

To evaluate the quality of a predicted structure S, for an RNA ω of known structure $S^\star$, we considered the true/false positive/negative (see section 1.9) base pairs, such that:

$$\text{VP} := |S \cap S^\star| \quad \text{FP} := |S \setminus S^\star| \quad \text{VN} := |\{(i,j)\} \setminus (S \cup S^\star)| \quad \text{FN} := |S^\star \setminus S|.$$

The *sensitivity* is then derived, defined as the proportion of pairs from the reference $S^\star$ that are actually predicted by a given algorithm; conversely, the *positive predictive value* (PPV) is the proportion of pairs from S, predicted by the algorithm, that are found in the reference, and finally the *Matthews correlation coefficient* (MCC), an agglomeration of the different measures, such that:

$$\text{Sens.} = \frac{\text{VP}}{\text{VP} + \text{FN}} \qquad\qquad \text{PPV} = \frac{\text{VP}}{\text{VP} + \text{FP}}$$

$$\text{MCC} = \frac{\text{TP} \times \text{TN} - \text{FP} \times \text{FN}}{\sqrt{(\text{TP} + \text{FP})(\text{TP} + \text{FN})(\text{TN} + \text{FP})(\text{TN} + \text{FN})}} \approx \sqrt{\text{Sens.} \times \text{PPV}}$$

With respect to these metrics, as can be seen in Figure 6.10, the Turner model produces predictions that are far superior to those obtained with the simplified model, regardless of the measure being considered. For this reason, despite its sophistication and the technicality of its implementation, the Turner model can be found in virtually all the predictive methods in the state of the art (described in the next section).

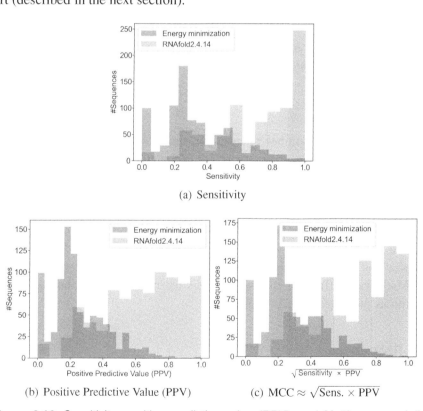

(a) Sensitivity

(b) Positive Predictive Value (PPV)   (c) $\text{MCC} \approx \sqrt{\text{Sens.} \times \text{PPV}}$

Figure 6.10. *Sensitivity, positive predictive value (PPV), and Matthews correlation coefficient (MCC) of energy minimization-based prediction in two energy models: simplified model based on base pairs (blue) and Turner model (orange). For a color version of this figure, see www.iste.co.uk/chateau/graphs.zip*

Task	Section	Tool/command	Package/Ref.
Energy minimization	6.2.1	RNAfold	ViennaRNA
		Fold	RNAStructure
Suboptimal folding	6.2.2	RNAsubopt	ViennaRNA
		AllSub	RNAStructure
Comparative folding	6.2.3	LocARNA	ViennaRNA
		dynalign	RNAStructure
		FoldAlign	Sundfeld et al. (2015)
Partition function	6.3.1	RNAfold -p	ViennaRNA
		partition	RNAStructure
Statistical sampling	6.3.2	RNAsubopt -p	ViennaRNA
		stochastic	RNAStructure
Boltzmann probabilities	6.3.3	RNAfold -p	ViennaRNA
		partition	RNAStructure
Multiple folding	–	RNAalifold	ViennaRNA

Table 6.1. *Reference implementations of the algorithms considered in this chapter (Turner energy model)*

6.4.2. *Tools*

There are a large number of available tools for predicting the structure of RNA sequences. Among the most popular implementations is the `ViennaRNA` software suite (Lorenz et al. 2011). It contains an extensive set of options and variations on folding/alignment, in addition to `Python` and `Perl` interfaces which can be easily integrated within an analysis pipeline. It is one of the most complete, and highly popular, tools in RNA bioinformatics due to these features. The `RNAstructure` package also offers many features, and provides a myriad of options, as well as a Java graphical interface (Reuter and Mathews 2010). Table 6.1 summarizes the main implementations of the algorithms presented in this chapter.

6.5. References

Berman, H.M., Westbrook, J., Feng, Z., Gilliland, G., Bhat, T.N., Weissig, H., Shindyalov, I.N., Bourne, P.E. (2000). The protein data bank. *Nucleic Acids Research*, 28, 235–242.

Ding, Y. and Lawrence, C.E. (2003). A statistical sampling algorithm for RNA secondary structure prediction. *Nucleic Acids Research*, 31, 7280–7301.

Ding, Y., Chan, C.Y., Lawrence, C.E. (2005). RNA secondary structure prediction by centroids in a boltzmann weighted ensemble. *RNA*, 11, 1157–1166.

ENCODE, C. (2007). Identification and analysis of functional elements in 1% of the human genome by the ENCODE pilot project. *Nature*, 447(7146), 799.

Findeiß, S., Etzel, M., Will, S., Mörl, M., Stadler, P.F. (2017). Design of artificial riboswitches as biosensors. *Sensors*, 17(9), E1990.

Gotoh, O. (1982). An improved algorithm for matching biological sequences. *Journal of Molecular Biology*, 162, 705–708.

Huang, L. and Chiang, D. (2005). Better k-best parsing. *Proceedings of the Ninth International Workshop on Parsing Technology*, Association for Computational Linguistics, Vancouver, 53–64.

Kalvari, I., Argasinska, J., Quinones-Olvera, N., Nawrocki, E.P., Rivas, E., Eddy, S.R., Bateman, A., Finn, R.D., Petrov, A.I. (2017). Rfam 13.0: Shifting to a genome-centric resource for non-coding RNA families. *Nucleic Acids Research*, 46(D1), D335–D342.

Lai, D., Proctor, J.R., Meyer, I.M. (2013). On the importance of cotranscriptional RNA structure formation. *RNA*, 19(11), 1461–1473.

Lari, K. and Young, S.J. (1990). The estimation of stochastic context-free grammars using the inside-outside algorithm. *Computer Speech and Language*, 4, 35–56.

Lorenz, R., Bernhart, S.H., Höner Zu Siederdissen, C., Tafer, H., Flamm, C., Stadler, P.F., Hofacker, I.L. (2011). ViennaRNA package 2.0. *Algorithms for Molecular Biology: AMB*, 6, 26.

Lu, X.-J., Bussemaker, H.J., Olson, W.K. (2015). DSSR: An integrated software tool for dissecting the spatial structure of RNA. *Nucleic Acids Research*, gkv716.

Mathews, D.H. (2004). Using an RNA secondary structure partition function to determine confidence in base pairs predicted by free energy minimization. *RNA*, 10(8), 1178–1190.

Mathews, D.H. and Turner, D.H. (2002). Dynalign: An algorithm for finding the secondary structure common to two RNA sequences. *Journal of Molecular Biology*, 317(2), 191–203.

McCaskill, J.S. (1990). The equilibrium partition function and base pair binding probabilities for RNA secondary structure. *Biopolymers: Original Research on Biomolecules*, 29(6–7), 1105–1119.

Michel, F. and Westhof, E. (1990). Modelling of the three-dimensional architecture of group I catalytic introns based on comparative sequence analysis. *Journal of Molecular Biology*, 216(3), 585–610.

Mückstein, U., Tafer, H., Hackermüller, J., Bernhart, S.H., Stadler, P.F., Hofacker, I.L. (2006). Thermodynamics of RNA–RNA binding. *Bioinformatics*, 22, 1177–1182.

Nussinov, R., Pieczenik, G., Griggs, J.R., Kleitman, D.J. (1978). Algorithms for loop matchings. *SIAM Journal on Applied Mathematics*, 35(1), 68–82.

Ponty, Y. (2008). Efficient sampling of RNA secondary structures from the Boltzmann ensemble of low-energy: The boustrophedon method. *Journal of Mathematical Biology*, 56(1–2), 107–127.

Reuter, J.S. and Mathews, D.H. (2010). RNAstructure: Software for RNA secondary structure prediction and analysis. *BMC Bioinformatics*, 11(1).

Sankoff, D. (1985). Simultaneous solution of the RNA folding, alignment and protosequence problems. *SIAM Journal on Applied Mathematics*, 45(5), 810–825.

Sundfeld, D., Havgaard, J.H., de Melo, A.C.M.A., Gorodkin, J. (2015). Foldalign 2.5: Multithreaded implementation for pairwise structural RNA alignment. *Bioinformatics*, 32(8), 1238–1240.

Turner, D.H. and Mathews, D.H. (2010). NNDB: The nearest neighbor parameter database for predicting stability of nucleic acid secondary structure. *Nucleic Acids Research*, 38(Database issue), D280–D282.

Wang, L. and Jiang, T. (1994). On the complexity of multiple sequence alignment. *Journal of Computational Biology*, 1(4), 337–348.

Waterman, M. (1978). Secondary structure of single-stranded nucleic acids. *Advances in Mathematics: Supplementary Studies*, 1, 167–212.

Waterman, M. and Byers, T.H. (1985). A dynamic programming algorithm to find all solutions in a neighborhood of the optimum. *Mathematical Biosciences*, 77(1–2), 179–188.

Waterman, M. and Smith, T.F. (1986). Rapid dynamic programming algorithms for RNA secondary structure. *Advances in Applied Mathematics*, 7(4), 455–464.

Will, S., Joshi, T., Hofacker, I.L., Stadler, P.F., Backofen, R. (2012). LocaRNA-p: Accurate boundary prediction and improved detection of structural RNAs. *RNA*, 18, 900–914.

Will, S., Otto, C., Miladi, M., Möhl, M., Backofen, R. (2015). Sparse: Quadratic time simultaneous alignment and folding of RNAs without sequence-based heuristics. *Bioinformatics*, 31, 2489–2496.

Wuchty, S., Fontana, W., Hofacker, I.L., Schuster, P. (1999). Complete suboptimal folding of RNA and the stability of secondary structures. *Biopolymers: Original Research on Biomolecules*, 49(2), 145–165.

Xia, T., SantaLucia Jr., J., Burkard, M.E., Kierzek, R., Schroeder, S.J., Jiao, X., Cox, C., Turner, D.H. (1998). Thermodynamic parameters for an expanded nearest-neighbor model for formation of RNA duplexes with Watson–Crick base pairs. *Biochemistry*, 37(42), 14719–14735.

Zuker, M. (1989). On finding all suboptimal foldings of an RNA molecule. *Science*, 244, 48–52.

Zuker, M. and Sankoff, D. (1984). RNA secondary structures and their prediction. *Bulletin of Mathematical Biology*, 46(4), 591–621.

Conclusion

The question "How can it be done?" was the focus of this book. The objective was to present some of the diversity of methods existing in bioinformatics, and also to illustrate the importance of the choice of the data structure and the problem and how it can contribute to simplifying the methods for solving these problems. We have considered different questions, and the emphasis has been put on their meaning, analysis, formalization as mathematical problems, representation in discrete structure form and the algorithmic aspect of their resolution. By addressing the difficulties mentioned in the various chapters, we have merely scratched the surface of a small number of other operational aspects of bioinformatics. We dedicate a few lines to them here, in order to engage you in getting involved in continuing the exploration of this emerging discipline.

Therefore, to better understand the interaction between the representation and the choice of structures, on the one hand, and the data and problems, on the other hand, we must consider the visualization aspect. This involves proposing a graphical representation of the concepts and data not only upstream, but also at the level of the solutions constructed by the methods. As a result, for genome assemblies, the question regarding what we obtain as output, the sequences of contigs, proves to be more complex than it seems at first sight, and to be able to visualize the graphs of assemblies, rather than simply having the file of linear sequences corresponding to an organism, is extremely rewarding. Visualizing the parts of this graph with a higher complexity can lead us to provide tools to better understand them and better utilize them. The same idea applies for each question presented in this book, and each type of mathematical representation is accompanied by an "expected picture", allowing experts to

From Sequences to Graphs,
coordinated by Annie CHATEAU and Mikaël SALSON.
© ISTE Ltd 2022.

apply their knowledge a priori or, on the contrary, to experience something entirely new when coming across more exploratory topics. It is also the job of the bioinformatician to propose methods for visually representing structures and data. This part is not necessarily emphasized in this book, but we underline its importance in everyday practice.

Bioinformatics is a young discipline, but it relies on elder and illustrious siblings such as mathematics, physical sciences, chemistry, computer science and, of course, biology. From these elder siblings, it inherits their methods and adapts them to its problems. It may not appear in this book, but the part of the method that is concerned with reproducibility underlies, in a more or less expressed manner, the scientific approach illustrated throughout the chapters. This quality of the methods, which consists of being able to guarantee that the experiments presented to illustrate or validate them can be identically reproduced under similar conditions, equally implies that not only the data used will last for a long time, but also the implementation of the methods, and the documentation of the protocol that is used. Why would this be more sensitive in bioinformatics than in other scientific fields? Two reasons can be identified for this purpose. The first is the content and the nature of the data, which are often already "interpreted" data having undergone transformations that do not necessarily guarantee this reproducibility. When looking into genomes, for example, the primary data of interest in this field are the sequencing data. The samples that have enabled this sequencing are sometimes preserved, but rarely accessible, and are generally not considered as input data for the problem. However, these data are extremely dependent on the sequencing technology that was used, and on the parameters applied with this technology, notably, for example, the depth of coverage. Hence, the proposed methods are required to determine their limitations with respect to this variability and their conditions in applications: Are they rather adapted for short reads, long reads or a clever mixture of the two? Within this context, being able to reproduce the method with different types of data becomes a prerequisite for their use by those likely to need them. The second fundamental reason is the nature of the proposed solutions. These are essentially software programs, or sets of scripts, implemented in a computer language. This implies a modeling layer that we have not mentioned here, consisting of the choice of language, the degree of modularity of the tools and their functional analysis in terms of user needs. This also implies a careful analysis of the implementation of discrete data structures, which are mathematical objects but not computer objects. How can we represent a tree or a graph in computers? Likewise, how should data formats be addressed, both on input, with the syntactic and sometimes grammatical analysis of data files, and how should we propose output formats adapted to their needs? There is a myriad of possible answers to this set of questions and sometimes the tools that are most often used are not necessarily the most suitable for the problem, but simply the most ergonomic, the easiest to install, the most referred to in the literature or the ones that have been most "convincing". In this context, once again, it is essential to design these tools in such a way that they can be reused, as independently as possible of the evolution of technologies and languages. In this sense, a large number of principles are emerging to ensure this reproducibility both at the data level and at the software and scripting level. The issues in question involve the documentation, and articulation between human understanding and the automation of processes. Therefore, electronic laboratory notebooks that make it possible to integrate code and explanations, version control software, collaborative tools, public data warehouses, and encapsulation tools in minimal autonomous virtual systems to avoid versioning conflicts without inflating too much the necessary resources are too many concepts that are available to bioinformaticians to propose complete and long-lasting solutions to the problems that arise.

We hope that through this book, we have been able to open new avenues towards fundamental concepts, and also that we have succeeded in transmitting part of the enthusiasm that we can feel in our daily research practices in bioinformatics, as well as this sparkle that animates us when we find the "right method", the one that will bring "beautiful results", whose sharing is rewarding, and lead us into evolving and answering very concrete problems.

List of Authors

Annie CHATEAU
University of Montpellier
CNRS, UMR 5506 – LIRMM
France

Tom DAVOT-GRANGÉ
University of Montpellier
CNRS, UMR 5506 – LIRMM
France

Cervin GUYOMAR
GenPhySE
University of Toulouse
INRAE, ENVT
France

Dominique LAVENIER
IRISA / INRIA
Rennes
France

Thierry LECROQ
University of Rouen Normandy
LITIS
France

Claire LEMAITRE
University of Rennes
CNRS, INRIA
IRISA-UMR 6074
France

Laurent NOÉ
University of Lille
CNRS, UMR 9189 – CRIStAL
France

Yann PONTY
LIX UMR 7161
Polytechnic School
Polytechnic Institute of Paris
France

Vladimir REINHARZ
Department of Computer Science
University of Quebec
Montreal
Canada

Mikaël SALSON
University of Lille
CNRS, UMR 9189 – CRIStAL
France

Index

Printed and bound by CPI Group (UK) Ltd, Croydon, CR0 4YY

27/10/2024

14580732-0003